Social Context Reform

Currently, both the status quo of public education and the No Excuses Reform policies are identical. The reform offers a popular and compelling narrative based on the meritocracy and rugged individualism myths that are supposed to define American idealism. This volume refutes this ideology by proposing Social Context Reform, a term coined by Paul Thomas, which argues for educational change within a larger plan to reform social inequity—such as access to health care, food, higher employment, better wages and job security.

Since the accountability era in the early 1980s, policy, public discourse, media coverage, and scholarly works have focused primarily on reforming schools themselves. Here, the evidence that school-only reform does not work is combined with a bold argument to expand the discourse and policy surrounding education reform to include how social, school, and classroom reform must work in unison to achieve goals of democracy, equity, and opportunity both in and through public education.

This volume includes a wide variety of essays from leading critical scholars addressing the complex elements of social context reform, all of which address the need to re-conceptualize accountability and to seek equity and opportunity in social and education reform.

P. L. Thomas is Associate Professor of Education at Furman University, USA. He taught high school English in South Carolina before moving to teacher education. He is currently a column editor for *English Journal* (National Council of Teachers of English) and author of *Ignoring Poverty in the U.S.* (IAP). Follow his work at http://radicalscholarship. wordpress.com/ and @plthomasEdD.

Brad Porfilio is Associate Professor of Education at Lewis University, USA. Recent publications include *The Phenomenon of Obama and the Agenda for Education: Can Hope Audaciously Trump Neoliberalism?*, which received the American Educational Studies 2012 Critics' Choice Award.

Julie Gorlewski is Assistant Professor of Education at the State University of New York at New Paltz, USA, and co-editor of *English Journal*. Publications include *Power, Resistance, and Literacy: Writing for Social Justice* (2011), *Making it Real: Case Stories for Secondary Teachers* (2012) and *Theory into Practice: Case Stories for School Leaders* (2012).

Paul R. Carr is Professor in the Department of Education at the Université du Québec en Outaouais, Canada. His research focuses on political sociology, democracy, media studies, peace education, and the sociology of education. He is the author and editor of a number of books, including the recently published *Educating for Democratic Consciousness: Counter-hegemonic Possibilities* (2013), and *Educating for Peace in a Time of Permanent War: Are Schools Part of the Solution or the Problem?* (2012).

Routledge Research in Education Policy and Politics

The Routledge Research in Education Policy and Politics series aims to enhance our understanding of key challenges and facilitate on-going academic debate within the influential and growing field of Education Policy and Politics.

Social Context Reform

A Pedagogy of Equity and Opportunity

Edited by
**P. L. Thomas, Brad Porfilio,
Julie Gorlewski, and Paul R. Carr**

Routledge
Taylor & Francis Group

NEW YORK AND LONDON

First published 2014
by Routledge
711 Third Avenue, New York, NY 10017, USA

and by Routledge
2 Park Square, Milton Park, Abingdon, Oxfordshire OX14 4RN

First issued in paperback 2016

*Routledge is an imprint of the Taylor & Francis Group,
an informa business*

Library of Congress Cataloging-in-Publication Data
Social context reform : a pedagogy of equity and opportunity / edited by
    P. L. Thomas, Brad Porfilio, Julie Gorlewski, and Paul R. Carr.
        pages cm — (Routledge research in education policy and politics ; 5)
    1. Educational change—United States.   2. Social change—United
States.   I. Thomas, P. L. (Paul Lee), 1961– editor of compilation.
    LA217.2.S63 2013
    370.973—dc23
    2014001957

Typeset in Sabon
by IBT Global.

ISBN 13: 978-1-138-28698-6 (pbk)
ISBN 13: 978-1-138-78861-9 (hbk)

Contents

PART II
School-Based Reform for Equity and Opportunity

PART III
Classroom-Based Reform for Equity and Opportunity

Figures and Tables

FIGURES

TABLES

Foreword
Education and the Epochal Crisis

Peter McLaren

John Bellamy Foster (2013) argues that we are living in an "epochal crisis" (a term borrowed from Jason Moore), a tremulous period in which dire economic and ecological crises emerge inextricably entangled in each other. He cites systems ecologist Howard Odum's revelation that Latin Americans, in particular, are being systematically robbed of their environmental resources through an unequal exchange in trade and production in which "embodied energy" is being withdrawn from the global South to the benefit of the global North—a situation that Álvaro García Linera refers to as "extraterritorial surplus value." We are facing what Foster describes as the unlimited expansion of a capitalist system geared to a process of abstract wealth creation. We are witnessing the displacement of natural material use value by specifically capitalist use value, which does little more than enhance exchange value for the capitalist so that the production of use value ceases and money creates money.[1]

The "real economy" is being hijacked by the irrational logic of monopoly finance capitalism organized around financial asset appreciation, which is dependent on an endless series of financial bubbles. Big corporations and wealthy investors, according to Foster (2013), have "increasingly poured their surplus capital into the financial sphere in order to secure high speculative returns." The response to this additional demand for their products by financial institutions was to supply "an endless array of new, exotic speculative opportunities (junk bonds, derivatives, options, hedge funds, etc.)" that invariably leads to massive credit/debt. And all of this is occurring in the midst of human suffering, the magnitude of which is scarcely imaginable. According to Foster (2013),

> Behind the worldwide veil of capitalist value relations, hundreds of millions, even billions, of people are poor and destitute, often lacking the most basic prerequisites of material existence—adequate food, water, clothing, housing, employment, healthcare, and a non-toxic environment—due to the failures and contradictions of accumulation. Meanwhile, what ecologists call "real wealth," i.e., the product of nature itself, is being extracted from the environment on an ever-increasing

scale devoid of any concern for either the rationality of production or the sustainability of natural systems, thereby robbing both present and future generations. Since unequal exchange relations with respect to both nature and labor prevail within the international economy this robbery falls disproportionately on poorer nations, a portion of whose natural use values (and economic surplus) is systematically siphoned off to enrich nations at the apex of the global imperialist pyramid.

Here in Los Angeles, where I am writing this foreword, an estimated 254,000 men, women, and children experience homelessness during some part of the year. On any given night, 82,000 people are homeless in Los Angeles County, and 4,800 to 10,000 of them are young people. One-third of this population holds a bachelor's degree or higher, compared to 25% of the population as a whole (Wells, 2013). Throughout the U.S., 80% of the population faces poverty or near poverty (Yen & Naziri, 2013).

In the midst of the current epochal crisis, the U.S. Department of Education and its spokespersons in the corporate media are diverting us away from the central issues of the crisis of capitalism and the ecological crisis by turning our attention to the failure of public schools. They propose as a solution to smash public schools and the commons by privatizing education. Of course, this is not specific only to the U.S.; we are facing the imperatives of the transnational capitalist class, and so the challenge to public education is occurring on a transnational scale.

In the present age, characterized by the dominance of militarism, nationalism, imperialism, and aggressive forms of neoliberal globalization, critical pedagogy has led the way in efforts to discover the basis of a just and equitable social order. *Social Context Reform* is a book edited and written by educators within the tradition of critical pedagogy. They are writing *from* varied social contexts and *about* the importance of social context in school reform with an eye to the transformation of the larger social order. The book makes a powerful case for the need for a determined opposition to what the editors call "no excuses reformers," who have become the standard bearers of the "blame and shame" policies of standardized testing, grade retention, charters and cybercharters, high-stakes testing, merit pay, school choice, Teach for America, value-added methods of teacher evaluation, and now—of course—the Common Core. We are encouraged to fight the Sam Walton–and Bill and Melinda Gates–financed reform efforts, the attack on teachers' unions, and the assault on public schools in general.

We know that federal programs such as No Child Left Behind and Race to the Top have largely been disastrous, resulting in teachers being labeled failures and, ultimately, fired if their students underperform. The problem with all of these reform efforts is that they ignore the context of neoliberal globalization, taking this context for granted and assuming it is irreproachable. In Europe there are similar moves to bring educational standards into line with the imperatives of the global economy and the logic of neoliberal capitalism (and its emphasis on competitive markets) with the Bologna Accords designed to ensure comparability in the standards and quality of higher education qualifications. We also have the Programme for International Student Assessment, a test created by the Organisation for Economic Co-operation and Development for evaluating the knowledge and skills of the world's 15-year-olds in which more than 510,000 students in 65 economies have already participated, with a focus on mathematics, reading, and science. *Social Context Reform* presents us with a determined opposition to the standards/efficiency movement that is designed to further the integration of social knowledge produced in educational contexts situated in the global commons into private dividends for capitalists and opposition to the monopolistic control of education by corporate capital. We are encouraged, in other words, to resist the privatization of what Karl Marx called the "general intellect" (Žižek, 2012).

Social Context Reform represents a noteworthy attempt to define the problems and failures of the neoliberal experiment, and plays an honored part in shaping the dissenting tradition of critical education. Critical educators such as the editors of and contributors to this volume have made important contributions to the sum total of our educational heritage through their exemplification of the possibility of combining practical results in reshaping individuals and communities with the development of a philosophy of praxis, their championship of the cause of the oppressed, and their leadership in the fields of community activism and social service. Only a worldwide proclamation, recognition, and application of the principles of social justice and the struggle for a historical transition to a new mode of production can meet head on the danger of the current epochal crisis of the capitalist economy and the ecology of the planet.

NOTES

1. The following explanation by John Bellamy Foster offers a useful summary of this process. Foster (2013) writes:

   Contrary to economic myth, the system of capitalist production and exchange does not take the form of simple commodity production, or the circuit C–M–C, in which a commodity (C), representing a definite, qualitative use value is exchanged for money (M), which is then exchanged for a another commodity (C), representing a different use value—to be simply consumed in the end. Rather, in line with what Marx termed the "general formula of capital," or M–C–M′, money (M) is exchanged for labor power and commodities with which to produce a new commodity (C), to be sold for more money (M′ = M + Δm or surplus value). Hence, it is not *use value*, fulfilling concrete, qualitative needs, that constitutes the aim of capitalist production, but rather *exchange value*, generating profit for the capitalist. The abstract, purely quantitative nature of this process, moreover, means that there is no end to the incentive of seeking more money or surplus value because M′ leads in the next circuit of production to a drive to obtain M″, followed by the drive to obtain M''' in the circuit after that, in an unending sequence of accumulation and expansion.

Characteristic of monopoly capitalism is a further warping of this process through the displacement of natural-material use value by *specifically capitalist use value*—the only real "use" of which is to enhance exchange value for the capitalist. Thus wasteful and destructive commodities increasingly dominate production, from military hardware to superficial car model-changes, to excessive packaging. Here Marx's general formula for capital, as it pertains to production itself, has metamorphosed into M–CK–M′, where CK stands for specifically capitalist use value.

At the more stratospheric level represented by contemporary finance, the general formula for capital, or M–C–M′, is being increasingly supplanted by the circuit of speculative capital, M–M′, in which the production of use values disappears altogether and money simply begets more money. What economists call "the real economy" or the realm of commodity production associated with GDP is thus being subordinated in the irrational logic of today's phase of monopoly-finance capital to a process of wealth generation organized around financial-asset appreciation and dependent on an unending series of financial bubbles. Financial capital more and more rules the roost, largely disconnected from the real economy of commodity production and use value.

REFERENCES

Foster, J. B. (2013). The Epochal crisis. *Monthly Review*, 65(5). Retrieved from http://monthlyreview.org/2013/10/01/epochal-crisis

Wells, M. (2013, November 30). Los Angeles moves toward restricting food distributions in public places. Retrieved from http://www.wsws.org/en/articles/2013/11/30/losa-n30.html

Yen, H., & Naziri, M. (2013, July 28). Shocking study: 4 out of 5 in USA face near-poverty and unemployment. Retrieved from http://politicalblindspot.com/shocking-study-4-out-of-5-in-usa-face-near-poverty-and-unemployment/

Žižek, S. (2012). Living in the time of monsters. In M. Nikolakaki (Ed.), *Critical Pedagogy in the New Dark Ages: Challenges and Possibilities* (pp. 32–44). New York: Lang.

Acknowledgments

P. L. Thomas wishes to thank all of the teachers and students who have built and continue to build the foundation upon which his teaching and scholarship are built. This volume as a coedited collection is a work of powerful collaboration; it is inspiring as a model of the call for community instead of competition in our pursuit of democracy, human agency, and a kinder, more patient world for all.

Brad Porfilio would like to thank his coeditors and the contributors to this volume. Their work has positioned me to think more deeply about what larger forces are behind the contemporary reform agenda for education.

Julie Gorlewski is grateful for the relentless encouragement of David Gorlewski, who provides enduring material, spiritual, intellectual, and emotional support. Thanks also to my family, especially Jeff, Jake, Jon, and Jennie, who simultaneously ensure that I am both grounded and inspired. Finally, I appreciate the collegial nature of my coeditors in the development of this volume. You have made this challenging work a joyful process of learning and growth.

Paul R. Carr acknowledges the unwavering support of Gina Thésée, who has been a source of inspiration throughout our shared academic journey. *Je te remercie pour tout, mon amour.* I would also like to thank my old friend, Richard Townsend, professor emeritus at the Ontario Institute for Studies in Education at the University of Toronto, who was extremely generous and empathetic when I was a young man.. Similarly, life would not be the same without my *deux petits travailleurs*, Noah and Luka, who have provided endless animation, excitement, joy, and love. Finally I would also like to thank my coeditors for their complicity, good nature, and critical engagement.

The editors are deeply indebted to the chapter authors and Routledge, as well as its editorial staff.

Introduction

Social Context Reform—A Pedagogy of Equity and Opportunity

Brad Porfilio, Julie Gorlewski,
Paul R. Carr, and P. L. Thomas

Asked to explain the many competing narratives of the religions of the world, comparative myth and religion scholar Joseph Campbell told Bill Moyers that he did not reject religion, as some scholars have, but instead reached this conclusion: "Every religion is true one way or another. It is true when understood metaphorically. But when it gets stuck to its own metaphors, interpreting them as facts, then you are in trouble" (Campbell & Moyers, 1988, p. 56).

As a number of education scholars and historians have noted (Berliner & Biddle, 1996; Bracey, 2004; Kliebard, 1995; Ravitch, 2010, 2013b; Tienken & Orlich, 2013), public education in the U.S. has suffered a long history of crisis narratives about the state of schools—narratives that have been coupled with a never-ending call for reform. The last 30 years of accountability-driven reform have been based on standards and high-stakes tests. Standards were initially generated by states; however, there is now a move toward national standards known as the Common Core. High-stakes assessments have followed a similar trajectory, situated first at the state level and now based on Common Core. During the past three decades, two competing narratives have emerged, what we label "no excuses" reform (NER) and social context reform (SCR):

> "No Excuses" Reformers insist that the source of success and failure lies in each child and each teacher, requiring only the adequate level of effort to rise out of the circumstances not of her/his making. As well, "No Excuses" Reformers remain committed to addressing poverty solely or primarily through education, viewed as an opportunity offered each child and within which . . . effort will result in success.
>
> Social Context Reformers have concluded that the source of success and failure lies primarily in the social and political forces that govern our lives. By acknowledging social privilege and inequity, Social Context Reformers are calling for education reform *within* a larger plan to reform social inequity—such as access to health care, food security, higher employment along with better wages and job security. (Thomas, 2011b, emphasis in the original)

A powerful but generally ignored irony of the accountability era involves No Child Left Behind (NCLB), which rhetorically codified the use of "scientifically based research" in education. The problem presented by NCLB is that three decades of evidence on the most popular and dominant reforms implemented by NER advocates and political leadership—grade retention, charter schools, school choice, value added methods of teacher evaluation, merit pay, Teach for America, high-stakes testing, and standards—have failed to support the effectiveness of these policies.

When faced with the competing narratives of NER and SCR, then, the public, the media, and political leaders must face the research base and consider the degree to which false narratives and ideological myths have been imbued within NER as well as the relevance and importance of SCR narratives to seek out more bone fide evidence-based directions. Notably, trends within the U.S. have also had varying levels of influence elsewhere, and most international jurisdictions now have significant educational policy related to standards, testing, assessment, and accountability. For this reason, the U.S. context is particularly important for understanding neoliberalism and globalization at a broader level, encompassing such universal concerns as social inequalities, accessibility, a societal focus on education, differentiated outcomes, and the role of teachers. Ultimately we find this debate to be fundamental in relation to democracy, and the place of education within a democracy (Carr, 2011).

OBAMA'S FAILED HOPE AND CHANGE

Writing in 1976 about the U.S. bicentennial, novelist John Gardner (1976/1994) challenges the 20th-century concern that "the American Dream is dead" (p. 96):

> The American Dream, it seems to me, is not even slightly ill. It's escaped, soared away into the sky like an eagle, so not even a great puffy Bicentennial can squash it. The American Dream's become a worldwide dream, which makes me so happy and flushed with partly chauvinistic pride (it was our idea) that I sneak down into my basement and wave my flag. . . .
>
> That idea—humankind's inalienable right to life, liberty, and the pursuit of happiness—coupled with a system for protecting human rights—was and is the quintessential American Dream. The rest is greed and pompous foolishness—at worst, a cruel and sentimental myth, at best, cheap streamers in the rain. (p. 96)

Gardner continues, addressing "majority rule" as "right even when it's wrong (as often happens)" because

> it encourages free men to struggle as adversaries, using established legal means, to keep government working at the business of justice for all.
>
> The theory was and is that is the majority causes too much pain to the minority, the minority will scream (with the help of the free press

and the right of assembly) until the majority is badgered or shamed into changing its mind. . . .

It's true that the system pretty frequently doesn't work. For decades, pollsters tell us, the American people favored gun control by three to one—law-enforcement officials have favored it by as much as nine to one—but powerful lobbies and cowardly politicians have easily thwarted the people's will. (p. 97)

About three decades later, voters in the U.S. elected the first biracial (often called simply African American) president in the country's history. At the time, some voted for Barack Obama primarily because the election was an important, symbolic moment for the U.S.; some bought his message of hope and change. Others remained skeptical that the Democratic Party establishment would allow a true champion of liberal and progressive ideas to assume the mantle of U.S. president. The sophisticated and compellingly influential rhetoric employed by Obama for two years prior to being elected, presenting "hope" and "change" as not only desirable but—more important—entirely achievable, laid the groundwork for an important juxtaposition between hegemonic forces and the will of the majority of people, who wanted a more humane, social justice–based orientation to public services and government (Carr & Porfilio, 2011b).

As public educators, academics, and scholars have discovered (Carr & Porfilio, 2011b), Obama is not the progressive he portrayed himself to be, much less the socialist that libertarians and Tea Party advocates claim. In fact, Obama's education policies are an extended version of the NCLB accountability agenda begun under president George W. Bush. The Obama education agenda has been committed to neoliberalism, not democracy, not justice for all, not protecting human rights:

> Barack Obama personifies the power of personality in politics and the value of articulating a compelling vision that resonates with many voters in the US and other global citizens. For Obama's presidential campaign, the refrain that worked was driven by two words and concepts, "hope" and "change." From healthcare, to war, to education reform, however, the Obama administration is proving that political discourse is more likely to mask intent—just as Orwell warned through his essays and most influential novel 1984, the source of the term "doublespeak" that characterizes well Obama's and Secretary of Education Arne Duncan's public comments on education reform. They mask the programs promoted and implemented by the Department of Education. (Thomas, 2011a, p. 68)

Despite Gardner's soaring optimism, the media is culpable in this failure to commit to the hope and change that was so eloquently and vociferously presented by Obama and his administration.

A powerful and disturbing example of how the Obama administration, through the U.S. Department of Education (USDOE) and its secretary Arne Duncan, masks the neoliberal agenda (see Carr & Porfilio, 2011a; Hursh, 2011) behind civil rights rhetoric and crisis discourse is an exchange between civil rights leaders calling for the removal of Duncan and a reply from Obama. Civil rights leaders include in their call the following:

National Journey for Justice Alliance demands include:

- A moratorium on school closings, turnarounds, phase-outs, and charter expansions
- Its proposal for sustainable school transformation to replace failed, market-driven interventions as support for struggling schools
- Resignation of secretary of education Arne Duncan. (Ravitch, 2013a)

In a letter to Atlanta education activist Ed Johnson that bears Obama's signature prominently, the language no longer masks his agenda; Obama is resolute in his commitment to "provid[ing] our children with the world-class education they need to succeed and our Nation needs to compete in the global economy." Not once in this two-page response does Obama mention democracy, or any of the ideals embraced by Gardner above. Obama, instead, offers "cheap streamers in the rain":

> Our classrooms should be places of high expectations and success, where all students receive an education that prepares them for higher learning and high-demand careers in our fast-changing economy. . . .
> In states that make it a priority to educate our youngest children, students grow up more likely to read and do math at their grade level, graduate high school, hold a job, and form stable families of their own. (Ravitch, 2013a)

The message is clear that education is a mechanism for building a competitive workforce; nothing else seems to matter. Obama's focus on education as training for workers is disturbing, but his relentless commitment to competition and punitive accountability policies in education is highly problematic when placed against democratic goals and the pursuit of equity.

Throughout the response, Obama mentions Race to the Top (a USDOE competitive grant process that awards federally funding for state-based education reform) twice, invokes "competition" three times, and twice endorses "reward" structures for raising teacher and school quality. But let's not forget the crisis: "America's students cannot afford to wait any longer." Even this crisis is driven by economic diction in the term "afford." The emphasis is clearly on the workforce, business, employment, and training and not on citizenship, social justice, critical engagement, and democracy.

Almost 40 years ago Gardner (1976/1994) argued, "The lie on the American left is this: that the American theory promised such-and-such and has sometimes not delivered, whereas We Deliver. The truth—a metaphysical truth, in fact—is that nobody delivers" (p. 99). With Obama's neutered education agenda before us as part of three continuous decades of failed accountability policies (Thomas, 2013), Gardner's analysis seems prophetic. Despite Gardner's rejecting cynicism ("But the myth of the mindless patriot is not worse than the myth of the cynic who speaks of America with an automatic sneer," p. 98), George Carlin (2010), comedian and social critic, appears to have a more accurate view of the American dream:

> But there's a reason. There's a reason. There's a reason for this, there's a reason education sucks, and it's the same reason it will never, ever, ever be fixed.
>
> It's never going to get any better, don't look for it, be happy with what you've got.
>
> Because the owners, the owners of this country don't want that. I'm talking about the real owners now, the big owners! The Wealthy . . . the real owners! The big wealthy business interests that control things and make all the important decisions.
>
> Forget the politicians. They are irrelevant. The politicians are put there to give you the idea that you have freedom of choice. You don't. You have no choice! You have owners! They own you. They own everything. They own all the important land. They own and control the corporations. They've long since bought, and paid for the Senate, the Congress, the state houses, the city halls, they got the judges in their back pockets and they own all the big media companies, so they control just about all of the news and information you get to hear. . . .
>
> They want more for themselves and less for everybody else, but I'll tell you what they don't want:
>
> They don't want a population of citizens capable of critical thinking. They don't want well informed, well educated people capable of critical thinking. They're not interested in that. That doesn't help them. That's against their interests.

This isn't simply biting social satire. This isn't easily discounted cynicism. Obama's education policies and his neoliberal agenda are solid proof that Carlin, not Gardner, is right: "It's called the American Dream, because you have to be asleep to believe it" (Carlin, 2010).

BUILDING A CASE FOR SOCIAL CONTEXT REFORM

This volume's three sections and 11 chapters seek ways in which we can confront the current in-school-only education reform driven by neoliberal ideologies that honor market forces while marginalizing the essential nature of public institutions and democratic ideals. This argument is not popular, and it is also complex. The political and public narrative for over a century has included a story of failing public schools; in the last three decades, that claim has been joined by charges of failing students and "bad" teachers. Simplistic and misleading use of state-by-state and international rankings based on standardized testing has supported these claims, creating an atmosphere hostile to nuanced arguments, teacher professionalism, and credible analysis of educational research.

In that context, the volume includes the following sections and chapters.

Part I: Social Reform for Equity and Opportunity

In Chapter 1, "Defying Meritocracy: The Case of the Working-Class College Student," Allison L. Hurst details the "social costs and repercussions" of U.S. educational policy makers enthusiastically adopting meritocracy as the chief "goal of social and educational policy." Hurst begins the chapter by highlighting the intellectual work of Michael Young, who was a British sociologist and Labour Party activist. Young coined the term "meritocracy" in the late 1950s. Hurst argues that examining Young's work helps scholars, educators, and citizens recognize why contemporary social and educational policy is "compatible with increased social inequality." Next, the author highlights her empirical work with working-class college students. Their stories and knowledge remind us of "the fatal faults of meritocracy." Meritocracy not only deeply affects "the texture" of working-class students' "educational experiences" but also keeps in place the economic and social structures that ensure many citizens "fail." Next, Hurst highlights "some of the ways that individual working-class college students resist cultural assimilation and hierarchization." She concludes the chapter by discussing "more systematic ways we can scrub our educational system of its hierarchizing tendencies by exploring the ideal university from the working-class person's perspective."

In Chapter 2, "Reforming the Schooling of Neoliberal, Perpetual Zombie Desire," William M. Reynolds argues that contemporary educational reform in the U.S. ought to be situated within the history of U.S. schooling. The author begins the chapter by pinpointing how "the recycling of the businessification of schooling in the U.S." has taken place for over 100 years. Next Reynolds looks more specifically at the contemporary educational reform movement, arguing that contemporary educational reform in the U.S. is more pernicious than it was in past reform movements because corporate leaders have infused consumer culture into today's neoliberal movement. Consequently, corporate ascendency over all aspects of social life has ensured that schools are unable to stand "outside of culture." Reynolds believes we may need to critique this culture, "but within the next hour even most of the staunchest critics are shopping online to find just that right bargain to purchase." After unveiling how contemporary U.S. politicians and business leaders have turned "our children into compliant zombielike purchasers who wait impatiently for the next new thing," the author concludes the chapter by providing a glimmer of hope that the "initial resistances to present schooling and testing are the beginning of more resistance and the real reform of the public schools and the neoliberal society in which they exist."

In Chapter 3 "ThePseudoaccountability of Education Reform: The Denial of Democracy, Citizenship, and Social Justice," Randy Hoover deals with "the fundamental metrics of the neoliberal school reform model and how the carefully constructed metrics lead to an extreme narrowing of the conversation about school reform that precludes discourse about social justice and democratic ideals." The author begins the chapter by providing a historical backdrop behind how the neoliberal reform model came to life in the U.S. educational system. Next, Hoover illustrates how the neoliberal educational reform agenda elides an "extremely important nuance inherent within the use and understanding of the concept of *accountability*." Supporters of the neoliberal educational agenda have ensured that teachers, schools, and citizens have little or no control over variables "upon which the accountability system is based." In a more authentic accountability system, educators would be *"responsible for their own professional decision making and professional actions within the context of the professional practice"* (Hoover's emphasis). Third, the author documents how the "number game" associated with neoliberal education reform has led us to a point where "anything about schools that cannot be seen in some way to be measurable as an explicit quantity is neither important nor of any value." Hoover concludes the chapter by reminding us that democracy, equity, and social justice will not be produced in U.S. schools until the "neoliberal reform's false proxy" is exposed. However, this will be extremely difficult because union leadership is currently embracing "the political capital of the false proxy."

In Chapter 4, "Teacher Education and Resistance within the Neoliberal Regime: Making the Necessary Possible," Barbara Madeloni and Kysa Nygreen name the policies and practices associated with "the neoliberal assault" on teacher education. After providing us their personal narratives and detailing how they have experienced the neoliberal assault on education, the authors detail more broadly how several neoliberal practices are narrowing "the possibilities of teacher education for social justice and critical consciousness" as well as infiltrating "the expectations of the students with whom we are working." Madeloni and Nygreen conclude their chapter by providing a clarion call to teacher educators and others who are concerned with promoting equity and social justice in our schools. They believe it is imperative to

> fight for what is most important, and we must be ready to accept the risks attendant to claiming our space. This requires solidarity. But this

is the work of education for liberation—under any system that works to silence and dehumanize us. If we claim this as our work, we must enact it in our practice and our programs.

Part II: School-Based Reform for Equity and Opportunity

In Chapter 5, "Changing the Colonial Context to Address School Under-performance in Nunavut," Paul Berger reminds us that there are additional forces, beside the neoliberal educational agenda, that are leading to marginalization of children in schools across North America. The author taps his empirical work "from interviews with 74 Inuit adults" and "with parents and students in the western Arctic" to argue that colonialism is at the heart of these children's educational and social struggles. Berger also believes that "neoliberal thinking provides a barrier to moving away from colonialism." The author concludes the chapter by urging Canadians to "push for changes" in the underlying relations that lead to some Inuit students "struggl[ing] with addictions themselves, and social problems ranging from overcrowded housing to violence make it difficult to learn." Sadly, this may be a "distant hope" given the political reality in Canada. Berger states,

> Canadian prime minister Stephen Harper visits the Arctic every year to assert its importance to Canada, but there has been no indication that the Inuit are important to him or his government. The Arctic, especially as it melts under the assault of global climate change, is strategically important and a major new arena for resource extraction. . . . When Canada's indigenous peoples are noticed at all by this government, it is usually in the context of getting them training (not education) to enable them to take part in resource extraction . . . . Unfortunately, most Canadians seem politically disengaged from any sort of action that might push the government to treat the Inuit fairly, or to even suggest that it should.

In Chapter 6, "An Injury to All? The Haphazard Nature of Academic Freedom in America's Public Schools," Robert L. Dahlgren, Nancy C. Patterson, and Christopher J. Frey argue the educational accountability movement that developed in the U.S. with the 1983 report *A Nation at Risk* (1983) has lead to devastating consequences for minoritized students and low-income communities across the U.S. The authors illustrate that the educational accountability movement has also impinged "upon the freedom of teachers to decide on academic and other curricular content." To ensure that educators do not lose further control over their teaching practices and the production of scholarship, the authors center their chapter on their study of a review of academic freedom contract language in select regions of two strong union states (Ohio and New York). The authors conclude the chapter by arguing that "teachers in unionized districts must be vigilant in negotiating their collective bargaining agreements," are "our best hope of ensuring academic freedoms in the context of the current accountability regime."

In Chapter 7, "Educating, Not Criminalizing, Youth of Color: Challenging Neoliberal Agendas and Penal Populism," Mary Christianakis and Richard Mora argue current neoliberal educational initiatives, "particularly the competitive Race to the Top initiative," are complicit in ensuring that there is "a great likelihood that youth of color, in general, will be fed into the school-to-prison-pipeline and experience further exclusion from our neoliberal society." After providing a backdrop to how neoliberalism "has made incarceration a profitable business" in the U.S., the authors unveil several forces that have led to the contemporary "populist response to crime." U.S. politicians and business leaders scapegoat Black and Latino youth for being "threats to the social order," rather than altering the structural arrangements responsible for cementing the elite's wealth and power and for hindering the life chance of low-income youth and youth of color. Next, the authors capture how "crime-control policies" in U.S schools "exclude urban students who cannot be 'responsibilized'" and pushes some low-income youth and youth of color to live life behind bars. The authors provide a call of action, asserting, "We must not accept the criminalization of our youth." This can only be done if we "counter the conservative and neoliberal policies that are perpetuating the expansion of prisons, dismantling the welfare state, and wreaking havoc on economically depressed and racially isolated communities."

Part III: Classroom-based Reform for Equity and Opportunity

In Chapter 8, "Pedagogies of Equity and Opportunity: Critical Literacy, Not Standards," P. L. Thomas calls attention to the fact that the contributors and editors of the present volume embrace "social and educational reform that addresses equity and opportunity" instead of embracing in-school-only policies that are designed to control educators' professionalism and amass wealth and power for the dominant elite. At the outset of the chapter, Thomas outlines the pernicious implications of embracing the "no excuses" reform (NER) agenda. For instance, by embracing the agenda, we support the false ideas that "[e]ducation is the one true way to overcome all of society's ills" and education reform is predicated on a national model steeped in "standards-and-testing accountability." After debunking additional claims associated with the NER agenda, Thomas confronts "the failure of traditional and progressive methods in order to embrace critical methods" that promote critical awareness and democracy in schools. The author details the nature of critical methods through his own instructional practice. Some of the broad guiding concepts of critical instruction include "collaboration and choice, reimagining content, de-testing and de-grading schools." They are predicated on honoring "the agency and autonomy of students and teachers."

In Chapter 9, "YouTube University: How an Educational Foundations Professor Uses Critical Media in His Classroom," Nicholas D. Hartlep documents how he, as young assistant professor at Illinois State University, employs YouTube to cultivate critical literacy with preservice teachers. After providing "a brief history of YouTube," the author explicates what is critical literacy and why he believes it to be a central skill to "captivate" in preservice education. The author concludes the chapter by sharing three sample lessons that have been successful in fostering critical literacy in his classroom.

In Chapter 10, "Developing a User-Friendly, Community-Based Higher Education," Rebecca Collins-Nelsen and Randle W. Nelsen provide a blueprint for how higher education institutions can implement "classroom-based reforms that take into account the diversity to be found among today's students in a manner that emphasizes equity and opportunity." The authors argue that these reforms have the ability to "empower students, creating classroom contexts that run counter to the current obsession with professionalism and accountability education." After analyzing "higher education as professional certification," the authors argue that the changing "demographic makeup" of university classrooms "reinforces the need for less-structured and more user-friendly classrooms." Next, Collins-Nelsen and Nelsen "offer details about teaching experiments in four courses that created a social context that in each case made the university classroom more user-friendly." The authors conclude the chapter by pinpointing the various ways the four courses provided learning experiences that empowered students through "self-revelatory and storytelling elements."

In Chapter 11, ""Transcending the Standard: One Teacher's Effort to Explore the World beyond the Curriculum," Christopher R. Leahey reveals how "bureaucratic accountability systems perpetuate the status quo, depriving students of opportunities to critically investigate the past and explore the social, political, and economic forces shaping their lives." However, the author documents that it its possible to find fissures amid the educational status quo so as to "humanize the world history curriculum, complicate the past, and create authentic opportunities to question dominant narratives and critically investigate the history of the world." The outset of the chapter reveals how neoliberal initiatives, including Race to the Top and No Child Left Behind, have limited value for "strengthening instruction or improving student outcome," and have concomitantly wrought "rationalization of teaching and learning" and attempt to standardize such disciplines as social studies education. Next, Leahey provides insight from his own pedagogical practices of how he successfully navigates the standard-based environment. He is able to build "a classroom dedicated to humanistic values" and capture for his students the "power and importance of social studies for democratic life." The author concludes the chapter by outlining what is needed for a "vigorous form of social studies education" that

> requires us to think deeply about the ways in which we present the curriculum, the manner in which we interact with students while engaging

the past, and the ways in which we allow students to interact as they develop a richer, deeper understanding of the curriculum and the complex world they have been given. Perhaps the truest, most significant measure of learning social studies may not be found in test scores but instead may be better demonstrated in students' willingness to unlock the past and draw upon one another to build a sophisticated understanding of the history of the world and a desire to apply what they have learned beyond the classroom.

•

During the final stages of drafting this book, politicians, reformers, the media, and the public once again rushed to inaccurate conclusions based on the release of National Assessment of Educational Progress and Program for International Student Assessment test scores. Few acknowledged the most powerful aspect of these scores: in the U.S. and throughout the world, standardized test scores remain overwhelmingly a reflection of out-of-school factors such as parental income and parental educational attainment.

And from that, those seeking educational reform have failed both the promise of universal public education and the possibility of genuine educational reform. In the second decade of the twenty-first century, we remain unable to admit that the achievement gap is a metric for the opportunity gap; we remain unable to admit that social reform must precede in-school reform; and we remain unable to admit that our schools tend to mirror and perpetuate the exact inequities the political leaders and pundits lament when they criticize schools and public school teachers.

As Gardner (1976/1994) proclaimed about the American Dream, it seems well past time that we admit that universal public education has not failed us, but that we continue to fail universal public education.

EDITOR'S NOTE

Some of this text has been adapted from Thomas (2013).

REFERENCES

Berliner, D. C., & Biddle, B.J. (1996). *The manufactured crisis: Myths, fraud, and the attack on America's schools.* New York: Basic Books.

Bracey, G. (2004). *Setting the record straight: Responses to misconceptions about public education in the U.S.* Portsmouth, NH: Heinemann.

Campbell, J., & Moyers, B. (1988). *The power of myth.* New York: Doubleday.

Carlin, G. (2010, September 25). George Carlin on the American dream (with transcript). Retrieved from http://shoqvalue.com/george-carlin-on-the-american-dream-with-transcript/

Carr, P. R. (2011). *Does your vote count? Critical pedagogy and democracy.* New York: Peter Lang.

Carr, P. R., & Porfilio, B. J. (2011a). The Obama education file: Is there hope to stop the neoliberal agenda in education? *Journal of Inquiry and Action in Education, 4*(1), 1–30. Retrieved from https://journal.buffalostate.edu/index.php/soe/issue/view/11

Carr, P. R., & Porfilio, B. J. (2011b). *The Phenomenon of Obama and the agenda for education: Can hope audaciously trump neoliberalism?* Charlotte, NC: Information.

Gardner, J. (1994). Amber (get) waves (your) of (plastic) grain (Uncle Sam). In *On writers and writing* (pp. 95–100). New York: Addison-Wesley. (Original work published 1976)

Hursh, D. (2011). Explaining Obama: The continuation of free market policies in education and the economy. *Journal of Inquiry and Action in Education, 4*(1), 31–47. Retrieved from https://journal.buffalostate.edu/index.php/soe/issue/view/11

Kliebard, H. M. (1995). *The struggle for the American curriculum: 1893–1958.* New York: Routledge.

Ravitch, D. (2010). *The death and life of the great American school system: How testing and choice are undermining education.* New York: Basic Books.

Ravitch, D. (2013a, August 25). Civil rights groups call for Duncan's ouster. Retrieved from http://dianeravitch.net/2013/08/25/civil-rights-groups-call-for-duncans-ouster/

Ravitch, D. (2013b). *Reign of error: The hoax of the privatization movement and the danger to America's public schools.* New York: Knopf.

Thomas, P. L. (2011a). Orwellian educational change under Obama: Crisis discourse, Utopian expectations, and accountability failures. *Journal of Inquiry and Action in Education, 4*(1), 68–92. Retrieved from https://journal.buffalostate.edu/index.php/soe/issue/view/11

Thomas, P. L. (2011b, December 30). Poverty matters! A Christmas miracle. Retrieved from http://truth-out.org/news/item/5808:poverty-matters-a-christmas-miracle

Thomas, P. L. (2013, August 19). What we know now (and how it doesn't matter). Retrieved from http://radicalscholarship.wordpress.com/2013/08/19/what-we-know-now-and-how-it-doesnt-matter/

Tienken, C. H., & Orlich, D. C. (2013). *The school reform landscape: Fraud, myth, and lies.* Lanham, MD: Rowman and Littlefield Education.

Part I

Social Reform for Equity and Opportunity

1 Defying Meritocracy
The Case of the Working-Class College Student

Allison L. Hurst

INTRODUCTION: THE RISE OF MERITOCRACY

Michael Young, British sociologist and Labour Party activist, coined the term "meritocracy" in a 1958 dystopic satire titled *The Rise of the Meritocracy*. In the novel, the ablest and most intelligent became the new rulers of society. One's place in society was a result of IQ plus effort. Young intended this as a serious critique of the shift away from egalitarian values, but most who read the book took it instead as a blueprint for the future. The new champions of meritocracy simply ignored his caution that hierarchy, no matter how artfully arranged, was a threat to democracy and equality. Today, educational policy makers and intellectuals seemingly endorse Young's narrator's assertion that "democracy can be no more than aspiration, and [we] have rule not so much by the people as by the cleverest people; *not an aristocracy of birth, not a plutocracy of wealth, but a true meritocracy of talent*" (Young, 1958/2008, p. 11, emphasis added). We take this for granted in the way we track students from birth, in our overuse of test scores to sort students, in our market-driven heavily stratified system of higher education, and even in the way we applaud *equal opportunity* policies to the exclusion of truly equal outcomes.

Perhaps Young's contemporaries did not finish reading the book. At the conclusion of *The Rise of Meritocracy*, the masses revolt against the new elite, killing the narrator (as the book's fake preface makes clear). What happened to this promising new social system? A brief look at how Young answered this question may inform us of the costs of our current obsession with meritocracy. Young's story highlights the ways in which such a system is compatible with increased social inequality. Not only does the gap widen, but the gap itself appears socially *deserved*, further increasing the social distance between those who "rise to the top" through the educational system and those many who do not. Bluntly speaking, "the gradual shift from inheritance to merit as the ground of social selection was making (and has finally made) nonsense of all their loose talk of the equality of man" (p. 105).

Second, a meritocratic system condones the existence of bad jobs, and the relegation of those who fail to advance educationally to those bad jobs. In Young's meritocratic future, domestic service (i.e., slavery) was restored "once it was again accepted that some men were superior to others" (p. 112). How better to explain our collective mockery of "burger flippers" and "Walmart greeters," or the rise of a host of personal service "jobs," including real-time bidding for running errands?

Finally, a meritocratic system prevents the forms of collective solidarity that Young saw as crucial for a good society. Moving up individually becomes the goal of each person, no matter his or her starting point. Whereas failure means internalized shame, perhaps some envy, and a life of demeaning and undervalued work, success can mean turning one's back on one's community. Young likens this to the "Mohicans who took away the best young men and women from a conquered tribe and reared them as members of their own families" (p. 140).

These three faults—greater class divisions, declining job opportunities for the majority of citizens, and the loss of collective solidarity in favor of a cult of individual mobility—proved fatal to Young's meritocracy. Reformers in Young's satire issued the *Chelsea Manifesto*, arguing for the opportunity for each "to develop his own special capacities for leading a rich life" instead of the opportunity to "rise up" (p. 159). Schools would then be "devoted to encouraging all human talents" and not simply marking a few students for occupational success. But the reformers were unsuccessful, and a fierce class war, brutish and violent, ensued:

> Without intelligence in their heads, the lower classes are never more menacing than a rabble, even if they are sometimes sullen, sometimes mercurial, not yet completely predictable. If the hopes of some earlier dissidents had been realized and the brilliant children from the lower classes remained there, to teach, to inspire, and to organize the masses, then I should have had a different story to tell. (p. 180)

I open this chapter with Michael Young's book as a reminder that the very things we say we want—expanded access to college, equal opportunity for all—may be at odds with such other socially desirable qualities as democracy, equality, and social justice. Our misguided obsession with test scores is more appropriate to the meritocracy so effectively satirized by Michael Young. Those who succeed—against the odds, no doubt—do not always benefit from their success. Academically successful working-class college students are on a path taking them away from their home communities into a new world of opportunities and experiences. These opportunities and experiences are linked to an unequal class structure. Their successes are thus premised on the failure of others. Pursuing the American dream now means, inevitably, that others will stumble by the wayside. This is a knowledge that many working-class college students carry with them, whether they can articulate it clearly or not. It can deeply affect the texture of their educational experiences. Their stories and knowledge are stark reminders of the fatal faults of meritocracy.

WORKING-CLASS COLLEGE STUDENTS

What is a working-class college student? When I first proposed to my dissertation committee in 2003 that I wanted to interview working-class college students, I was met with confused silence. Do we still have a working class? And, if we do, what does it have to do with college? Doesn't attendance at college mark one as *not* of the working class? In the 10 years since then, we have witnessed a flourishing of articles, books, and conferences dedicated to exploring the experiences of working-class college students. Awareness of rising inequality combined with greater scrutiny of out-of-control tuition have opened up new questions about college and those who attend it.

The first thing to note about working-class students in four-year colleges and universities is that they are in a unique and ambiguous position. Although the exact figure is hard to obtain, it is unlikely that *more than 3%* of children whose parents have working-class jobs (a majority of Americans) earn a bachelor's degree compared to a majority of youth from the upper middle class (Hurst, 2012). They are thus quite different in attainment from their before-college peers, and even more different in formative experiences from their in-college peers.

This unique and ambiguous position—no longer situated in the working class but not yet, if ever, part of the middle class (more properly, the upper middle class or the professional-managerial class) is key to understanding how class is working and reshaping itself today. Academically successful college students from the working class are the latest exemplars of the American dream, which has always posited, in one form or another, material success through hard work and high character. In the days of Horatio Alger, the upwardly mobile hero advanced through hard *physical* work and "pluck" as well as a healthy dose of luck. The 20th-century captains of industry advanced by starting and growing a business. Today, we are told that anyone can make it if he or she just stays in school long enough. Working-class college students are thus both proof of the continuing existence of the American dream and the power of education *and* stark reproofs of the same. The advance of these students will not and does not lead to advances for the working class, or the elimination of bad jobs, or greater social harmony. As the very few achieve, the vast majority are consigned to a failure allegedly of their own making that is attributed to a lack of either intelligence or perseverance (and sometimes, we simply blame the schools and their teachers). And, further, the very achievement of these students raises questions about what we most value in our society. Why should professionals and managers be the only ones whose standard of living has not seriously eroded in the past thirty years? What is wrong, after all, with being a mechanic, a plumber, or caring for children and the elderly? Our collective choices may be narrowing to "the reservation or Harvard—take your pick," as Carolyn Chute has so eloquently suggested in her story *Faces in the Hands* (Chute 2001, p. 43)

When I listened to working-class college students, I heard the class struggle internalized. A Latina student who started work picking strawberries with her mother and sister at age 13 told me she refused to blame her family for their poverty. She was in college because she was smart but also because she was tired of people's expectations that she would end her life in the fields. A handsome Latino student told me he wanted to prove to his own mother that he, the darkest-skinned of her five children, was the "best" one. A white man confessed the shame of growing up in a trailer, and then confessed his own classism against his former high school friends once he alone began college. A daughter of a union lineman swore to me she would never work in management. A Native American man stated his refusal to ever be anyone's boss. I wondered what kind of job he would find after college. He returned to the reservation to help other smart kids do well in school. I wondered, for what?

I suppose a confession is warranted here. I began my research because I was struggling to understand my own reasons for being in graduate school. Having always been that *one kid* who succeeded while my peers struggled futilely with nonsense tests, I was in a sociology graduate program without having any idea for what purpose. I had jumped through all the hoops thus far. What was next? I had seen my education increasingly alienate me from several members of my family, and I was often wistful for what would have been had I adopted a useful trade instead of taking the path that had been emblazoned with klieg lights for me since kindergarten.

As I listened to the students I interviewed, I heard two types of stories. Some shared with me stories of how their family worked together to survive, how they struggled to send money back to help out a younger brother or sister buy books for school, how they were committed to helping out those still tragically stuck in poverty. Others told a story of dysfunction—of parents who failed to make plans for the future, of educations cut short by early pregnancies or alcohol abuse, of sheer laziness or defeatism. I realized that what I was hearing from the students I interviewed may or may not be the literal truth but were instead *stories that working-class students told themselves* to explain their families and their own social mobility. I also realized that these stories were only necessary for students for whom higher education was something to be explained, something that defined them as different from their families and home communities. I understood what was asked of each and every one of us who was the first in our family to attend college. We had to choose between loyalty to our working-class roots or an adoptive faithfulness to the middle class to which we had long been led. The price of our success was the elimination of our collective identity in favor of the upwardly mobile individual prized by the middle class. We grow up hearing so much about the power of education that we are blinded to this underlying reality. The power of education *to change lives* is equally the power of education *to destroy lives.*

I was not the first person to recognize that working-class students must and do come up with different explanatory narratives and coping strategies, although I was the first to attempt to create a typology (Hurst, 2010). The contributions in *Strangers in Paradise*, perhaps the definitive collection of working-class academics describe in great detail the cultural dislocations of being first in the family to go to college (Ryan & Sackrey, 1984).[1] Although Paul Willis only focused on the "lads" in his well-known study, it is important to remember that the "ear'oles" (those who applied themselves at school and modeled themselves after their middle-class teachers) were primarily working-class boys as well (Willis, 1977). Closer to home, a startling book written by a college-educated working-class journalist located in Philadelphia asks the following questions:

> If you learn the language of the new world, can you still speak with the folks from the old country? Do you cross the border and try to pass for white collar, until you totally assimilate? Do you stay true blue and risk alienation and career stagnation among the middle class? Or do you blend town and gown, creating a hybrid who is, at the end of the day, at home in neither world? (Lubrano, 2004, p. 193)

In my topology, *loyalists* are those students who remain primarily identified with their class of origin, *renegades* are those who reconfigure their class identities so as to match up with the middle class toward which they are moving, and *double agents* are those happy and charismatic few who avoid the primary identification issue by fitting in with both class groups equally. I believe that these are strategies of class navigation in that they are complicated affiliations, allegiances, and stories that people tell themselves while (potentially) in the process of social mobility. The dichotomy between loyalists and renegades may also be seen as the difference between resistance to and accommodation of middle-class culture. It is important to be clear about what I mean when I use the term *middle-class culture*. Although all students may desire the advances and opportunities that come with earning a college degree, some do actively resist the accompanying cultural changes—in particular, the required shift in allegiances, values, and affiliations. Recent educational reforms have detrimentally focused on improving the chances of getting ahead; even if such reforms were working, which they have not been shown to be doing, issues of cultural integrity are ignored.

THE COLLEGE EXPERIENCE FROM THE PERSPECTIVE OF THE WORKING-CLASS STUDENT

Getting to College

To get to college in the first place (and here I am limiting the discussion to the traditional four-year post–high school college attendance), most working-class students will have to do something that sets them apart from their family and friends. Almost always a middle-class mentor will have provided guidance. Often the student will have engaged in reading as a form of escapism from his or her daily life. Against stereotype, perhaps, working-class college students are often *more* prepared for the academic side of college than their peers—after all, they are the ones whose talents in this area have marked them as worthy for advancement. As two authors on university life explain, "the upper-middle class child of moderate ability is today pushed into college no matter what; his working-class or lower-class age-mate is unlikely to go unless he has done well in high school, learns quite easily, and has come to regard books and classrooms as part of his turf" (Jencks & Riesman, 1968, p. 131). Patricia Gándara, exploring the mobility of low-income Chicano/a youth, found that those students who go on to college were great readers, generally placing a higher premium on ideas and information than did their peers (1995, p. 41). A love of reading is a recurrent theme in working-class academic autobiographies (Dews & Law, 1995; Ryan & Sackrey, 1984). This love of reading can be viewed as escapist. One such academic has remarked that books could themselves become "barricades," giving examples of how she idealized the middle class as it appeared in the novels she read (Clancy, 1997, pp. 45–46). Suzanne Sowinska, another working-class academic, describes the importance (and ambiguities) of reading:

> A deep passion for reading, *which is intricately connected to notions of escape, survival, and passing,* is part of the reality of almost all the poor and working-class women in academia that I know. . . . Where there are no family resources to provide us with the necessary financial or cultural prerequisites for our educations, we learn to do just about anything to be able to keep reading books. (1993, pp. 152–153, emphasis added)

Richard Hoggart (1957), Arthur B. Shostak (1969), and Gillian Plummer (2000) have all reflected upon the necessity for working-class academics to "reject" their working-class families and peers. This had led some theorists to argue that rejection of family and neighborhood peer groups is the sine qua non of the working-class academic. As one academically successful working-class student in an earlier study makes clear, rejection of former friends can be the price of success:

> I don't even like running into them now—I don't like seeing them. To be polite I'll stand there and talk to them and ask them what they're doing, because I don't want to seem like a jerk who just changed completely overnight. (Steinitz & Solomon, 1986, p. 185)

Severing ties and rejecting cultural norms can be particularly problematic for racial minorities. Gándara has pointed out that academically-successful

Chicano/a students had an "internal locus of control" that helped them avoid the influence of bad peers (1995, p. 76). On the other hand, she has also argued that the most successful students actually had "dual reference" groups; the fact that they could identify with both (Anglo) middle-class and (Chicano/a) working-class values gave them good practice in transitioning between cultures. Racial identities may sometimes mitigate the transition between classes. Because class is largely ignored in the public discourse at the same time that classist comments are ubiquitous ("white trash," for example) it may be harder for white working-class students to believe there is anything of value in their home culture to retain.

There is often intense pressure on working-class children to adopt middle-class notions of success and proper behavior. In fact, to the extent that middle-class teachers, counselors, and administrators become gatekeepers to higher education, students who fail to exhibit proper deference to the middle class may *not* be able to succeed academically (Brantlinger, 1993, 2003; Carnoy, 1974; Cusick, 1973; Everhart, 1983; Harry & Klingner, 2006; Jackson & Marsden, 1962; Lareau, 1989; Lightfoot, 1978; Valenzuela, 1999; Willis, 1977).

Because of the ambiguous position in which working-class students find themselves, mentorship can be an important factor in college attendance and success. Mentors crucially provide hope, confidence, knowledge of the importance of education, and knowledge about how to get into college (sometimes making calls, doing applications, etc.; Levine & Nidiffer, 1996, pp. 74–77). This last is especially important, given the low quality of college counseling in many low-income high schools (Bowl, 2003; Golden, 2006; Kadi, 1996; McDonough, 1997; Ogbu, 1974; Sacks, 2007). In the face of extreme naïveté surrounding college and the application process, mentorship can be crucial (Dews & Law, 1995; Gándara, 1995; Hurst, 2012). On the other hand, mentors can help drive the wedge between working-class children and their families (Hurst, 2007).

Experiences in College

Dropout rates for working-class college students are quite high, as these students struggle with both financing education and the psychological dislocations associated with social mobility. An early study of black college students in a two-year college located in a strong working-class community demonstrated some of the latter (Weis, 1985). In order to succeed, students were pressured to abandon local ties and friendships with people "of bad influence" (those who might want to borrow money or get high). Complicating this choice was the fact that the benefits of reorientation were doubtful:

> It is only the individual who escapes the underclass via the college. The college does not herald the destruction of a class society; it simply offers

a possible "way out" for those who are willing and able to break with the collective. Given generalized racism in the United States, breaking with the collectivity and obtaining dominant cultural capital may lead to very little (Weis, 1985, p. 127).

The students who succeeded were those who were willing to change aspects of their own culture; they were also those who expressed closeness with faculty mentors. Greater assistance and facilitation by faculty can encourage a reorientation to individualistic notions of success. This raises the interesting question of whether having faculty more aware of these issues might allow students to flourish without rejecting home cultures.

A great deal of literature attests to the middle-class nature of academia. "College life is lived in a middle-class space with middle-class rules," notes Alfred Lubano. "People from the working class must change themselves—or, at least, important parts of themselves—to fit" (2004, p. 81). Most of this has been written with an eye toward explaining the pressures placed upon working-class students and students of color. Some theorists have asserted that these students must conform to middle-class values and norms of behavior in order to succeed academically (Bowl, 2000; Brint & Karabel, 1989, p. 117; Hinchey & Kimmel, 2000, p. 87; Jencks & Riesman, 1967; Jensen, 2004, p. 178; MacKenzie, 1998; Newton, 1971; Sullivan, 2003; Weis, 1985). "Most of the education [that working-class students] receive in university settings will serve only to perpetuate dominant values," notes Donna Langston. "Most privileges are the result of class advantage, and in order to gain these privileges, the working-class students must be willing to become middle-class impersonators" (1993, p. 69). Other theorists (and they have all been working-class academics themselves) agree on the class biases of college culture but argue that students can resist this. Working-class students and students of color are mercilessly pressured to conform to white middle-class values, bell hooks argues, but they need not do so to succeed—hooks herself being a good example of this (hooks, 1994, p. 180) Echoing this, Janet Zandy has argued that working-class academics must do all in their power to resist class cooptation:

> According to the book of success, a working-class identity is intended for disposal. In order to "make it" into the dominant society, one "overcomes" the class circumstances of birth, and moves into the middle and then upper class. Not only is this projected trajectory becoming economically *less* feasible as job opportunities shrink and downward mobility increases, but it is an assumption that reduces human interaction and potential to mere commodity exchange and personal enhancement. (1995, p. 1, emphasis in the original)

Many working-class students thus experience college as a hostile environment. It is important to stress that this is not simply a matter of *difference* but of *hierarchy*, and that conformity to middle-class values of competitive individualism *requires* a ceding of working-class values of collectivity. Langston found the basic operating procedures of academia "offensive" because they were "based on competitive game playing, which in working-class settings would make you an outcast" (1993, p. 67) "We struggle to resist the colonizing capacities of the dominant culture—of succumbing to the lure of the master codes or being trapped as gatekeepers for the owning class," comments Zandy (1995, 11). Similarly, hooks writes,

> One of the clear and present dangers that exists when we move outside our class of origin, our collective ethnic experience, and enter hierarchical institutions that daily reinforce domination by race, sex, and class, is that we gradually assume a mind-set similar to those who dominate and oppress, that we lose critical consciousness because it is not reinforced or affirmed by the environment" (hooks, 1993, p. 105).

Sharon O'Dair (1993, pp. 246–247) has accused colleges of training working-class people to oppress other working-class people. I do not want to diminish the very real and valuable educative qualities of the modern university but merely point out here that colleges have played an historic role in supporting and spreading middle-class ideals and values—ideals and values that some working-class students experience not only as alien but as oppositional to themselves and their families (Cappello, 1995; Charlesworth, 2000).

Working-class college students recognize their peers, faculty, and the academy in general to be of a different class from themselves (Brookfield & Preskill, 1999; Dews & Law, 1995; Ryan & Sackrey, 1984). Michelle M. Tokarczyk and Elizabeth A. Fay ask the question, "We know where the rich can go to learn to understand their lives and their place in society. They can go to Harvard. Where can the poor go?" (1993, p. 18). Paul Rogat Loeb interviewed several hundred college students around the country, some of them from the working- class, and found that, for them, "peers with similar experiences are rare. Intellectual and social codes are foreign. Fellow students talk differently, wear different clothes, cite different cultural references, take distant vacations. Day-to-day discussions remind these students, by their simple unfamiliarity, that their right to belong is tenuous" (1994, p. 64).

Studies also indicate that working-class students are particularly concerned with issues of language (Dews & Law, 1995, p. 5). This is especially marked regarding what is appropriate discourse for classrooms. According to Brookfield and Preskill, the following are middle-class forms of discourse: richness of language, precision of definition, frequent use of authors' names or of specialized terms, fluidity of sentence construction, use of subclauses. Note that all of these are class-based linguistic styles and all are habitually used by middle-class teachers as *evidence of intelligence* (Brookfield & Preskill, 1999, p. 145). Psychologist Barbara Jensen argues that "working class people must do psychosocial back flips through a maze of new rules, new values, and new language" (2004, p. 171).

A major difference between working-class college students and middle-class college students, then, is that "upper class students have a seamless quality to the worlds of friends, family, and school; for working-class students, on the contrary, going to college meant [a break]" (McDonough 1997, p. 137). As English professor Renny Christopher describes it, the experience can be disheartening:

> I suddenly realized what I had been so stolidly ignoring: that all my feelings of displacement came from having traveled from a class that is not supposed to enter higher education . . . right into what was for me a great heart of darkness, out of which eventually came the light of understanding but never any warmth or comfort. (Christopher, 1993, p. 206)

Educators and policy makers must realize that our "college for all" mantra is pushing many bright youth into this "great heart of darkness." This is so fundamentally different from what college and upward social mobility is *supposed* to be that perhaps we should pause a moment and consider why this is so. Much, I believe, comes down to the implicit meritocratic assumptions underlying our educational system. Rather than recognizing an increasingly unequal society for what it is, we patch over injustice by assuming education to be a choice, freely equal and available to all. The fact that college attainment is skewed continuously along the class ladder, that what is normal for the middle class is abnormal for the working class, is ignored. I am reminded of the difference between the emphases, "*anyone* can make it in America" (meaning: birth doesn't matter) and "anyone *can* make it" (meaning: not likely, but anything's possible). We seem to have moved from the former to the latter without realizing the shift in emphasis and meaning.

Working-class college students experience college as foreign territory; some also experience it as *enemy* territory. Whichever one, it is alien and alienating, as Valerie, one of my interviewees, noted:

> They hold out a dream. Come, they told me. It is yours. You are chosen. They didn't tell me, however, that for years, I would no longer feel any sense of belonging, nor any sense of safety. That I didn't belong in the new place, any more than I now belonged in the old. So around every corner of apparent choice lurked doubt and uncertainty.

Given this underlying class frisson that exists in college, what are the actual differences between working-class and middle-class students? What are the specific barriers that working-class students must overcome in order to succeed academically and socially, according to the literature? We've already seen one study suggest that working-class African American students do not enter college with a spirit of possessive individualism; on the contrary, "they live within and survive because of a lived ethic of cooperation" (Weis, 1985, p. 115). Elizabeth A. Armstrong and Laura T. Hamilton (2013) found social isolation and marginality among less privileged college students. Part of this is linked to the need to work. Unlike middle-class families, most working-class families do not have a strong belief that parents should pay for the college education of their children—working-class students are thus "on their own" financially when in college (McDonough, 1997, p. 143). Connected to this, too, is the fact that middle-class parents tend to include college as a natural aspiration for their children, whereas it is something out of the ordinary for working-class parents (Gándara, 1995, pp. 44–45).

Social isolation of less privileged students on college campuses has long been noted by researchers. In the 1960s Harvard University was so aware of the acute differences between what it called "risk-gamble" undergrads and the rest of the student body that it made elaborate arrangements to "break down the communication barriers" that *almost inevitably separate*" the two groups (Ellis & Lane, 1967, p. 252, n. 21, emphasis added). Shostak (1969, pp. 157–158) argued that "the price of social mobility is social isolation."

DEFYING MERITOCRACY

So far we have seen the difficulties experienced by working-class college students. At an earlier time, these difficulties would have remained hidden. This is no longer the case. Even though they are the minority graduates, working-class academics have begun talking among themselves, recognizing the collective nature of their experiences. This has reduced social isolation to some extent. More colleges are running programs specifically designed for first-generation college students, and many of these programs now include insights learned from these discussions. Whereas in the past such a program might have focused exclusively on remedial scholarship, many now attempt to raise awareness about class privilege. This is a revolution—the change from seeing first-generation students as a group with problems to seeing the campus as problematic for some groups. Still, we are far from a national recognition of the effects of inequality on our campuses. In this section I would like to highlight some of the ways that individual working-class college students resist cultural assimilation and hierarchization. I will provide examples of insights that can help us move forward. The final section will then discuss more systematic ways in which we can scrub our educational system of its hierarchizing tendencies by exploring the ideal university from the working-class person's perspective.

One of the ways working-class college students resist co-optation is by rejecting the conceptual hierarchy of mental and manual labor. This is a bit tricky to do, as college is understood as a place of the intellect, preparing students for lives and careers that make use of mental abilities rather than physical ones. Ask any liberal arts professor about the value of vocational training and you will likely hear a "tut-tutting" of disapproval. I once heard a liberal arts dean describe the disfavor with which even "preprofessional" programs such as "law and society" were met with on her campus. To those students whose parents are engaged in "mental labor" careers (i.e., the majority), this distinction is one not commented upon. But to students whose parents work with their hands, this distinction is striking. Often there is a rejection of the idea that people who work with their hands are less smart than those who work in offices. Classist comments about the aptitude, character, and cultural habits of working-class people abound both in and out of the classroom, as abundant examples in the literature attest.

Working-class students may also be silenced, especially when they attempt to describe their own experiences in a way that is against the "universalizing abstract" form appreciated by teachers. Furthermore, they are sometimes made to feel that their experiences are "alien" to everyone else's, and thus, in some ways, not "right." One such student recounted her experiences to Vivyan C. Adair:

> I would actually feel sick to my stomach when I would enter the Sociology of Poverty class that I had enrolled in so that I could understand the social conditions of my own experience. I was made to feel as though I had nothing of value to say, that my experiences and evaluations of class readings were worthless, and even that I was a worthless student who was doomed to failure. (2003, p. 260)

Working-class students notice these things. They also may notice, in a visceral way, arguments and presentation supportive of the employing class. Although many students may take offense at some of the assumptions of the bell curve, several working-class academics have reacted personally to professors' assertions about individual (e.g., genetic) causes of inequality (Megivern, 2003; Mitchell, 2003). To an economics professor who remarked in class, "You have to admit, capitalism is still the best economic system in the world," a working-class student muttered to herself, "It is, if you are not the one dragging your leg across the pavement" (Almanza, 2003, p. 158).

Even if they are aware of middle-class jobs (and many are not), working-class college students may actively reject those job paths. If constantly confronted by "us versus them," some simply choose to remain "us." In interviews I conducted, this was especially the case with students who had prior experience with what I will call "bad bosses"—employers who treated their workers with disdain—and those who had positive experiences with labor unions. Loyalist students in particular are likely to reject a great many possible middle-class occupations. For example, a female student I interviewed had stood on the picket line with her father when she was ten years old. Although she had always loved school, she absolutely rejected any ideas of seeking a job in management. Fortunately for her, she found a job working at a local radio station as a sports announcer. Similarly, the Native American student who chose to teach (for little pay) at a reservation did so after an explicit rejection of the notion of being a boss.

A loyalist who was also considering teaching told me the problem was not being a manager itself but what that means in our society. Having worked many years as an heating, ventilation, and air-conditioning installer for a "bad boss," he was unable and unwilling to put himself in such a position of relative privilege and ease:

> Even if I were to get a professional job—I think the difference between doing a job and feeling a job, I think there's a difference there. And if I were working in an office and I saw the boys come through who were out working on houses I think I would feel guilty. Guilty that I wasn't out there working. Making the money. Doing the work. Yeah, I do have a hard time trying to figure out what class is. I'm not sure there is or isn't one, the working class, but I know there are people out there who break their backs to do the work so other people don't have to.

Not all students want to become part of the middle class, and it is important to recognize that not all students have the same expectations or understandings of "success." Too often, well-intentioned policy makers from more privileged backgrounds fail to differentiate between the desire to get a good education for its own sake and the desire to "move up" in class. The latter is intimately tied in with the meritocratic scheme. Thus, working-class students who define success as education for its own sake are defying meritocracy.

Elsewhere (Hurst, 2010b) I have introduced the loyalist notion of "school-craft." Rather than seeing mental labor as superior to manual labor, these working-class college students argued for a vision of academe as one path among equals, whether this be carpentry, massage therapy, or nineteenth-century German poetry. They did not want college to be a "party place" and social rite of passage for young adults. Instead, they invariably described an ideal academic setting that would be both rigorous and exclusive. The students' understanding of exclusivity was based on interest, not the needs of the job market. College would ideally be free and available to all, but would not economically reward those who participated. That is, the carpenter, the massage therapist, and the person studying nineteenth-century German poetry would all be equally valued and rewarded. In other words, college should have absolutely nothing to do with one's class position (either coming in or going out). This is the antithesis of our current meritocratic ideal.

Unlike our "college for all" mantra, which serves to mask our deep and profound inequality, this ideal college would not be for everyone, even though it would be a real option for anyone. I was at first taken aback when a young woman I was interviewing expressed frustration at an instructor's comment that "everyone should go to college." Why was she frustrated? *By saying that everyone should go, those who don't go are going to be devalued.* Although she herself enjoyed academic work, she was also sure that this was not the case for everyone. These students agreed that having a college degree did not make you "better" than those without one. They were quite adamant about this point and gave several examples of friends and family members who did not go on to college but were "smarter," "more talented," or "better people." Or as one interviewee, Calder, points out, perhaps just more fun to be around:

> I don't see a certificate automatically making someone anything. . . . So you can hold up your degree and you shouldn't be knocked for it, but it doesn't mean that you are better than the guy holding the shovel over there. I mean, no way. Because that guy over there he is probably a lot funnier, and better to be around than you!

CAN WE SAY NO TO MERITOCRACY?

In our headlong rush to educate everyone to the maximum degree, ignoring the many casualties along the way, we are creating a system highly supportive of and responsive to class divisions. As others in this volume ably demonstrate, our obsession with testing narrows considerably what we teach and what we learn. But we should also recognize that the gross distortions produced by our testing regime are not mistakes; they are in fact the way a meritocratic system operates, to the advantages of some at the expense of the many. We are losing sight of the guy with the shovel who is "funnier and better to be around." A classless society would not use tests to sort people. Deserved sorting, even if we could achieve it, is no less stigmatizing than undeserved sorting. At the heart of Young's satire is the *Chelsea Manifesto* of the revolutionaries who would bring down the meritocracy. It is perhaps useful to end with its vision of the classless society as a reminder of how very far we have strayed:

> *The classless society would be one which both possessed and acted upon plural values. Were we to evaluate people, not only according to their intelligence and their education, their occupation and their power, but according to the kindliness and their courage, their imagination and their sensitivity, their sympathy and generosity, there could be no classes. Who would be able to say the scientist was superior to the porter with admirable qualities as a father, the civil servant with unusual skill at gaining prizes to the lorry driver with unusual skill at growing roses? The classless society would also be the tolerant society,*

in which individual differences were actively encouraged as we all passively tolerated, in which full meaning was at last given to the dignity of man. Every human being would then have equal opportunity, not to rise up in the world in the light of any mathematical measure, but to develop his own special capacities for leading a rich life. (Young, 1958/2008, p. 159, italics in the original)

NOTES

1. "Working-class academic" has become the preferred designation of professors with working-class origins. The term has been used and popularized in collections of working-class academic biographies edited by Adair and Dahlberg (2003), Dews and Law (1995), Mahony and Zmroczek (1997), Muzzatti and Samarco (2006), Ryan and Sackrey (1984); Tokarczyk and Fay (1993), and Welsch (2005). It is also the term used by the \Association of Working-Class Academics\, an international organization whose members were once working-class college students.

REFERENCES

Adair, V. C. (2003). Disciplined and punished: Poor women, bodily inscription, and resistance through education. In V. C. Adair & S. L. Dahlberg (Eds.), *Reclaiming class: Women, poverty, and the promise of higher education in America* (pp. 25–52). Philadelphia: Temple University Press.

Adair, V. C., & Dahlberg, S. L. (Eds.). (2003). *Reclaiming class: Women, poverty, and the promise of higher education in America*. Philadelphia: Temple University Press.

Almanza, L. (2003). Seven years in exile. In V. C. Adair & S. L. Dahlberg (Eds.), *Reclaiming class: Women, poverty, and the promise of higher education in America* (pp. 157–168). Philadelphia: Temple University Press.

Anson, R. S. (1987). *Best intentions: The education and killing of Edmund Perry*. New York: Random House.

Aronson, A. (1999). Reversals of fortune: Downward mobility and the writing of nontraditional students. In S. Linkon (Ed.), *Teaching working class* (pp. 39–55). Amherst: University of Massachusetts Press.

Bourdieu, P., & Passeron, J.-C. (1979). *The inheritors: French students and their relations to culture*. Chicago: University of Chicago Press.

Bourke, J. (1994). *Working-class cultures in Britain, 1890–1960: Gender, class, and ethnicity*. London: Routledge.

Bowl, M. (2003). *Non-traditional entrants to higher education: "They talk about people like me."* Stoke-on-Trent, England: Trentham.

Brantlinger, E. A. (1993). *The politics of social class in secondary school: Views of affluent and impoverished youth*. New York: Teachers College Press.

Brantlinger, E. A. (2003). *Dividing classes: How the middle class negotiates and rationalizes school advantage*. New York: Teachers College Press.

Brint, S., & Karabel, J. (1989). *The diverted dream: Community colleges and the promise of educational opportunity in America, 1900–1985*. New York: Oxford University Press.

Brookfield, S., & Preskill, S. (1999). *Discussion as a way of teaching: Tools and techniques for democratic classrooms*. San Francisco: Jossey-Bass.

Cappello, M. (1995). Useful knowledge. In C.L.B. Dews & C. L. Law (Eds.), *This fine place so far from home: Voices of academics from the working class* (pp. 127–136). Philadelphia: Temple University Press.

Carnoy, M. (1974). *Education as cultural imperialism.* New York: D. McKay.

Charlesworth, S. J. (2000). *A phenomenology of working class experience.* Cambridge: Cambridge University Press.

Christopher, R. (1993). Teaching working-class literature to mixed audiences. In S. Linkon (Ed.), *Teaching working class* (pp. 203–222). Amherst: University of Massachusetts Press.

Chute, Carolyn. (2001). Faces in the Hands. In J. Zandy (Ed.), *What we hold in common* (pp. 32–45). New York: Feminist Press.

Clancy, K. (1997). Academic as anarchist: Working-class lives into middle-class culture." In P. Mahony & C. Zmroczek (Eds.), *Class matters: Working-class women's perspectives on social class* (pp. 44–52). London: Taylor and Francis.

Cusick, P. A. (1973). *Inside high school: The students' world.* New York: Holt, Rinehart and Winston.

Dahlberg, S. L. (2003). Families first—But not in higher education: Poor, independent students and the impact of financial aid. In V. C. Adair & S. L. Dahlberg (Eds.), *Reclaiming class: Women, poverty, and the promise of higher education in America* (pp. 169–195). Philadelphia: Temple University Press.

Dews, C.L.B., & Law, C. L. (Eds.). (1995). *This fine place so far from home: Voices of academics from the working class.* Philadelphia: Temple University Press.

Ellis, R. A., & Lane, W. C. (1967). Social mobility and social isolation: A test of Sorokin's disssociative hypothesis. *American Sociological Review, 32*(2), 237–252.

Everhart, R. B. (1983). *Reading, writing and resistance: Adolescence and labor in a junior high school.* Boston: Routledge and Kegan Paul.

Gándara, P. (1995). *Over the ivy walls: The educational mobility of low-income Chicanos.* Albany: State University of New York Press.

Golden, D. (2006). *The price of admission: How America's ruling class buys its way into elite colleges—And who gets left outside the gates.* New York: Crown.

Harry, B., & Klingner, J. (2006). *Why are so many minority students in special education? Understanding race and disability in schools.* New York: Teachers College Press.

Heller, D. E. (2002). *Condition of access: Higher education for lower-income students.* Westport, CT: Praeger.

Hinchey, P., & Kimmel, I. (2000). *The graduate grind: A critical look at graduate education.* New York: Falmer.

Hoggart, R. (1957). *The uses of literacy: Changing patterns in English mass culture.* Fair Lawn, NJ: Essential Books.

hooks, b. (1993). Keeping close to home: Class and education. In M. M. Tokarczyk & E. A. Fay (Eds.), *Working-class women in the academy: Laborers in the knowledge factory* (pp. 99–111). Amherst, MA: University of Massachusetts Press.

hooks, b. (1994). *Teaching to transgress: Education as the practice of freedom.* New York: Routledge.

Hurst, A. L. (2007). Telling tales of oppression and dysfunction: Narratives of class identity reformation. *Qualitative Sociology Review, 3*(2), 82–104.

Hurst, A. L. (2010a). *The burden of academic success: Managing working-class identities in college.* Lanham, MD: Lexington.

Hurst, A. L. (2010b). Schoolcraft vs. becoming somebody: Competing visions of higher education among working-class college students. *Qualitative Studies, 1*(2), 76–91.

Hurst, A. L. (2012). *College and the working class: What it takes to make it.* Rotterdam, Netherlands: Sense.

Jackson, B., & Marsden, D. (1962). *Education and the working class: Some general themes raised by a study of 88 working-class children in a northern industrial city.* London: Routledge and Kegan Paul.

Jencks, C., & Riesman, D. (1968). *The academic revolution.* Garden City, NY: Doubleday.

Jenkins, R. (1983). *Lads, citizens, and ordinary kids: Working-class youth lifestyles in Belfast.* London: Routledge and Kegan Paul.

Jensen, B. (2004). Across the great divide: Crossing classes and clashing cultures. In M. Zweig (Ed.), *What's class got to do with it?* (pp. **168**). Ithaca, NY: Cornell University Press.

Kadi, J. (1996). *Thinking class: Sketches from a cultural worker.* Boston: South End.

Langston, D. (1993). Who am I now? The politics of class identity. In M. M. Tokarczyk & E. A. Fay (Eds.), *Working-class women in the academy: Laborers in the knowledge factory* (pp. 60–72). Amherst, MA: University of Massachusetts Press.

Lareau, A. (1989). *Home advantage: Social class and parental intervention in elementary education.* London: Falmer.

Levine, A., & Nidiffer, J. (1996). *Beating the odds: How the poor get to college.* San Francisco: Jossey-Bass.

Lightfoot, S. L. (1978). *Worlds apart: Relationships between families and schools.* New York: Basic Books.

Loeb, P. R. (1994). *Generation at the crossroads: Apathy and action on the American campus.* New Brunswick, NJ: Rutgers University Press.

Lubrano, A. (2004). *Limbo: Blue-collar roots, white-collar dreams.* Hoboken, NJ: John Wiley and Sons.

Lynch, K., & O'Neill, C. (1994). The colonization of social class in education. *British Journal of Sociology of Education, 15,* 307–324.

MacKenzie, L. (1998). A pedagogy of respect: Teaching as an ally of working-class college students. In A. Shepard, J. McMillan, & G. Tate (Eds.), *Coming to class: Pedagogy and the social class of teachers* (pp. **94**). Portsmouth, NH: Boynton/Cook.

MacLeod, J. (1995). *Ain't no makin' it: Aspirations and attainment in a low-income neighborhood.* Boulder, CO: Westview.

Maguire, M. (1997). Missing links: Working-class women of Irish descent. In P. Mahony & C. Zmroczek (Eds.), *Class matters: Working-class women's perspectives on social class* (pp. 87–101). London: Taylor and Francis.

Mahony, P., & Zmroczek, C. (Eds.). (1997). *Class matters: Working-class women's perspectives on social class.* London: Taylor and Francis.

McDonough, P. (1997). *Choosing colleges: How social class and schools structure opportunity.* Albany: State University of New York Press.

Megivern, D. (2003). Not by myself alone: Upward bound with family and friends. In V. C. Adair & S. L. Dahlberg (Eds.), *Reclaiming class: Women, poverty, and the promise of higher education in America* (pp. 119–130). Philadelphia: Temple University Press.

Mitchell, T. (2003). If I survive, it will be despite welfare reform: Reflections of a former welfare student. In V. C. Adair & S. L. Dahlberg (Eds.), *Reclaiming class: Women, poverty, and the promise of higher education in America* (pp. 113–118). Philadelphia: Temple University Press.

Newton, R. M. (1971). *An exploratory study of a small group of disadvantaged students' first year on a college campus* (Doctoral thesis, University of Oregon).

O'Dair, S. (1993). Vestments and vested interests: Academia, the working class, and affirmative action. In M. M. Tokarczyk & E. A. Fay (Eds.), *Working-class women in the academy: Laborers in the knowledge factory* (pp. 239–250). Amherst: University of Massachusetts Press.

Ogbu, J. U. (1974). *The next generation: An ethnography of education in an urban neighborhood.* New York: Academic Press.

Plummer, G. (2000). *Failing working-class girls.* Stoke-on-Trent, England: Trentham.

Reay, D. (1997). The double-bind of the "working-class" feminist academic: The success of failure or the failure of success? In P. Mahony & C. Zmroczek (Eds.), *Class matters: Working-class women's perspectives on social class* (pp. 18–29). London: Taylor and Francis.

Rose, M. (1989). *Lives on the boundary: The struggles and achievements of America's underprepared.* New York: Free Press.

Ryan, J., & Sackrey, C. (1984). *Strangers in paradise: Academics from the working class.* Boston: South End.

Sacks, P. (2007). *Tearing down the gates: The class divide in American education.* Berkeley and Los Angeles: University of California Press.

Sennett, R. & Cobb, J. (1972). *The hidden injuries of class.* New York: Knopf.

Shostak, A. B. (1969). *Blue-collar life.* New York: Random House.

Smith, D. N. (1974). *Who rules the universities? An essay in class analysis.* New York: Monthly Review Press.

Sowinska, S. (1993). Yer own motha wouldna reckanized ya: Surviving and apprenticeship in the "knowledge factory." In M. M. Tokarczyk & E. A. Fay (Eds.), *Working-class women in the academy: Laborers in the knowledge factory* (pp. 148–164). Amherst: University of Massachusetts Press.

Steinitz, V. A. & Solomon, E. R. (1986). *Starting out: Class and community in the lives of working-class youth.* Philadelphia: Temple University Press.

Sullivan, N. (2003). Academic constructions of "white trash," or how to insult poor people without really trying. In V. C. Adair & S. L. Dahlberg (Eds.), *Reclaiming class: Women, poverty, and the promise of higher education in America* (pp. 53–66). Philadelphia: Temple University Press.

Tokarczyk, M. M., & Fay, E. A. (Eds.). (1993). *Working-class women in the academy: Laborers in the knowledge factory.* Amherst: University of Massachusetts Press.

Valenzuela, A. (1999). *Subtractive schooling: U.S.-Mexican youth and the politics of caring.* Albany: State University of New York Press.

Weis, L. (1985). *Between two worlds: Black students in an urban community college.* Boston: Routledge and Kegan Paul.

Welsch, K. (2005). *Those winter Sundays: Female academics and their working-class parents.* Lanham, MD: University Press of America.

Willis, P. E. (1977). *Learning to labor: How working-class kids get working-class jobs.* Farnborough, England: Saxon House.

Wray, M., & Newitz, A. (1997). *White trash: Race and class in America.* New York: Routledge.

Young, M. (2008). *The rise of the meritocracy.* New Brunswick, NJ: Transaction. Original work published 1958

Zandy, J. (1995). *Liberating memory: Our work and our working-class consciousness.* New Brunswick, NJ: Rutgers University Press.

2 Reforming the Schooling of Neoliberal, Perpetual Zombie Desire

William M. Reynolds

[T]he highest mission and overriding purpose of schooling was to prepare students at different levels, to take their places in the corporate
order. The banking or transmission theory of school knowledge, which
Freire identified more than thirty years ago as the culprit standing in
the way of critical consciousness, has returned with a vengeance

—Stanley Aronowitz, "Introduction," in Paulo Freire, *Pedagogy of
Freedom: Ethics, Democracy, and Civic Courage*

Ours is a consumers' society, in which culture, in common with
the rest of the world experiencedby consumers, manifests itself as a
repository of goods intended for consumption, all competing for the
unbearable fleeting and distracted attention of potential clients, all
trying to hold that attention for more than just the blink of an eye.

—Zygmunt Bauman, *Culture in a Liquid Modern World*

Zombies don't read. They ain't hooked on phonics. So give it a rest.

—*House of the Dead 2* (Michael Hurst, director)

INTRODUCTION

Despite all of the discussions, programs, and governmental intrusion over
the last hundred years, there has only been a type of recycling rather than
a bone fide reform in—or reform of—education. The primary purpose of
recycling in school is and has remained the production of worker/consumer
citizens (workers can be defined in the traditional sense of material production or immaterial production; see Hardt & Negri, 2000). Business ideology has been inherent in these recycled programs from social efficiency
efforts in the early 1900s to "life adjustment" programs, to career education, to teacher effectiveness programs, to Madeline Hunter lesson plans,
to outcome-based education, to standardization and high-stakes testing.
Contemporary schooling, which is not education, has resulted in students
with a rather zombielike desire to consume products of all kinds, from
cell phones to fast food burgers. American schooling has become a process of information exchange and accumulation. Schooling holds students

responsible for remembering discrete bits of information in the same form in which they were given that information. They are held responsible for demonstrating their memorization of this information on standardized exams. This is not education that fosters imagination, creativity, critical thinking, or any type of complicated conversations. Even this schooling is viewed as a commodity to be consumed.

This chapter outlines the history of the recycling of the "businessification" of schooling. The consequences of this recycling on the attitudes, abilities, dis/positions and desires of 21st-century students are explicated. There is, indeed, need for educational reform, not the continual recycling of the same neoliberal agenda.

Oftentimes at this historical and global moment of neoliberal "free market fundamentalism" (a term coined by George Soros), with its cruelty, surveillance, and greed, I believe I am witnessing the dismantling of education.[1] I dwell these days in disbelief and anger. As Peter McLaren's (2006) book title so aptly states, I am filled with rage and hope. The U.S. is engaging successfully in moving public education with standardized curriculum, standardized tests, standardized or scripted lesson plans, and standardized objectives to a place at which schools develop, at best, into training camps for the global corporate economy. "Shopocalypse" now describes American schools as well as the global society.[2] It is ironic that at least one of the many zombie films, *Dawn of the Dead* (2004), is set in a shopping mall. Insatiable consumers are portrayed in the setting of the cathedral of consumption. The mall has become the center of our postmodern existence:

> Meanwhile we live in the present historical conjuncture that is corporatized and our cathedrals of spiritual fulfillment are the shopping malls. Families now ritually travel on Saturday or Sunday to their local malls or outlet malls not only to partake of the products of consumer culture, but also to acquire the lifestyle and ambiance that the brand names have to offer. (Reynolds, 2004, p. 20)

This consumer culture has led to consequences for education as well. No one or no institution stands outside consumer culture. We may critique it, but within the next hour even most of the staunchest critics are shopping online to find just the right bargain to purchase. No one stands outside the hegemony of consumer culture.

As Henry A. Giroux notes, "Conservative policies have systematically disinvested in public schools, turning them largely into dull testing centers for middle-class students and warehousing units and surveillance centers for working-class and poor youth of color" (2009, p. 14). This is done all in the effort for some type of continual monitoring in the name of accountability that wallows in its praise of high scores on high-stakes tests of which schools and teachers can be judged as being successes or failures. Schools and universities have become insidious corporations whose grandiose goal is to make a profit—whether that profit manifests itself in public schools with increased funding because of high test scores or in the universities by increasing the number of student credit hours. Universities have shining buildings, beautiful lawns, and soulless organization. Of course, efficiency at achieving these goals is praised, and ideas that stray from this path are condemned and in many cases punished. Heinz Sunker and Hans-Uwe Otto write,

> Conformist behavior is established far more by the withdrawal of autonomous control over practical and cultural resources, without which personal expression is impossible. These resources of self-expression are to an increasing extent subordinated to the regularities of capitalist development. (1997, pp. 9–10)

As a result of this development, students view schooling as a path to a job and view the world with a consumer consciousness. Schooling at all levels is exclusively viewed as something to be consumed, whether it is in terms of points, grades, courses, degrees, or even pizzas. Schooling becomes the memorization of discreet bits of information to be regurgitated on tests and then in most cases forgotten. It becomes something to be consumed and endured, not a haven for critical thought and discussion. Absent is a devotion to study, learning, erudition, complicated conversations, and reading for the sake of their transformative powers. Studying and reading become focused on only one goal—better test scores or the accumulation of information. Curriculum constructed by the state has become a lifeless information artifact to be downloaded into the students and recited by them. Paulo Freire has described it as the epitome of banking; it is banking with strict accountability for the deposits. The passive role students accept maintains their thinking in the magical conforming stage, and a critical consciousness is not developed. As Freire suggests, it is a fragmented view of reality:

> The more students work at storing the deposits entrusted to them, the less they develop the critical consciousness which would result from their intervention in the world as transformers of the world. The more completely they accept the passive role imposed on them, the more they tend simply to adapt to the world as it is and to the fragmented view of reality deposited in them. (2000, p. 73)

SCHOOLING IN THE PRESENT TENSE

As William F. Pinar asserts, "The present historical conjuncture in education is a nightmare" (2004, p. 3). This nightmare exists as standardized state-developed curriculum, scripted lesson plans, predetermined state objectives, computerized reading tests (constructed by the Accelerated

Reader brand of software), and state-mandated tests (developed by very lucrative textbook/testing corporations such as Pearson) to make sure that teachers are compliantly implementing and depositing what they are told to implement and deposit:

> In recent years, the creation and scoring of K–12 tests has become big business. Between 1955 and 1970, sales of standardized tests grew gradually from $5 million to $25 million (both in 1988 dollars). Since then, sales have increased dramatically, reaching $130 million in 1990 and jumping to $234 million in 2000. Even these figures understate the industry's size. A 1993 Boston College study estimates that the K–12 standardized testing industry may be four to six times larger—perhaps as much as $1.5 billion a year—when scoring and score reporting are include, along with customized tests produced under contract with individual states. (Gluckman, 2002, p. 1)

There is even the suggestion, and various implementations of, rewarding teachers monetarily for achieving higher test scores or on different forms of student achievement—that is, pay for performance. On January 12, 2010, the governor of the state of Georgia, Sonny Perdue, announced his plans to "enhance" the method in which teachers would be compensated. In this new plan there was the concept that teachers could and should be rewarded on the basis of a "performance-based pay" option. According to the plan, this would enable teachers to earn much higher salaries based on their students' "growth" (State of Georgia, 2010a). This, of course, translates into the students' scores on high-stakes tests. The business ideology is evident in this concept, and Perdue stated this in his initial announcement. There is an obvious anti-intellectual orientation to this plan; the value is in the product:

> "Our current system only incentivizes the degree, not the degree to which students learn," said Governor Perdue. "We must encourage our best and brightest to enter the teaching profession and must reward effective teachers in order to retain them in Georgia classrooms. Student achievement must be our driving force and our compensation model must reflect that focus." (State of Georgia, 2010a)

This is pay based on information, not knowledge. Gilles Deleuze speaks to this concept of information:

> And then there is the second idea, to do with information. Because here again, language is presented to us a basically informative, and information as basically an exchange. Once again, information is measured in abstract units. But it is doubtful whether the schoolmistress, explaining how something works or teaching spelling is transmitting information.

> She's instructing, she's delivering precepts. And children are supplied with syntax like workers being given tools, in order to produce utterances conforming to accepted meanings. (1995, p. 41)

Instruction, information and performance compensation are the manner in which we school. All of us are being immersed in the proper, correct, and accountable utterances. Perdue made this evident in his address to the Georgia state legislature and in his education legislation. The emphasis on information is clearly evident; valid data is essential:

> We must ensure integrity in our tests. This becomes even more important when we tie teacher evaluations to student improvement, said Governor Perdue. Valid data is the key to making good public decisions and developing a credible system of rewarding our top educators. (State of Georgia, 2010b)

This "control" is evident in all aspects of schooling, from zero-tolerance discipline policies to the textbooks. Another example of this pay-for-information-retention plan can be found in the New Jersey Department of Education. In May 2010, commissioner of education Bret Schundler determined that he would actively pursue merit pay as a way of rewarding teacher performance. As was reported later that year,

> The Governor [Chris Christie] has made it clear that student performance, and the ability of teachers to drive it, are what matter when we make decisions about who we hire to instruct our children. He's also made it clear that student performance data is a critical component of measuring the success of our teachers. This stance is unprecedented in recent New Jersey history. Great teachers are essential to turning around New Jersey's broken schools. The Governor's focus on hiring and compensating excellent teachers, and removing underperformers, puts kids first, treats teachers like professionals accountable for their performance, and helps pave the way for an aggressive reform agenda. (State of New Jersey, 2010)

Even President Obama is pushing the agenda of pay for performance:

> Obama Tuesday declared it's time to start "rewarding excellence" in the classroom and pushed for performance-based pay for deserving teachers—and giving the hook to educators who fail. "It is time to start rewarding good teachers and stop making excuses for bad ones." (Bazinet, 2009)

It is rather apparent that the factory notion of quality control is at work. Teachers will be rewarded based on their compliance to the testing regime and their unquestioning allegiance to it. And their pay will be determined by the quality of their product. Even the very textbooks in use are correlated with the elaborately constructed high-stakes system. This evolves, no doubt, from the fact that most of the major testing companies are also textbook publishers. Of course, school districts buy into these textbooks and tests and spend enormous sums of money on them. This phenomenon is also in its initial stages in undergraduate teacher education programs—that is, the movement toward standardization. In this chapter, however, I want to focus on public schooling. This chapter is not written out of some type of misguided nostalgia for what never was, but with hope about the ways education could and ought to be. In fact, getting into debates about the high-stakes testing phenomenon is unproductive. The point is to deconstruct the current milieu of zombie consumer education to allow for the possibility to create something new. These dead-end debates usually return to whether the poor results on a certain test can be traced back to incompetent teachers, slow students, certain questions on the test, or inadequate schools. There is rarely a discussion of the whole nature of the meaning of schooling and testing. The discussion of the meaning of education is nowhere to be found in the current frenzied rush to accountability and free market ideology. As William F. Pinar notes,

> Accountability is the face of fascism in America today. Using the business model, politicians and others have made the common-sensual (if anti-educational) argument that all that matters is the "bottom line"—scores on standardized tests—and in the process converted the school into a business, a skill-and-knowledge factory (or corporation), but a business—not an educational institution—nonetheless. (2004, pp. 163–164)

Patricia Burch discusses this idea that neoliberal free market economics has permeated schooling. Her book *Hidden Markets: The New Education Privatization* (2009) sheds new light on the extent of the intrusion of the market into education. Education is subsumed in a free market fundamentalism of sorts. As Soren Ambrose notes,

> The basic tenet of free market fundamentalism is that the most efficient way to deliver services and goods, to keep an economy humming, to provide for members of society, and even, in its more advanced formulations, to maintain social order, is to conceive of virtually all human activity in commercial terms, with values negotiated between the contracting parties without outside interference, according to the laws of supply and demand. The market fundamentalist seeks to solve any imbalance by trying to reduce the role of government and expand the options of those operating in the market."
>
> The neo-liberal agenda of reducing the size of the federal government has more to do with disallowing government intervention in business

than with concerns about the cost of big government. Market funda-
mentalists insist that failures to provide adequately for people result
not so much from imbalances in wealth or power, but in restrictions
placed on the 'invisible hand' of market logic—restrictions created by
governments becoming economic actors who do not obey market logic,
or through government's efforts to regulate private economic actions.
(Soren Ambrose, quoted in Reynolds and Webber, 2009, p. 2)

Schooling has become ingrained in this free market ideology. The needs
of the market are paramount. "The center of gravity in public policy is
shifting," writes Burch. "Ideologies of neo-liberalism are remaking educational policy to fit the needs of the market. The ideas are pushed as helping public education although the arguments have little empirical basis"
(Burch, 2009, p. xii).

One of the masks of the free market is privatization. The movement
toward privatization in American society is widespread, from discussions
of privatizing social security, health care, and other social services to the
use of private corporations in the war in Iraq. Private companies took over
health services, food services and, in the case of Blackwater, combat services in that war. Schooling has not escaped this market-driven phenomenon. Private companies are making inroads into public education. So, the
testing craze is conjoined with private companies that infiltrate the public
schools. Most of these privatization efforts occur unnoticed by the general
public. Burch identifies some of the major companies that are involved
with education, describing them as "specialty service companies"; these
companies are also involved in textbook and test publication. There are
the established companies: Houghton Mifflin (1832), Kaplan (1938), and
the Princeton Review (1981). New companies have emerged in the late
1990s and into the 21st century: Blackboard (1997), K12 (1999), Connections Academy (2001), and Educate (2003; Burch, 2009). The companies
divide public schooling into market segments. Burch classifies these segments as test development and preparation (Harcourt Education, Riverside
Publishing, NCS Pearson, Houghton Mifflin, Kaplan, McGraw-Hill, and
the Princeton Review);[3] data management and analysis (Houghton Mifflin
and Pearson);[4] remedial services (Educate/Sylvan Educational Solutions),
Huntington Learning Centers, Club 2, and Kuman North America);[5] and
online content (Connections Academy, Renaissance Learning, K12, eCol-
lege, and Blackboard; see Burch, 2009, p. 24).[6] So privatization of schooling is yet another link with the free market corporatization of schooling.
Even in the 2008 presidential election both candidates demonstrated that
they had become part of the discourse of standards, accountability, and
the market.

The 2008 presidential election between Barack Obama and John
McCain manifested the entrenchment of the banking, testing, and information model of education. Both candidates discussed the importance of

"standards" (read: standardization) and testing. Obama's plan for federal assistance to schools was interlaced with the language of business:

> They will promote the use of performance metrics—including student achievement, college and high school graduation rates and school report cards—to evaluate discretionary federal education spending programs. Independent performance teams will be tasked with analyzing and reforming underperforming federal programs, and will have the authority to demand improvement reviews within 30 days, make necessary reforms, fire bad managers and replace them with high-performing managers from other agencies, or shift the program's budget to other programs if necessary. And successful programs will have their funding expanded, in partnership with Congress. (Obama & Biden, 2007, p. 4)

McCain's educational agenda did not shrink from the accountability and standards mantra:

> We must continue to set standards and hold schools accountable for their performance. . . . We should never shrink from the truth, or seek to soften accountability where schools are failing in their most basic responsibility. Where schools fail to meet Annual Yearly Progress, they have failed students, parents and communities. (McCain, 2007, p. 1)

In 2008 Americans were left with little choice when it came to the vision of schools in the 21st century. Schools were businesses.

Clearly, the appointment of Arne Duncan to the position of secretary of education is a clear indication that the agenda is the business of schooling. Duncan's former position with Chicago Public Schools was that of chief executive officer; this is clearly the intermingling of business language with the public school system. His degree from Harvard University was in sociology; apparently an education degree is not sufficient or worthwhile. Duncan's agenda for schooling is clear: he supports the notions of higher standards for public schools. But in a speech given at the Teachers College of Columbia University on October 22, 2009, titled "Teacher Preparation: Reforming an Uncertain Profession," Duncan emphasized the need for accountability and standards to be infused into teacher education programs:

> In the end, I don't think the ingredients of a good teacher preparation are much of a mystery anymore. Our best programs are coherent, up-to-date, research-based, and provide students with subject mastery. They have a strong and substantial field-based program in local public schools that drives much of the course work in classroom management and student learning and prepares students to teach diverse pupils in high-needs settings. And these programs have a shared vision of what constitutes good teaching and best practices—including a single-minded

focus on improving student learning and using data to inform instruction. (Duncan, 2009, p. 1)

In his 2010 State of the Union address, President Obama stressed the importance of education. The White House website assures the public that new emphasis in education will promote *excellence* (a rather overused term in education) and reform. As part of this reform, a new framework is proposed for the Elementary and Secondary Education Act that will stress testing and accountability. President Obama has also called for major changes to the No Child Left Behind Act; in this new agenda the focus will be on defining the standards that students "need to learn in earlier grades to advance successfully toward high school graduation" (Dillon, 2010, p 2). This is in line with the Race to the Top program unveiled in July 2009, the major focus for the Obama educational agenda:

> The centerpiece of the Obama administration's education reform efforts is the $4.35 billion Race to the Top Fund, a national competition which will highlight and replicate effective education reform strategies in four significant areas: Adopting internationally benchmarked standards and assessments that prepare students for success in college and the workplace; Recruiting, developing, rewarding, and retaining effective teachers and principals; Building data systems that measure student success and inform teachers and principals how they can improve their practices; and Turning around our lowest-performing schools. (U.S. Department of Education, 2009)

The State of Georgia received $400 million over four years to implement its Race to the Top plan. Georgia's plan elaborated on the criteria of the Race to the Top agenda—in particular, the pay-for-performance agenda:

> Recommendations [that] focus on strengthening traditional and alternative preparation programs for teachers and leaders, supporting teachers more effectively in the classroom, evaluating teachers and leaders with consistent and objective criteria that inform instruction, and rewarding great teachers and leaders with performance-based salary increases. (Georgia Department of Education, 2010)

This testing, accountability, and standards fetish is part of a larger issue—that of the globalization of corporate capitalism and its extended power relations. Teachers in this standardized testing phenomenon are, as Michael Apple has discussed, "deskilled":

> In other words, [deskilling] is to separate conception from execution. The control of knowledge enables management to plan; ideally, the worker

should merely carry these plans out to the specifications, at the pace set by people away from the actual point of production. (1995, p. 130)

As Giroux stated so succinctly in *Teachers as Intellectuals: Toward a Critical Pedagogy of Learning*, teachers have become "clerks of the empire" (1988, p. 91). Teachers who presently implement a state-developed curriculum that is assessed via a testing agency–or state-developed test and are held increasingly accountable for student performance on such tests are serving in a role that has certainly become clerk-like.

THE PERSISTENCE OF THE FACTORY MODEL

Amazingly, this tinkering with business ideology and management in the "new" educational agenda harkens back to the turn of the 20th century and industrialization with the concepts developed by Fredrick Winslow Taylor (1911) known as scientific management. Applying business principles to education is nothing new (see Reynolds, 2003). These educational reforms of the 21st century are not only about business but also about schemes of management and control of the very labor processes and the intellectual abilities of teachers—and, consequently, their students. The concept of management has morphed into a more all-encompassing and consistent-presence in the current historical moment with corporate competitiveness seizing upon education. Deleuze warned us about business and education in the 1990s:

> Even the state education system has been looking at the principle of "getting paid for results": in fact, just as businesses are replacing factories, *school* is being replaced by *continuing education* and exams by continuous assessment. It is the surest way of turning education into a business. (1995, p. 179, emphasis in the original)

Deleuze certainly foreshadowed the daily experiences of teachers and students in American schools at the present time. But again, there is a haunting presence or trace of old management ideology in the present, particularly with the continued application of Taylorian notions of management. It is ironic that Taylorism would be discussed in the 21st century, because Taylor's principles were discussed in the early 20th century and applied to factories and the management of workers. The irony here is that we and our students are living in a postmodern culture and yet we are schooling them in a modernist paradigm, which is completely inappropriate for our time.

Taylor attempted to make it appear as if scientific principles were being applied to management, whereas in actuality his methods were positing ideas for more effective covert and overt control. As Harry Braverman writes,

[Taylorism] does not attempt to discover and confront the case of this condition but accepts that it is an inexorable given, a "natural" condition. It investigates not labor in general, but the adaption of labor to the needs of capital (global corporate economy). It enters the workplace (read education) not as a representative of science, but as the representative of management masquerading in the trappings of science. (1974, p. 86)

Taylor wanted to do more than simply maintain authoritative control over the worker (the teacher/student); he also wanted to take any decision about the work away from the worker (the teacher). Braverman makes this point:

Management, he insisted, could only be a limited and frustrated experience as long as it left to the worker (teacher) any decision about the work. His system was simply a means for management to achieve control over the actual mode of performance of every labor activity from the simplest to the most complicated. (1974, p. 90)

Taylor wanted control over the workforce by having control over the "decisions that are made in the course of work."

Braverman distills Taylor's ideas into three basic principles. There is an eerie similarity to the present orientation in education. These three basic principles are obvious in the 21st century agenda(s), both at the state and federal levels in education. The parallels are obvious and striking:

1. The dissociation of the labor process from the skills of the workers
2. The separation of conception from execution
3. Use of monopoly over knowledge to control each step of the labor process (Braverman, 1974, pp. 113–119)

The first principle of the process of scientific management is that the knowledge of the labor process should be taken out of the hands and minds of the laborers and kept in the hands and minds of management. I would suggest that *state* can be substituted for *management* in all of the following examples. So the process depends less on workers than on management Braverman writes, "The managers assume the burden of gathering together all of the traditional knowledge which in the past has been possessed by the workmen and then classifying, tabulating, and reducing this knowledge to rules, laws, and formulae" (1974, p. 112)

The second principle takes all the conception, planning, and brainwork away from the laborer and places it in the hands of management. This is because, as Braverman so aptly states, "If the workers' execution is guided by their own conception, it is not possible, as we have seen, to enforce upon them either the methodological efficiency or the working place desired by capital" (p.113). As a direct result of this, the laborers not only lose control of the instruments of production but also their own work and the manner of its performance:

> The final and most insidious principle of management (control) is that every single step of the laborer's work is manipulated. The work of every workman is fully planned out by the management at least one day in advance, and each man receives in most cases complete written instructions, describing in detail the task which he is to accomplish, as well as the means to be used in doing the work. This task specifies not only what is to be done, but how it is to be done and the exact time allowed for doing it. (p. 118)

The worker (teacher/student) has become controlled. She is simply carrying out a type of prepackaged task. The managers (the state) become, then, the taskmasters (see Reynolds, 2003). When we examine the scripted materials (lesson plans), the premade PowerPoint presentations, the scripted curriculum packages, the performance salary benefits, the standardized tests, and the packaged test preparation materials, it is obvious that a Taylorian ghost haunts 21st-century education. Freire writes, "The development of the so-called teacher-proof materials is a continuation of experts' authoritarianism, of their total lack of faith in the possibility that teachers can know and create" (2005, p. 15).

This business ideology was deployed through the majority of the 20th century and into the 21st. The only deviations were in the 1930s, with a slight detour with progressives in education, and in the 1960s, during an era of experimentation in schooling and curriculum. The plethora of consumer-orientated, corporate laced, market-driven programs and curricular developments in the schools morphed through the 1950s (life-adjustment education); the early 1960s (post-Sputnik education, including the "new math"); the 1970s (president Richard Nixon's agenda of career education and "back to basics"); the 1980s (the post–Nation at Risk era and the "new basics"); the 1990s (Goals 2000, developed by governors and business leaders), and into the 21st century (No Child Left Behind and Race to the Top).[7]

It is the industrial factory model of labor; Fordism has been replaced by global corporatism or transnational capitalism (Giroux, 2004). The system has also been named the prison-industrial complex. This results in a situation in which corporations and management have slipped the bonds of nation-state regulation. It has become part of the process that Giroux (2004) discusses that shifts regulation and management to a type of capitalist hegemony over all aspects of our everyday lives. Giroux states,

> Part of this shift has to be understood within the emerging forces of transnational capitalism and a global restructuring in which the economy is separated from politics and corporate power is largely removed

from the control of nation-states. Within the neoliberal register, globalization represents the triumph of the economy over politics and culture
. . . and the hegemony of capital over all other domains of life. (Giroux,
2004, p. 59)

Meanwhile, American schooling dwells with apparent stubborn steadfast-
ness to the factory notion of production and the consequent factory notion
of quality control. We manage to produce global consumers, not critical
citizens. We produce citizens of the global empire who are mostly concerned with the newest item they can consume rather than understanding
and challenging the complete envelopment of society into a type of zombie
buyer. We have become consumers who are bargain smart, but cluelessly
so. We approach schooling the same way—consuming it, always looking
for a bargain, like an online sale. Educational experts are obsessively concerned with "valid data" in terms of test results and national standards and
not about the ability to critically think about ourselves and the society in
which we live.

AN EMPIRE OF PERPETUAL ZOMBIE
CONSUMERS AND HOPE

It is schooling's collusion in the building of empire, the phenomenon discussed by Michael Hardt and Antonio Negri, who claim that *empire* is the
name given to the center of the globalization of all productive networks
because it

> casts its widely inclusive net to try to envelop all power relations within
> its world order—and yet at the same time it deploys a powerful police
> function against the new barbarians and the rebellious slaves who
> threaten its order. (2000, p. 20)

It is schooling as the preparation of students as global consumers in and
of the empire. Contemporary schooling is not concerned with the development of human beings with critical consciousness, but with inculcating
the necessary dispositions and attitudes that maintain and continue capitalist consumerism. It is the fetishization of testing and memorization to
perpetuate the continuation or perhaps recovery of contemporary power
relations and privilege. In a 2007 interview, Joe L. Kincheloe addressed
these issues, stating,

> What's going on in education around the world is part of what I
> oftentimes call a recovery movement—a recovery of dominant power;
> whether it be colonial power with new forms of colonialism; whether
> it be gendered power with new forms of patriarchy; racial power with

new forms of the recovery of white supremacy; whether it be class power, with new forms of class elitism and of global empire that exist, and unfortunately no matter where we go now, education plays the role of helping to support that empirical behemoth. (Kincheloe, 2007)

Finally, it is what Zygmunt Bauman discusses in a chapter on fashion in *Culture in a Liquid Modern World*. Fashion can be used as an example of what I want to call *perpetual consumerism*. Whereas Bauman is discussing fashion, his thoughts are applicable to all consumer items and to school program recycling and the students it "produces." This schooling in perpetual zombie consumerism is never-ending:

> Today's tokens of "being ahead" have to be acquired quickly, while those of yesterday must be just as swiftly confined to the scrapheap. The injunction to keep an eye on "what has already gone out of fashion" must be observed as consciously as the obligation to keep on top of what is (at this moment) new and up to date. (Bauman, 2011, p. 22)

These are the zombie consumers that our schooling and the free market ideology of neoliberalism produce; they are not active citizens who engage in the process of democracy and social justice but insatiable buyers who want the latest products. Schooling, with its test-driven, factory-model ideology, turns our children into compliant zombielike purchasers who wait impatiently for the next new thing. The free market depends on them. Those who would propose reform of the present system of schooling have to understand the historical and contemporary dilemma that years of recycling has produced. Reforming schooling toward education for critical consciousness, complicated conversations, and social justice is a daunting task. But there are glimmers of hope in the resistances on the part of teachers who refuse to give standardized tests, students who refuse to take them, and parents who support both the teachers and the students. These initial resistances to the present forms of schooling and testing are the beginning of more resistance and the real reform of the public schools and the neoliberal society in which they exist.

NOTES

1. See the discussion of free market fundamentalism in Giroux (2013) and Reynolds (2004).
2. The term "Shopocalypse" is discussed in Sandlin and McLaren (2010, p. 16): "The 'Shopocalypse'—a combination of "Shopping" and "Apocalypse"—is a term coined by anti-consumption social activist Bill Talen, who takes on the persona of "Reverend Billy." Reverend Billy, along with the "Stop Shopping Gospel Choir," stage "Retail Interventions" inside big box stores, chain stores, traffic jams and other monuments of our current mono-culture."
3. The vendors mentioned account for sales between $100 million and $600 million. Sales have increased steadily since the adoption of the No Child Left Behind Act.

4. These companies also make preloaded curriculum for teachers, giving suggestions on what and how materials should be taught.
5. Burch notes, "Now a growing number of districts are relying on outside for- profit vendors to provide remedial instruction to academically struggling students who continue to attend regular classrooms during the day. With services paid for by the district, the students attend after-school or summer-school programs located on of off school grounds and designed and staffed by outside firms" (2009, p. 26).
6. Renaissance Learning is the company that provides the software for the Accelerated Reader Program.
7. For extended discussions of this historical development of curriculum, see Pinar et al. (1995); Kleibard (2004); and Schubert et al. (2002).

REFERENCES

Altman, M. A., & Gottwald, M. (Producers), & Hurst, M. (Director). (2005). *House of the dead 2* [Motion picture]. United States: Lionsgate.

Ambrose, S. (2004, April). Resisting market fundamentalism! Ending the reign of extremist neo- liberalism. Retrieved from http://www.rootsie.com/blog/?p=28

Apple, M. (1995). *Education and power* (2nd ed). New York: Routledge.

Aronowitz, S. (1998). Introduction. In Paulo Freire, *Pedagogy of freedom: Ethics, democracy, and civic courage* (pp. 1–19). Lanham, MD: Rowman and Littlefield.

Bauman, Z. (2011). *Culture in a liquid modern world*. Alden, MA: Polity.

Bazinet, K. (2009, March 11). President Obama education plan calls for performance-based pay, firing poorly performing teachers. *New York Daily News*. Retrieved from http://www.nydailynews.com/news/politics/2009/03/10/2009–03–10_president_obama_education_plan_calls_for-1.html

Berstein, A., Bliss, T. A., & Jones, D. E. (Producers), Snyder, Z. (Director). (2004). *Dawn of the dead* [Motion picture]. United States: Universal Studios.

Braverman, H. (1974). *Labor and monopoly capital: The degradation of work in the 20th century*. New York: Monthly Review Press.

Burch, P. (2009). *Hidden markets: The new education privatization*. New York: Routledge.

Deleuze, G. (1995). *Negotiations 1972–1990* (M. Joughin, Trans.). New York: Columbia University Press.

Dillon, S. (2010, January 31). Obama to seek sweeping change in 'No Child' law. *New York Times*. Retrieved from http://www.nytimes.com2010/02/01/education/01child.html?sq=educ

Duncan, A. (2009, October 22). Teacher preparation: Reforming the uncertain profession. Retrieved from http://www.ed.gov/news/speeches/teacher-preparation-reforming-uncertain-profession

McCain, J. (2007). *John McCain on Education*. Retrieved from http://web.archive.org/web/20111130053924/http://www.education.com/magazine/article/John_McCain/?page=2

Freire, P. (2000). *Pedagogy of the oppressed* (30th anniversary ed.) (M. Bergman Ramos, Trans.). New York: Continuum.

Freire, P. (2005). *Teachers as cultural workers: Letters to those who dare teach*. Cambridge, MA: Westview Press.

Georgia Department of Education. (2010, August 24). Georgia Wins Race to the Top. Retrieved from http://archives.gadoe.org/pea_communications.aspx?ViewMode=1&obj=1969

Giroux, H. A. (2004). *The terror of neoliberalism: Authoritarianism and the eclipse of democracy.* Boulder, CO: Paradigm.

Giroux, H. A. (2009). *Youth in a Suspect Society: Democracy or disposability?* New York: Palgrave Macmillan.

Giroux, H. A. (2011). *Zombie politics and culture in the age of casino capitalism.* New York: Lang.

Giroux, H. A. (2013). *America's education: Deficit and the war on youth.* New York: Monthly Review Press.

Gluckman, A. (2002). Testing . . . testing . . . one, two, three: The commercial side of the standardized-testing boom. *Dollars and Sense.* Retrieved from http://www.dollarsandsense.org/archives/2002/0102gluckman.html

U.S. Department of Education. (2009). *President Obama, U.S. secretary of education Duncan announce national competition to advance school reform.* Retrieved from http://www2.ed.gov/news/pressreleases/2009/07/07242009.html.

Hardt, M., & Negri, A. (2000). *Empire.* Cambridge, MA: Harvard University Press.

Kincheloe, J. L. (2007). Interview with Joe L. Kincheloe by the Freire Project [Video]. Retrieved from http://vimeo.com/72834466

Kliebard, H. M. (2004). *The struggle for the American curriculum 1893–1957* (3rd ed.). New York: Routledge.

McLaren, P. (2006). *Rage and hope: Interviews with Peter McLaren on war, imperialism, and critical pedagogy.* New York: Lang.

Obama, B., & Biden, J. (2007). Reforming and Strengthening America's Schools for the 21st Century. Retrieved from http://obama.3cdn.net/3297d77a034ada10f5_hpdhmvj1s.pdf

Pinar, W. F. (2004). *What is curriculum theory?* Mahwah, NJ: Erlbaum.

Pinar, W. F., Reynolds, W. M., Slattery, P., & Taubman, P. M. (1995). *Understanding curriculum.* New York: Peter Lang.

Reynolds, W. M. (2003). *Curriculum: A river runs through it.* New York: Lang.

Reynolds, W. M. (2004). To touch the clouds standing on top of a Maytag refrigerator: Brand name postmodernity and a Deleuzian in-between. In W. M. Reynolds and J. A. Webber (Eds.), *Expanding curriculum theory: Dis/positions and lines of flight* (pp. **19–35**). New York: Lang.

Reynolds, W. M., & Webber, J. A. (2009). *The civic gospel: A political cartography of Christianity.* Rotterdam, Netherlands: Sense.

Schubert, A.L.L., Thomas, T. P., Schubert, W. H., & Carroll, W. M. (2002). *Curriculum books: The first hundred years* (2nd ed.). New York: Lang.

Sandlin, J. A., & McLaren, P. (Eds.). (2010). *Critical pedagogies of consumption: Living and learning in the shadow of the "shopocalypse."* New York: Routledge.

State of Georgia. (2010a). Governor Perdue announces plan to transform teacher pay. Retrieved from http://sonnyperdue.georgia.gov/00/press/detail/0,2668,780 06749_154885747_155353123,00.html

State of Georgia. (2010b). Governor Perdue introduces education legislation. Retrieved from http://sonnyperdue.georgia.gov/00/press/detail/0,2668,78006749_ 132830663_132830675,00.html http://gov.georgia.gov/00/press/detail/ 0,2669,78006749_78013037_.

State of New Jersey. (2010). Education reform leaders: Governor Christie's reforms will "make New Jersey a national leader In education reform." Retrieved from http://www.state.nj.us/governor/news/news/552010/approved/20100928c.html.

Sunker, H., & Otto, H.-U. (Eds.). (1997). *Education and fascism: Political identity and social education in Nazi Germany.* Washington, DC: Falmer.

Taylor, F. W. (1911). *Principles of scientific management.* New York: Harper Brothers.

3   The Pseudoaccountability of School Reform

Injustice by (False) Proxy

Randy L. Hoover

Far from improving education, high-stakes testing marks a major retreat from fairness, from accuracy, from quality, and from equity.

—Senator Paul Wellstone, *High-Stakes Tests: A Harsh Agenda for America's Children*

This chapter deals with the fundamental metrics of the neoliberal school reform model and how the carefully constructed metrics lead to an extreme narrowing of the conversation about school reform that precludes discourse about social justice and democratic ideals. The metrics are viewed as the technical means for a *false proxy* that is used to justify the rhetoric of no-excuses reform and to lock out possibilities for any reasoned, thoughtful dialogue. The technical means of the false proxy shape a closed metanarrative within which neoliberal school reform operates.

The chapter discusses the evidence that the current accountability-based public school reform model *does not work* as it claims; it explicates how the metrics themselves act as a proxy for school improvement that precludes any and all development of curriculum to provide students the opportunities to learn the efficacy of content knowledge or the value of social justice. It also attempts to show why the technical metanarrative promotes an effective, popular ideological war against public schools by imposing and enforcing a system of *pseudoaccountability* on students, educators, and public school performance.

HISTORICAL CONTEXT

The history of contemporary school reform, from No Child Left Behind (NCLB) through today's Common Core State Standards Initiative, is replete with controversy, contradiction, and claims. Indeed, the *no-excuses, will-not-tolerate-failure, one-size-fits-all* accountability model initiated by the neoconservatives and later co-opted by the neoliberals has established a model of schooling that has, arguably, become a tail wagging a dog at the expense of commonsense justice and democratic schooling.

Historically in the U.S., the primary responsibility for establishing public schools and school reform systems belongs to each state government. Whereas, in its radical design, NCLB requires states to comply with federal mandates, the exact system of accountability employed is left to the states. NCLB, however, sets the ideological tone for what the states implement for their metrics—metrics designed to *prove* the point that public schools and public school educators are failures for the most part, failures because the data from massive use of standardized achievement tests tell us so.

Lost in the shuffle is the reality that the reform initiatives, bundled as the mandates of the federal requirement, have been so intrusive that the very essence of public schooling has been exorcised and firmly replaced with a form of *government schooling* as opposed to *public schooling* (Hoover & Shook, 2005). Local control as a hallmark of traditional public schooling has been replaced with severely limited local decision latitude in which raising standardized achievement test scores is the only significant mission (and mandate) for local boards of education (Hursh, 2013; Winerip, 2012).

Requisite to understanding the arguments and evidence that the test-driven accountability-based school reform model *does not work* and *why it does not work* is accepting the particular ideological nature of the reform progenitors and their policies. David Hursh puts it succinctly:

> I will situate high-stakes testing within the rise of neoliberal policies in the USA. Neoliberals advance a particular vision of society that promotes reducing the size of government by replacing governmental organizations with private corporations, establishing markets as the model for all economic and social transactions, and creating the entrepreneurial individual who only relies on her or himself rather than society (Olssen, Codd, and O'Neill 2004; Peters 1994). In education, neoliberal policies have focused on expanding high-stakes testing, as reflected in both state and federal policies such as No Child Left Behind (NCLB) and Race to the Top, increasing school privatization and school choice and competition. These educational reforms aim to transform education from a publicly to privately provided good. (2013, p. 2)

The reform movement's mantra of *accountability* has lost any standing as a credible signifier of professional practice and has instead become a narcotic substitute for equity and social reform by legitimizing the metrics it uses as the be-all, end-all truth of school performance. By sheer force of neoliberal ideological will, the school-reform metrics used to portray school, student, and educator performance stand essentially unquestioned and unexamined. Indeed, conspicuously absent from the discourse against the pseudoaccountability systems have been the two major union groups—the National Education Association and the American Federation of Teachers. Both organizations have strongly supported most of the neoliberal initiatives, Race to the Top being the most conspicuous among them. Politically, the differences between Republicans and Democrats on school reform have been nominal when they have existed at all.

The extent to which the Democrats have been silent or even supportive of the reform legislation is enigmatic to an extent when we realize that the American Legislative Exchange Council (ALEC), better known as the extreme right-wing coalition of corporate and religious right interests,[1] has been the primary source of all legislation dealing with school reform. ALEC produces model legislation that serves to transform public education "from an institution that serves the public into one that serves private for-profit interests" (Fischer, 2013). The values that motivate the efforts of ALEC have nothing to do with reforms that improve public schooling for a democratic society; indeed, the metrics endorsed by ALEC legislation initiatives are those that perpetuate the capitalization and corporatization of public schools and demonization of public school educators as a means of garnering public support for their actions.[2]

No matter the particular real-world conditions of any school, student, teacher, or community, the metrics of school reform are fundamentally driven by once-a-year standardized test scores.[3] The categorization of school districts, buildings, and educators all flows from the mandated standardized test results and the spurious metrics used to manipulate the data.

The mantra power of such school reform slogans as *no excuses, high standards*, and *accountability* is hegemonic power that is used to sedate the public to preempt any questioning of the legitimacy, validity, or credibility of accountability claims. The fundamental requirements of NCLB and the particular state requirements legislated to meet the NCLB requirements implicitly misuse the concept of accountability; ignore virtually all research on learning, assessment, and human development; and apply metrics that ultimately yield highly spurious conclusions—conclusions that are seemingly, but not actually, valid results.

Understanding the concept of professional accountability requires understanding the concepts of professional responsibility and professional decision latitude as they apply to professional practice. It also requires examination of the reform movement's inherent assumptions about children, teaching, and learning that embrace the banking model of schooling (Freire, 1993). But challenging the current accountability system is not the same as rejecting any principle of professional accountability whatsoever; *it is questioning the validity of the measures and metrics used to rate performance and the credibility of the conclusions drawn.*

AUTHENTIC ACCOUNTABILITY VERSUS PSEUDOACCOUNTABILITY

> "Accountability" has become the fundamental tool for instituting changes in public schools. In most states and districts and through the federal No Child Left Behind (NCLB) Act, accountability means using standardized test results to trigger labels, sanctions, rewards or interventions for districts, schools, educators or students. This approach has been both insufficient and has had undesirable side effects.
>
> —National Center for Fair and Open Testing,
> "Authentic Accountability"

Few people recognize that there is an extremely important nuance inherent within the use and understanding of the concept of *accountability*, a very important nuance missing from the neoliberal reform movement's use of the term. That nuance is distinguishing between accountability wherein the one being held accountable has clear opportunity to significantly control the variables upon which the accountability system is based and accountability wherein the one being held accountable has little or no control over those variables.

For any accountability system to be credible (worthy of belief), it must be *authentic*. In most simple terms, *authentic accountability means that the subjects of the accountability system are being held responsible for their own professional decision making and professional actions within the context of the professional practice.* Authentic accountability seeks out and excludes any and all forces and factors affecting performance that are not within the sphere of control by the performer (Hoover, 2004).

For accountability to be authentic and, hence credible, the system must contain an integral operational vigilance in consideration of both equity and opportunity. Without vigilance toward extraneous variables affecting performance, the performer is denied fairness and the opportunity for decision making.[4]

For example, if the state or federal government were to hold local meteorologists accountable for each day's actual weather, any fair-minded person would think that to be unjust and uninformed because the weather reporters have no control over the meteorological conditions they encounter; they can control only the things they do in determining their forecast. Should a meteorologist's forecasts be consistently wrong, then and only then can we hold the meteorologist authentically accountable.

Therefore, to be fair and to generate accurate and credible accountability reports to stakeholders, it is only right and proper to hold educators accountable for only those things within their decision latitude—only things over which practitioners have control and the power to affect. To hold anyone accountable for something over which they have neither control nor decision latitude is *pseudoaccountability*. Likewise, in a functioning democracy, where equity and participation are valued, stakeholders have a right to warranted and credible accountability reports.

ACCOUNTABILITY AND VALIDITY

In the matter of the pseudoaccountability systems of neoliberal reform, the source of the credibility problem rests with the notion of validity in terms of standardized achievement tests and in terms of metrics used within the accountability system itself.[5] As Eva Baker and Robert Linn emphasize, "There are, however, broader validity issues for accountability systems, which go beyond those normally thought of in connection with tests" (2002, p. 4). To address the broader issues of accountability as well as the basic issues of standardized testing, the Standards for Educational Accountability Systems were produced for the National Center for Research on Evaluation, Standards, and Student Testing (CRESST) by a consortium comprised of the American Educational Research Association, the American Psychological Association, and the National Council on Measurement in Education.[6] They consist of 22 standards that represent rigorous guidelines for all accountability systems. The test standards are widely recognized as the most authoritative statement of professional consensus regarding expectations on matters of validity, fairness, and other technical characteristics of tests (Baker & Linn, 2002). Adherence to all of the 22 standards is a requirement for any given accountability system to be credible.

Technically, test validity is not solely an attribute of the test by itself. Rather, test validity is an attribute of the test *in conjunction with the use(s)*—meanings and interpretations—intended for the test to serve. A test may be valid for one use but not for another. This point about validity may seem trivial, but it is not. It is a subtle point with tremendous ramifications for mistaken interpretations and misleading meanings to be promulgated.

Whereas any internet search for the term *validity* will yield a number of types of validity, the primary function of standardized test validity in terms of school reform accountability models is to secure evidence through formal, rigorous analysis that (1) the test questions cover a fair and representative sample of the academic standards it is intended to test, and (2) the test content and language do not unfairly disadvantage any students because of such identities as ethnicity, race, class, or gender, among others (American Institutes for Research, 2008).

The first of the two criteria above relates to what is essentially content validity; it answers the question as to what degree the test reflects the breadth and depth represented by the academic standards of the grade level and subject. Content validity can be thought of as subject matter integrity and is extremely important for any test. In this vein, it is regularly referred to as *internal validity*. However, given the evidence that the content validity of the achievement tests used in the accountability models appears to be well documented, it is not seen as a major threat to the overall system. Nonetheless, a state can have robust content or internal validity evidence but still have a test that fails to assess what it claims to assess.

Given that virtually all of the school accountability systems in the U.S. are based on standardized achievement test scores, the system becomes a house of cards when test validity is examined in terms of the group membership of the student—the socioeconomic environment defining the lived experiences of the child taking the test. The reality of standardized achievement test performance for K–12 and above is that the scores are determined primarily by the lived experience of the test taker (Hoover, 2000, 2008; Newton et al., 2010). Diane Ravitch observes that "unfortunately, every testing program—be it the SAT, the ACT, NAEP, or state scores—shows a tight correlation between family income and scores. Children from affluent families have the highest scores, and children from poverty have the lowest scores" (2010, p. 286). Middle-class children have the middle scores. Ravitch also reveals the same is true of international tests such as the Programme for International Student Assessment.

Overall, the more advantaged and enriched the lived experience of the child, the better the child's performance on the tests will be. When looking at the number of children passing proficiency tests as analyzed by school districts, student scores correlate significantly with the living conditions associated with the socioeconomic level of the districts. My own empirical studies of test performance in Ohio across all school districts and all tests (Hoover, 2000, 2008) show definitive statistically significant correlations between the lived experience of the child and test performance. When in these two studies I indexed median family income, the percentage who received free and reduced lunch subsidies and numbers of single-parent families in each district, the correlation between this *lived experience index* and achievement test scores reached $r = 0.80$, an extremely high correlation coefficient.

These data are extremely robust, and by virtue of their statistical significance, they clearly provide powerful evidence that Ohio's achievement tests violate the requisite standard for validity previously discussed. The tests are extremely sensitive to *cultural capital* (Bourdieu & Passeron, 1990), assessing the particular language, meanings, and signifiers of the lived experience of the child. The tests advantage students and schools that exhibit greater fluency in the dominant cultural capital and greatly disadvantage those who lack a fluency, as is borne out in the extremely high correlations between test performance and advantaged living found in my research (Hoover, 2000, 2008).

Betty Hart and Todd R. Risley have presented an amazingly powerful empirical study titled "The Early Catastrophe: the 30 Million Word Gap by Age 3" (2003). This study of childhood vocabulary acquisition deals with the vast differences in language experience and family support mechanisms among lower-, middle- , and upper-class children. When their conclusions are seen in conjunction with the empirical reality that the greater the advantage, the higher the standardized test scores, *the gross injustice of the no-excuses mentality and the way it powerfully serves to create inequity are conspicuous.* The tests and the accountability system unfairly disadvantage (or advantage) students because of their *group membership,* the term used in the Standards for Educational Accountability Systems to refer to disaggregate test takers by demographic characteristics. Ignoring bias in group memebership is not only a violation of a basic form of test validity but also a violation of the Standards for Educational Accountability Systems developed by the National Center for Research on Evaluation, Standards, and Student Testing (2002).

The critical insight here is that the tests are demonstrably invalid: they do not assess what they claim to assess. Test validity is the single most important criterion for a test to meet. If a test and the use of that test are shown to be valid, then the test results of those taking the test are credible—worthy of belief. For any system of accountability to be credible, the assessments used must be demonstrably valid through empirical analysis in terms of the interpretations to be made based upon the test scores.

Accountability systems and their summary findings are complex mixtures of standardized test scores and other data such as attendance rates, dropout rates and graduation rates, all combined through specific metrics to create summative, categorical ratings or rankings for the system performers. System performers can be students (individually or disaggregated into subgroups,) teachers, principals, districts, buildings, and grade levels.

Validity, as legitimacy in how the tests are used and what they are used for, plays out across the tests and the accountability system as a primary factor in determining the accuracy of the conclusions. Similarly, *measurement error,* inherent in all tests and accountability systems, also affects the accuracy of conclusions. Measurement error may be thought of as the degree of sloppiness in any given aspect of assessment; it is a caveat for how much confidence (credibility) there can be in the accuracy of any given measure. Classifications for district, school, or teacher effectiveness made by accountability systems are tremendously affected by the inherent limitations of measurement error.

Trying to enumerate and explicate all of the measurement threats to accountability system accuracy is impossible within the limits of one chapter, but three additional psychometric understandings are vital to deconstructing the system's truth claims. First is the notion of *inference level* as the degree to which any summary quantitative determination is precise. The higher the inference level of a mathematical determination, the more there is left to the imagination. The lower the inference level, the more precise the results. For example, the height of someone is a low inference conclusion if he or she has been measured using a standard measure, whereas a given value-added score for a teacher is an extremely high inference due to measurement error complexities and thus is, if anything, a numeric conclusion leaving much to the imagination (inference) and very little to certainty. We must understand that given the metrics of educational accountability systems, the entire array of statistical conclusions are extremely imprecise.

The second important understanding is the notion of test *reliability*— the degree to which a test yields stable and consistent scores from the test takers—as a most critical factor in shaping inference levels. If a test is not valid, its reliability is moot and no inferences can be made. This is so because if a test does not assess what it claims to assess, the accuracy of its mismeasure is ordinarily of no value. But given that the achievment tests are used without any regard for their absence of validity, and given the data showing the emperically-demonstrable invalidity of the achievement tests, test reliability error only adds to increasing the inference level of student scores to such a point that scores are rendered psychometrically and academically meaningless.

The third notion is *confidence interval* as an aspect affecting inference level for any test score. Confidence interval is determined by the degree of reliabilty calculated for a test. The lower the test reliablity, the broader the confidence interval is for any given score. What this means is that for any standarized test score, we cannot have confidence in the specific score itself, but, we can have confidence that the score is within the range (interval) immediately above and below it as determined by the relaibility coeficient for that particular test. In other words, any specific achievment test score is a only a midpoint in the interval of scores immediately above and below it. We can say with reasonable certainty that the score is somewhere within the interval.

Remembering that at the root level school reform targets students by requiring them to pass achievement tests, the notion of measurement error takes on even greater relevance in the form of each score being only as accurate as the confidence interval of the score as a function of test reliablty. Baker and Linn comment on how this may play out and mislead:

> The use of performance standards to determine whether a student is proficient or not (passes or fails) reduces test scores to a dichotomy. Measurement error that is associated with any test score results in classification errors. That is, a student whose true level of achievement should lead to a passing score earns a score that is below the passing standard and vice versa. Valid inferences about student proficiency are undermined by measurement errors that result in misclassification of students. Hence, it is critical that the probability of misclassification is evaluated and the information is provided to users of the performance standards results. The precision of test scores can be enhanced by increasing test length. As Rogosa [1999] has shown, however, even tests that have reliability coefficients normally considered to be quite high (e.g., .90) result in substantial probabilities of misclassification. For example, if the passing standard is set at the 50th percentile for a

test with a reliability of .90, the probability is .22 that a student whose true percentile rank is 60, and who therefore should pass, would score below the cut score and therefore fail on a given administration of the test. Even a student whose true percentile rank is 70, a full 20 points above the cut score, would have a probability of failing of .06 [Rogosa, 1999]. (Baker and Linn, 2002, p. 9)

This example from Baker and Linn shows what happens at the root level of the accountability systems in terms of confidence intervals. The confidence interval for a test score is the calculated range of the score, not a precise single value as is suggested by the accountability system. But whether the tests in the example are no-stakes, low-stakes, or high-stakes makes a tremendous difference. Typically, test scores like those in the example *are* the primary sources of data for high-stakes categorization of teachers,[7] individual schools, and districts.[8]

The higher the stakes, the greater the issues of invalidity and measurement error are compounded. State accountability systems are notorious for obfuscating the 22 CRESST standards in order to cover both the misuse of test scores and the tremendous amount of measurement error. The hidden uncertainty of these dual threats goes into the reports and conclusions. The higher the stakes for students or educators, the greater the need for transparency and vigilance in accountability systems through mechanisms such as the CRESST Standards. Without a high level of vigilance, democratic equity is sullied for educators, and the citizenry is horribly mislead.

When student test scores are used as data for overall accountability systems, the likelihood of any accuracy or clear meaning is lost. Value-added models are the epitome of this. Mathew Di Carlo, senior research fellow at the Albert Shanker Institute, writing about the work of Sean Corcoran (2010) of the Annenberg Institute for School Reform, notes how using value-added models (VAM) greatly amplifies the role of measurement error:

Interpreting a teacher's VAM score without examining the error margin is, in many respects, meaningless. For instance, a recent analysis of VAM scores in New York City shows that the *average* error margin is plus or minus 30 percentile points. That puts the "true score" (which we can't know) of a 50th percentile teacher at somewhere between the 20th and 80th percentile—an incredible 60 point spread (though, to be fair, the "true score" is much more likely to be 50th percentile than 20th or 80th, and many individual teacher's error margins are less wide than the average). If evaluation systems don't pay any attention to the margin of error, the estimate is little more than a good guess (and often not a very good one at that). Now, here's the problem: Many, if not most teacher evaluation systems that include VAM—current, enacted or under consideration—*completely ignore this*. (Di Carlo, 2010)

It is important to note that in many states—Ohio being one of them—there is great controversy over the percentage that value-added should represent in the overall teacher evaluation system. There is also controversy about the fairness and accuracy of using fewer than three years of value-added scores because of the effects of random error.[9]

The categorical rating of teacher effectiveness using standardized test score data manipulated by value-added metrics takes the notion of pseudo-accountability deep into the rabbit hole of the reform movement. Yet the controversies over teacher evaluation systems in Los Angeles, New York, and Chicago, among many other cities, lead us into realizing that Alice's world has become our own regardless of the absurdity of it. One of the realities of educational research is that teacher impact on student achievement is extremely small and extremely difficult to measure with any precision (McLeod, 2013). When the notion of determining the precise academic effect of teachers on students is examined rationally, the conclusions are explicit. Scott McLeod captures this well:

> Another issue worth noting is that even if teacher effects could be teased out, decades of peer-reviewed research show that teachers only account for about 10% of overall student achievement (give or take a few percentage points). Another 10% or so is attributable to other school factors such as leadership, resources, and peer influences. The remaining 80% of overall student achievement is attributable to non-school factors such as individual, family, and neighborhood character-istics. A few exceptional 'beating the odds' schools aside, these ratios have remained fairly stable (i.e., within a few percentage points) since they were first noted by the famous Coleman Report of the 1960s. Given the overwhelming percentage of student learning outcomes that is attributable to non-teacher factors, it is neither ethical nor legally defensible to base teacher evaluations on factors outside of their con-trol. (McLeod, 2013)

I find it worth noting that McLeod's commentary supports my own con-clusions (Hoover, 2000, 2008) as to the limited extent to which teachers can have academic impact against the lived experience of the student as measured by achievement tests. However, the primary point is that good science clearly indicates *it is simply impossible to credibly categorize the performance of educators because the issues of test validity, the high mea-surement error, and the inability to know the precise impact teachers have on students separate from what the child enfleshes from lived experience.*

Educator evaluation via the pseudoaccountability reaches the upper limit of high-stakes consequences when we consider the latest application of the flawed reform metrics by the newly created Council for Accredita-tion of Education Preparation (CAEP), an organization strongly dom-inated by the neoliberal establishment. Included in the new standards used by CAEP (2013) is the use of the value-added scores of classroom teachers to evaluate the performance of schools and colleges of education. The encroachment of typical neoliberal elements of accountability into higher education is indicative of the political power behind it. In spite of continued research to the contrary, value-added and scientifically dubious metrics continue to power pseudoaccountability systems, now into higher education.

Given what we know from the science of parametric statistics, from learned educational researchers, and from learned societies about the basic metrics and principles for creating fair and just testing and accountability systems,[10] we ponder why political power trumps reflectively derived knowledge so consistently and effectively when it comes to equity in the treatment of students and educators and credibility for our citizenry.

INJUSTICE BY (FALSE) PROXY

> The more any quantitative social indicator is used for social decision-making, the more subject it will be to corruption pressures and the more apt it will be to distort and corrupt the social processes it is intended to monitor.
>
> —Donald T. Campbell, *Assessing the Impact of Planned Social Change*

Campbell's (1976) thesis speaks to the issue of the numbers game in neoliberal reform. Through Campbell (1976) we can begin to see how the quantitative indicators of school and educator effectiveness have distorted the reality of schools and corrupted the process of change. We have reached the point at which anything about schools that cannot be seen in some way to be measurable as an explicit quantity is neither important nor of any value.

The evidence that the neoliberal reform movement has brought us to view schooling through distorted, indeed corrupt lenses of pseudoaccountability is replete. High-stakes consequences, once considered only in terms of student sanctions, have morphed into sanctions now primarily only for schools, school districts, and the educators who staff them. The mandated use of standardized achievement test scores as the basis for reform has taken on a life of its own: *The scores and the metric-produced numbers flowing from them that are used to rate and rank schools and educators have become a proxy supplanting actual reform.*

The notion of the false proxy appeared in a blog by Seth Godin (2012), a marketing guru and entrepreneur:

> Once you find the simple proxy and decide to make it go up, there are lots of available tactics that have nothing at all to do with improving the very thing you set out to achieve in the first place. When we fall in

love with a proxy, we spend our time improving the proxy instead of focusing on our original (more important) goal instead.

The important point is to recognize that the proxy always represents a very simplistic form of valuation and may have little or nothing to do with the original issue or project. The more unrelated it really is to the original phenomenon, the more it becomes a *false* proxy. But because it is easily understood, especially by the public, it becomes a complete surrogate. In the case of school reform, it becomes the entire focus even though it is demonstrably invalid and therefore a false proxy.

Whereas Campbell (1976) takes the stance that it is the numbers that seduce the people in charge of the process of change, the case of school reform and its evolution starting with the administration of President Ronald Reagan and the publication of *A Nation at Risk* (1983) would suggest otherwise. Terrell Bell, Reagan's secretary of education, writes in his memoirs that they were seeking a "Sputnik-type event" (1988, p. 30) that would evoke a highly emotional response to the crisis in education to serve to animate Reagan's right-wing reform agenda. Alas, no event was available , so as Bell fully confesses, they conspired to make one up. *A Nation at Risk* was born, and America's public schools were given as the reason the nation was not competing well with foreign competition for world markets, especially the auto industry. It was completely untrue but politically effective in launching the school reform movement. NCLB (2001) may be seen as the point where neoliberalism melded with neoconservatism to give birth to the current school reform system and formalize the false proxy of the numbers game.[11]

It is interesting to note that Campbell intimates the proxy notion and unknowingly takes aim at the current basis for the numbers-based reform:

> From my own point of view, achievement tests may well be valuable indicators of general school achievement under conditions of normal teaching aimed at general competence. *But when test scores become the goal of the teaching process, they both lose their value as indicators of educational status and distort the educational process in undesirable ways.* (1976, pp. 51–52, emphasis added)

Ironically, his point here concerns precisely what has become our reality, with standardized achievement testing fueling the goal for the whole system.

The ease with which the numbers proxy established itself is seen when we consider that specific outcomes of schooling have never really been the subject of much public or professional dialogue.[12] Likewise, the numbers proxy comes from a system of accountability that is blind to the tremendous complexities of schools (the organization) and schooling (the teaching and learning process). Aaron Regunberg (2012), writing about the false proxy of school reform, speaks directly to this issue:

Unfortunately, the world of education is not a simple one. Schools are incredibly complex places, and school districts are more complicated still. Teaching is an intricate art, and learning is not such a straight-forward task either, so it's tough to come up with straightforward but comprehensive measurements in any or all of these areas. What's more, the very purpose of education remains an incessantly dense and knotty question that we seem reluctant to ask, let alone answer. Is the goal of education only to give students the skills and knowledge they need to survive economically (a.k.a. get a job), or do we also expect schools to help prepare children to thrive emotionally and socially?

Clearly the neoliberal agenda is tightly locked into standardized achievement tests as the sole indicator of school and educator effectiveness. Yet we know well that these achievement tests are *incredibly invalid* at assessing academic achievement and *incredibly valid* at assessing the cultural capital acquired (or not) from the student's lived experience. Therefore, we know that any possibility of authentic, democratic school reform is impossible because the system does not consider any other outcome for schooling other than test scores. Democratic reform designed to do right by the students and the democracy does not fit into the numbers game.

The machinations of the reform movement are as insidious as they are tightly locked into metrics that are designed to preclude thoughtful, reflective judgments about effectiveness or reform.[13] It has become a rigid, numbers-based system; the no-excuses mentality prevails over any consideration of the weakness of the test-based numbers. The system now treats educators like unskilled, uncredentialed labor as the numbers game, conjured from spurious metrics, has been used to eliminate collective bargaining, salary schedules based on experience, and advanced graduate study. Ultimately, this numbers game is used to hire more and more Teach for America individuals to replace teachers educated in professional education at accredited institutions.

The numbers game has closed schools and fueled voucher and charter school expansion at the expense of public schools. What this numbers game proxy has not done is secure a curriculum affording students the opportunity to learn social justice, equity, or critical reflectivity. Indeed, because the reform movement proxy is rooted in test scores, students are denied the opportunity to learn how to think with and apply the subject area knowledge. The goal of schooling is to do well on the tests—no more and no less. The idea that a student should be able to know where, when, why, and how to apply subject area concepts to real world problems and issues is precluded.

When speaking about my research on the lack of validity of the tests, I constantly have to remind people that the tests are invalid across the continuum of socioeconomic levels. That wealthy, advantaged students do well on them does not mean that they know why, how, where, and when to apply the knowledge. When a group is asked how many got an A or B in algebra, most of the hands go up. When asked to name one use for certain concepts in algebra, such as binomial multiplication, it is rare if even one hand is raised.

As in the traditional algebra class, students can score well on standardized tests yet not have an inkling about what the knowledge means or how it is used in authentic, real-world contexts. Such is it that the reform system denies empowerment across all socioeconomic groups, not just to disadvantaged students.

The metrics of no-excuses accountability *game* the system to parcel billions of dollars of public school (taxpayer) money into corporate bank accounts. When we consider the range of cost items directly created by the accountability system (tests, test materials, curriculum materials, private consultants, standards books, charter schools,[14] and vouchers, among others) in light of what these special interest groups contribute to political candidates who support the reform movement, the idea of a false proxy becomes even more understandable as a very valuable political and ideological means to an end.[15]

The metrics also deny clarity to the public, misleading them at the expense of students and educators. For example, when we see summary data for a given school or district, we cannot discriminate between a low-performing staff and low-performing students. In their current form, the accountability system's validity failure and gamed metrics guarantee that regardless of why students may be performing poorly on the tests, their educators are *always* given as the cause. An example of this injustice is highlighted by Di Carlo (2012) in his study of Florida's school system:

> So, according to Florida's system, almost every single low-performing school in the state is located in a higher-poverty area, whereas almost every single school serving low-poverty students is a high performer. This is not plausible. There is a very *big difference* between being a low-performing school and being a school that happens to serve lower-performing students.

Not only is this implausible, it is impossible. In all states using the NCLB school performance report cards, we see the same phenomenon, showing the tests to be sensitive measures of lived experience, not of academic achievement. The accountability metrics are gamed to prevent there ever being any case of a school having good educators and low-performing students yet we know this to be true across schools of urban and rural poverty (Hoover, 2000, 2008).

THE END GAME

Because the tests measure the cultural capital of lived experience instead of academic achievement, we can now understand why the accountability system is a system of *pseudoaccountability* as opposed to a system of *authentic accountability*: *to hold either students or educators accountable for the lived experience of the student is holding them accountable for something not within their control. Children can no more choose their parents and their living conditions than the educator can. Holding either accountable in the manner of neoliberal school reform is truly an injustice.*

Such slogans as *academic accountability, school accountability, teacher accountability, failed schools,* and, especially, *no excuses* have taken on the attributes of a political battle cry rather than those of credible signifiers of professional practice. Since the beginning of NCLB mandates, these slogans have been used to freeze the arguments of those questioning school accountability—especially its metrics. To argue against neoliberal school reform is seemingly to argue against common sense. The reform claims seem intuitively correct, and the data is there for everyone to see, but close examination shows that the system has been gamed, and the data are highly questionable at best.

To game the system is to manipulate the rules and procedures to achieve surreptitious outcomes while maintaining the facade and supporting the rhetoric that the system is honorable and forthright in what it is claiming to do. The numbers game of school reform has created a very powerful false proxy, but, worse, it greatly affects the lives of *all* students in our schools— none more so than the already disadvantaged:

> What's worse, these negative effects are not distributed evenly among America's children. On the contrary, high-stakes testing *discriminatorily and inequitably hurts low-income youth and youth of color.* These are the young people who are most likely to be held back or pushed out of schools for having low scores. And research has shown that schools with higher percentages of students of color have greater narrowing of curriculum, more scripted curriculum, and more focus on rote skills instead of creative, higher-order thinking—so the students who often have the greatest need for wraparound services, extracurricular enrichment, and engaging and individualized learning are the ones who end up losing it all. (Regunberg, 2012)

If we view curriculum as being *what the students have the opportunity to learn* (McCutcheon, 1995), the cultural hegemony produced by the power of the false proxy effectively limits curriculum to teach-to-the-test opportunities. Opportunities for learning the instrumental value of content knowledge, social justice, and democratic civics are denied.

Until we can expose neoliberal reform's false proxy, there is likely to be no remedy. Political reality tells us that advocacy for exposé must come from the primary special-interest groups serving public school educators— the national unions. But without the rank and file forcing the leadership to redefine accountability authentically, little is likely to change given the culpability of union leadership in supporting strongly those who embrace the political capital of the false proxy. Both the National Education Association and the American Federation of Teachers have steadfastly supported President Barack Obama's investment in the politics of the proxy with Race to the Top. They have done so at great cost to the educators who pay the price both in membership dues and in the costs of being subjected to the horrendously unfair and unjust effects the pseudoaccountability their leaders support. Fair play for students is impossible until there is fair play for their educators.

NOTES

1. It is impossible to understand the insidious nature of neoliberal public school reform without understanding the role of ALEC in the process; see Fischer (2013).
2. In the first six months of 2013, 139 ALEC education bills had been introduced in 43 states; 31 were enacted (Fischer, 2013).
3. Most states claim to use *multiple measures* in calculating accountability reports. The reports simply use different grade levels or subject area scores from the same test, but this is one measure used multiple times, not the use of multiple measures.
4. The National Center for Research on Evaluation, Standards, and Student Testing's *Standards for Educational Accountability Systems* (2002) contains several standards that relate directly to eliminating external and extraneous variables.
5. School accountability systems are by no means uniform across the 50 states. However, those based in standardized achievement tests; district, school, and teacher categorization; and value added are all subject to the same psychometric weaknesses.
6. Respectively, these are the American Educational Research Association, the American Psychological Association, and the National Council on Measurement in Education.
7. A recent analysis of VAM scores in New York City shows that the average error margin is plus or minus 30 percentage points. That puts the "true score" (which we can't know) of a 50th percentile teacher at somewhere between the 20th and 80th percentile—an incredible 60-point spread (Di Carlo, 2010).
8. In my 2000 study, when I controlled for the lived experience factor (socioeconomic status), I found many apparently high-performing districts to be performing below their state ratings and many low-performing districts actually performing far above.
9. The U.S. Department of Education reports of error rates in measuring teacher and school performance using student test score gains as value-added estimates for teacher-level analyses are subject to a considerable degree of random error. If three years of data are used for estimation, more than one in four teachers who are average in performance will be erroneously identified for special sanctions (Schochet, P. & Chiang, H., 2010).
10. The following professional groups and learned societies have all raised significant questions about accountability models using value-added metrics in particular: the National Education Policy Center (Rothstein & Mathis, 2013); the American Educational Research Association and the National Academy of Education (Darling-Hammond, et al., 2011); the Economic

Policy Institute (Baker, E. et al., 2010); the U.S. Department of Education (Schochet & Chiang, 2010); the Annenberg Institute for School Reform (Corcoran, 2010); the National Research Council (Haertel, E. et al., 1999); and the Educational Testing Service (Braun, 2005).

11. Senators Hillary Clinton and Ted Kennedy, serving on the U.S. Senate Education Committee, were major supporters of NCLB and its numbers requirements.
12. See Silberman (1971), in which he comments about educators not really knowing why they are doing what they do.
13. One of the most egregious machinations is the use of the Education Value-Added Assessment System format in light of the precise calculus being considered as proprietary knowledge and therefore not open to public or professional scrutiny.
14. At the time of this writing, the Associated Press is reporting that it has obtained e-mails showing that former Indiana state superintendent Tony Bennett changed the grading system to make sure a particular charter school got an A. The school belongs to a major Republican Party donor who has contributed more than $2.8 million since 1998, including a contribution of $130,000 to Tony Bennett's campaign.
15. The proxy is also used to demonize the role of the unions in schooling.

REFERENCES

American Institutes for Research. (2008). *Validity evidence based on internal structure: Examination of the factor structure of the Ohio achievement tests.* Report TR 2008–02, to the Ohio Department of Education. Retrieved from http://education.ohio.gov/getattachment/Topics/Testing/Ohio-Graduation-Test-OGT/TR-2008-2-OGT-Validity-Study-2007.pdf.aspx

Baker, E. et al. (2010). Problems with the use of student test scores to evaluate teachers. Retrieved from http://epi.3cdn.net/b9667271ee6c154195_t9m6iij8k.pdf

Baker, E., & Linn, R. (2002). *Validity issues for accountability systems.* Los Angeles: Center for the Study of Evaluation, National Center for Research on Evaluation, Standards, and Student Testing.

Bell, T. (1988). *The thirteenth man: A Reagan cabinet memoir.* New York: Free Press.

Bourdieu, P. & Passeron, J. (1990). *Reproduction in education, society, and culture.* (Trans. R. Nice). London: Sage Publications.

Braun, H. (2005). Using student progress to evaluate teachers: A primer on value-added models. Retrieved from http://www.ets.org/Media/Research/pdf/PIC-VAM.pdf

Campbell, D. T. (1976). *Assessing the impact of planned social change.* Hanover, NH: Public Affairs Center, Dartmouth College.

Corcoran, S. (2010). Can teachers be evaluated by their students' test scores? Should they be? The use of value-added measures of teacher effectiveness in policy and practice. Retrieved from http://www.scribd.com/doc/37648467/The-Use-of-Value-Added-Measures-of-Teacher-Effectiveness-in-Policy-and-Practice#download

Council for Accreditation of Education Preparation. (2013). *CAEP standards.* Retrieved from http://caepnet.org/accreditation/standards/

Darling-Hammond, L. et al. (2011). Getting teacher evaluation right: A background paper for policy makers. Retrieved from http://www.aera.net/Portals/38/docs/New%20Logo%20Research%20on%20Teacher%20Evaluation%20AERA-NAE%20Briefing.pdf

Di Carlo, M. (2010). The war on error. Retrieved from http://shankerblog.org/?p=1383

Fischer, B. (2013). Cashing in on kids. Retrieved from http://www.prwatch.org/news/2013/07/12175/cashing-kids139-alec-bills-2013-promote-private-profit-education-model

Freire, P. (1993). *Pedagogy of the oppressed* (new rev. 20th-anniversary ed.). (M. Bergman Ramos, Trans.) New York: Continuum, 1993.

Godin, S. (2012). Voiding the false proxy trap. Retrieved from http://sethgodin.typepad.com/seths_blog/2012/11/avoiding-the-false-proxy-trap.html

Hart, B., & Risley, T. R. (2003). The early catastrophe: The 30 million word gap by age 3. *American Educator, 27*(1), 4–9.

Haertel, E. et al. (2009). National Research Council Letter report to the U.S. Department of Education on the Race to the Top fund. Retrieved from http://www8.nationalacademies.org/onpinews/newsitem.aspx?RecordID=12780

Hoover, R. (2000). *Forces and factors affecting Ohio proficiency test performance: A study of 593 Ohio school districts.* Retrieved from http://people.ysu.edu/~rlhoover/OAT-OGT/index.html

Hoover, R. (2004). *(Re)understanding educator accountability: Pseudo vs. authentic accountability.* Retrieved from http://people.ysu.edu/~rlhoover/OAT-OGT/index.html

Hoover, R. (2008). *A Re-examination of forces and factors affecting Ohio school district OAT and OGT performance.* Retrieved from http://people.ysu.edu/~rlhoover/OAT-OGT/index.html

Hoover, R., & Shook, K. (2005). School reform and accountability: Some implications and issues for democracy and fair play. *Democracy and Education, 14*(4), 81–86.

Hursh, D. (2013). Raising the stakes: high-stakes testing and the attack on public education in New York. *Journal of Educational Policy.* Retrieved from http://dx.doi.org/10.1080/02680939.2012.758829

McCutcheon, G. (1995). *Developing the curriculum.* White Plains, NY: Longman.

McLeod, S. (2013). Value-added measures (VAM). Retrieved from http://dangerouslyirrelevant.org/resources/value-added-measures

National Center for Research on Evaluation, Standards, and Student Testing (CRESST) (2002). *Standards for educational accountability systems.* Los Angeles: CRESST.

Newton, X., Darling-Hammond, L., Haertel, E., & Thomas, E. (2010). Value-added modeling of teacher effectiveness: An exploration of stability across models and contexts. *Education Policy Analysis Archives, 18*(23). Retrieved from http://epaa.asu.edu/ojs/article/view/810

Olssen, M., Codd, J., & O'Neill, A. M. (2004). *Education policy: Globalization, citizenship and democracy.* Thousand Oaks, CA: Sage.

Peters, M. (1994). Individualism and community: Education and the politics of difference. *Discourse: Studies in the Cultural Politics of Education, 14*(2), 65–78.

Ravitch, D. (2010). *The death and life of the great American school system.* New York: Basic Books.

Regunberg, A. (2012). Education's false proxy trap. Retrieved from http://www.golocalprov.com/news/aaron-regunberg-educations-false-proxy-trap

Rogosa, D. (1999). *Accuracy of individual scores expressed in percentile ranks: Classical test theory calculations.* (CSE Technical Report No. 509.) Los Angeles: National Center for Research on Evaluation, Standards, and Student Testing.

Rothstein, J & Mathis, W. (2013). Review of Two Culminating Reports from the MET Project. Retrieved from http://nepc.colorado.edu/thinktank/review-MET-final-2013

Schochet, P. & Chiang, H. (2010). Error rates in measuring teacher and school performance on test score gains. NCEE 2010–4004. Retrieved from United States Department of Educations http://ies.ed.gov/ncee/pubs/20104004/pdf/20104004.pdf

Silberman, C. (1971). *Crisis in the classroom: The remaking of American education.* New York: Vintage.

U.S. National Commission on Excellence in Education. (1983). *A Nation at risk: The imperative for educational reform. A report to the nation and the secretary of education.* Washington, DC: U.S. Department of Education.

Wellstone, P. (2000). *High-stakes tests: A harsh agenda for America's children.* Retrieved from http://www.fairtest.org/high-stakes-tests-harsh-agenda-americas-children

Winerip, M. (2012, January 22). In race to the top, the dirty work is left to those on the bottom. *New York Times.*

4 Teacher Education and Resistance within the Neoliberal Regime
Making the Necessary Possible

Barbara Madeloni and Kysa Nygreen

The neoliberal assault on public education impacts children, schools, and teachers at every level, often in explicitly devastating ways. From school closings, to teacher firings, high-stakes testing, high-control charters and the school-to-prison pipeline, teachers, students, and parents experience the violence of this assault each day. It can be difficult, if not sometimes impossible, to find our way toward not only resisting the attack, but also toward claiming a space and vision for the public schools we want. These same "no excuses" reforms that are crippling K–12 public education have come to teacher education. Fast-track programs, with excessive regulation on the one hand, deregulated alternative certification programs on the other, and surveillance through hyperaccountability, not only threaten the space we have, but distract us from critical reflection and the development of teacher education as liberatory practice.

In this essay we name the practices and policies that are undermining teacher education and look to imagine how our resistance can be part of the enactment of radical teacher education. Resisting the neoliberal assault on education requires a social movement. It requires teachers and teacher educators who have both political consciousness and the will to act. Teacher educators must not only name the dangerous impact of neoliberal policies, but reveal how they work to distract us from essential questions of economic and racial justice and of our participation in creating more just and democratic communities. We must redefine what counts as educational justice to include antipoverty social reform such as universal health care, job creation, and higher wages (Anyon, 2005) and align our practice with this broader, more contextualized understanding. This means preparing new teachers not only for the classroom, but also for community engagement and activism. In this way, the enactment of critical social justice teacher education is part of the struggle for social context reform (SCR).

WHO WE ARE

Barbara Madeloni

I am a white woman who entered teacher education motivated by a desire to support the development of new teachers into a critical consciousness that is attentive to racism, classism, and the multiple forms that oppression takes in schools and society and prepared to engage a pedagogy of liberation. I see public education as the soil in which we till the promise of the democratic project, and believe that in order to move toward this promise we must examine current and historical relationships of power, and schools as either reproductive of oppressions or as sites of liberation. I became an educator as one facet of the struggle for justice.

I am not naive. I understand that the hope of public education is confounded by institutionalized racism and classism. Public education is a site of contestation and contradiction; it has often served to reproduce injustice. I understand that my efforts toward liberation mean working to find spaces within a system that has long marginalized and silenced those teachers who act from knowledge of teaching as political work. Still, my commitment is to making real the vision of schools and society as a socially just, creative, loving, and liberatory project.

Kysa Nygreen

I am a white woman trained as an educational anthropologist, committed to pedagogy and scholarship that question, problematize, and challenge taken-for-granted assumptions and ideologies in education. I came to teacher education steeped in the literature of critical theory and critical ethnography, and was excited to engage with preservice teachers in exploring big questions of social justice: What is democracy? What is educational justice? How do we engage our teaching practice from within this understanding? It is my hope that exploring such questions will support new teachers in developing a more critical pedagogy and a sense of themselves as public intellectuals. As well, I hope these explorations will prompt a commitment in new teachers to help build and sustain a public educational system for democracy and social justice.

In order to engage a practice of critical social justice teacher education, we both knew we would have to reflect on our own privileges as white middle-class professionals and as a women engaged in work that bears a low status in the context of higher education (Labaree, 2009), what Daniel P. Liston refers to as the "domestic labor" of the academy (1995, p.89). Educators who ask students to be reflective must themselves be open to the vulnerability of reflection and uncertainty, notes bell hooks:

> When education is the practice of freedom, students are not the only ones who are asked to share, to confess. Engaged pedagogy does not seek simply to empower students. Any classroom that employs a holistic model of learning will also be a place where teachers grow, and are empowered by the process. That empowerment cannot happen if we refuse to be vulnerable while encouraging students to take risks. (1994, p. 21)

We came to the work of teacher education ready to grow into and be challenged by this work, and hopeful that within a professional context that espoused a commitment to social justice education we would find partners in the struggle.

WHAT WE HAVE EXPERIENCED: THE NEOLIBERAL ASSAULT

Teacher education is subject to the oversight of the state, and is often conservative in how it imagines its work. Virginia Lea notes that "most of us who fill the role of teachers in public schools today are important frontline agents in the reproduction of the corporate-military capitalist state" (2011, p. 34). Under the accountability and standards regime, teacher educators are "cast as implementers of curriculum," social justice teacher education is marginalized (Sleeter, 2008), and theoretical, political, and ethical knowledge are cast aside in the name of "outcome measures" (Delandshere & Petrosky, 2004, p. 12). Still, even given these forces, social justice teacher educators have developed courses, research, and programs that ask future teachers to read deeply into educational history, policy, philosophy, and theory to examine the ways education and schools as institutions emerge from and embody our country's racist and classist history, and to know themselves, their students, and their communities within these histories with the goal of naming injustice and developing the skills, empathy, courage, and solidarity to fight for justice (Katsarou, Picower, & Stovall, 2010).

But teacher education, like K–12 education, is under enormous pressure to conform to programs and policies promulgated within the context of neoliberal paradigms of efficiency and competition, and technocratic views of knowledge and human experience (Apple, 2001; Hill, 2007). These include the proliferation of fast-track teacher education programs (Baines, 2010; Labaree, 2010; Zeichner, 2012), the surveillance of hyperaccountability measures (Madeloni and Gorlewski, 2013b; Taubman, 2009; Varenne, 2007), and the decoupling of teacher education from higher education (Zeichner, 2012). These practices narrow the possibilities of teacher education for social justice and critical consciousness. Furthermore, the neoliberal ideology from which they emerge has infiltrated the expectations of the students with whom we are working. Together, these are working to reduce teacher education and teaching to technical, dehumanizing experiences, silencing the voices of critical pedagogy and liberation, and denying the broader contexts in which we teach and learn.

The Proliferation of Fast-Track Teacher Education Programs

Whereas the five-week programs of Teach for America (TFA) are subject to much critique (Labaree, 2010; Miner, 2010), in response to TFA as a *competitor*, higher education institutions are offering shorter programs (Sleeter, 2008) and fast-track one year masters of education programs (Baines, 2010). Like TFA, these programs are based upon an efficiency model of learning to teach. These high-intensity programs often begin with summer classes, followed by student teachers entering K–12 classrooms in the fall semester while taking required graduate courses after full days in the classroom. Like TFA, these programs frequently place student teachers in high-need, mostly urban, schools with populations comprising mostly students of color. Although alternative certification programs have more candidates of color, most candidates, like the majority of teachers, are white (Feistrizter, 2011).

Fast-track programs by their very design include messages about the nature of teaching, learning to teach, and who we are as teachers. As teacher educators we need to ask ourselves what is lost when we create programs in which speed to licensure is the goal. What messages are sent about the nature of the knowledge of teaching and the value of both long-term experience in the classroom and the study of philosophy, theory, and research? Further, whereas these programs might espouse praxis, the high-intensity versions leave little room for the kinds of deep discussion, reading, and reflection that expand knowledge beyond the immediate demands of the classroom. Student teachers, who often enter programs with a technical view of teaching (Smagorinsky, 2010), suddenly find themselves faced with the complicated intellectual, social, and emotional demands of students. The students we have taught in one-year programs came to class exhausted, barely had time for preparing their own lessons, were often far behind in completing course readings, and struggled to balance graduate work, teaching, and home life. The high intensity of the program often left them vulnerable, emotionally depleted, and needing extra attention and care. They often did not have the psychic energy or the actual time to reflect on themselves or their practice, let alone to meet the needs of students.

In this situation, teaching becomes action decontextualized from thought, history, and theory. Whereas teaching *is* about doing, teaching is also about reflecting, about waiting and not doing, about reading, talking, watching, and listening—not only to students but to colleagues and parents, even to ourselves. The classroom as it is currently constructed is already a very difficult place in which to learn to think. Under neoliberal efficiency models, teaching is being constructed as technical work, as doing without deep thoughtfulness. Fast-track programs reinforce this technical focus when student teachers find themselves needing to just get the job done without any time for reflection. Learning to teach is devalued as a process, and teacher education programs are more than ever simply a hurdle to overcome in order to get the sought-after certification. There is no time or space for questions, such as those posed by Britzman:

> What are our obligations, not in the sense of getting work done, but in the way we can even image our work and how our workings affect our capacity to think beyond what we do. What inhibits our capacity to respond ethically to others, to learn something from people we will never meet and to be affected by histories that we may never live? (2000, p. 22)

Fast-track programs merge well with neoliberal constructs of what it means to work and to create a life. Neoliberal ideology posits human life as dominated by how we know ourselves and are valued within the market. Human beings are, according to neoliberal ideology, in constant competition for goods and value on the market (Harvey, 2005). As inequality rises and workers compete for dwindling resources and opportunities, our lives are marked by fear of job loss, work intensification, fewer protections, and lower compensation (Hill, 2007). Neoliberalism is undemocratic in how it constructs work and our relationship to it, and in how it limits the time we have available to build democracy both inside and outside of the workplace. The sink-or-swim culture of fast-track programs reinforces this idea of what it means to teach and to be a working person. Students in the fast-track programs in which we have worked describe being under incredible pressure to perform in the classroom, being overwhelmed by the demands of preparation, school administration, and graduate courses, and becoming alienated from students, parents, and themselves. "We do not have enough time," is the chorus from these students. Fast-track programs contribute to the construction of workplaces as sites where we are overwhelmed, cannot take good care of ourselves or those we care about (including our students), and must respond to authoritarian demands. As new teachers enter the workplace under these high-pressure "survival" systems, their teacher identities are formed and their imaginations for what is possible in classrooms, and as teachers, is narrowed. The work—alienated and technocratic, measured by numerical data and rubrics—becomes the focus of life, leaving little room for other ways of being with people. This insidious process reinforces the acceptance of inequities as natural rather than as constructed.

Whereas K–12 and teacher education have rightly been criticized for reproducing inequalities of race and class, fast-track programs represent a new low in how they perpetuate institutionalized racism and white supremacy, often while espousing the rhetoric of civil rights. As critical social justice educators, we believe teacher education programs have an obligation to attend to the institutional racism that is deep in our schools and other public institutions. The work of coming to consciousness about racism that our primarily white teaching staff must do—never mind the extended work of imaging and enacting new communities and ways of being within this privilege in order to overturn it—takes time. Fast-track programs challenge us to name and claim what it means to do antiracist, anticolonial work. The pressures that our students experience in fast-track programs interfere with their ability to confront their privilege, name institutional racism, and feel empowered to act to enact critical pedagogy in their classrooms.

Unmasking white supremacy doesn't end with a weekend workshop or intensive summer course; nor does it stop with naming one's privilege (Applebaum, 2004). Whereas schools can be sites of liberation, they have traditionally served to sort students by race and class and reproduce hierarchies of power and access. There are many layers, from the personal to the political to the social-cultural aspects of schools as institutions, that must be uncovered in antiracist teacher education (Gay, 2010; Ladson-Billings, 2000; Nieto, 2000:). For those of us who are white, the work is ongoing and uncertain. Ours must be a position of constant openness to new, often unsettling, insights into how we are constructed and how we construct others. White supremacy and settler colonialism are deeply embedded in our theories of knowledge, teaching, learning, communicating, and school (Tuck, 2013). Student teachers need to not only know their personal privilege, but be prepared to challenge all of our institutional structures as enactments of white supremacy. To the degree that fast-track programs suggest that teaching Black and Brown children is something whites can learn with speed and efficiency, we are both denying the long-term struggle of antiracist work and reproducing white colonial ideologies.

The high intensity survival mode of fast-track programs makes it both psychologically and politically more difficult for student teachers to engage in this level of reflection, particularly that which requires them to examine their own privilege or question taken-for-granted assumptions about teaching, learning, and schooling. Student teachers are charged with meeting testing demands, "managing" classrooms, and "delivering" instruction. Each of these must be interrogated for what it means and looks like within our current systems and how it reproduces white supremacy. In a context of profound vulnerability, student teachers look for safety and certainty. Part of our struggle, then, is to help student teachers know that what we offer— antiracist knowledge and critical pedagogical practice—is the path to connecting with students and connecting students with learning. But that work takes trust, and trust takes time that fast-track programs do not allow.

The Surveillance of Hyperaccountability

The accountability regime is a critical tool in the reduction of teaching and learning, and learning to teach to technocratic work. From the tests our student teachers are expected to teach to in the schools where they are practicing, to the rubrics, data systems, and reports based upon numerical data that teacher educators are told to prepare, how we think about knowledge, the work of teaching and ourselves is narrowed and dehumanized (Au, 2009; Kohl, 2009; Leahey, 2013).

Teacher educators experience the accountability regime in teacher education within our own courses and departments and in the schools where our students teach. In the K–12 schools, especially but not only in high-poverty districts, the focus on preparing students to take state mandated tests often overrides other goals of teaching, creating profound challenges for faculty and K–12 teachers looking to develop classrooms as sites of critical consciousness (Kesson, 2004). Time and again, the student teacher who is curious about the possibilities of facilitating classroom experiences that give students voice, grow from the knowledge and experiences of the students, and involve rethinking and reimagining their lives report that "there just isn't enough time" or that the "instructional coach is upset about my ANET [Achievement Network] scores" and is inhibiting the student teacher's experiments in teaching and learning. Barbara recalls observing a student teacher at the same time as the district math coach. She watched this new teacher realize that the students were struggling with a concept; the teacher reset the frame and began again to mark success, but the math coach viewed the classes' ANET scores on a computer and commented at the end of the lesson about how poor the scores were. There was no space for this new teacher's development; time was marching on toward more testing. New teachers such as this one are not coming to know themselves within the context of nurturing supportive and challenging relationships, but within the context of surveillance and numerical data as the representation of one's value.

Teacher educators have to act to support student teacher learning when the practices demanded of them in K–12 schools is contrary to the possibilities for democratic and liberatory practice (Aronson and Anderson, 2013). How long can we try to work within the margins of possibility, and when do we agitate for refusing testing that we know to be destructive? What are the deeper lessons of our work when we name the violence of testing, but do not work with student teachers and K–12 teachers to actively resist it?

These questions could remain abstract for teacher educators as long as the accountability demands were restricted to K–12 schools. But the neoliberal ideology that reduces all work to quantitative data and has as its goal the privatization of all public spaces has shifted its focus to teacher education (Apple, 2001; Taubman, 2009). With the blessing of professional organizations, teacher educators are now measuring student "outcomes" using rubrics, data points, web-based data management systems and, soon, the test scores of the students who our graduates teach (Council for the Accreditation of Educator Preparation, 2013). Just as Labaree (1992) warned us, teaching and teacher education are subject to technical rationalization and loss of democratic control. The choices we face about how to respond are now much more immediate. But, just as happened in K–12 education, the danger is not always evident to those whose work is being so profoundly disrupted.

The first thing that the accountability regime has done to teacher education is change the words we use to describe the work we do (Berlak, 2010; Kornfeld et al., 2007). Conversations about critical pedagogy, teaching as political work, teaching as intellectual work, teaching as imaginative and creative, teaching as never fully known work, and teaching as uncertainty are pushed aside as we determine observable measures upon which to collect data about student teacher effectiveness in a range of discrete events that may or may not be part of a classroom practice (Taubman, 2009; Varenne, 2007). The very struggle we know in our courses, where student teachers tell us that our ideas are all fine and good but do not work in the "real world" of data-driven instruction, now enters our department meetings. Quantitative data comes to define the "real world" and, in defining it, comes to define us as subjects.

Whereas words construct us, we live in our bodies and actions. In the struggle to maintain our commitment to our values in the context of neoliberalism, we promise ourselves to work within the margins to create resistance and the possibility of something new. But the power of the neoliberal project is its ability to control the ways we use our bodies, the processes that we enact, and the material reality of our lives. The specific demands of accountability regimes change the work we do; they occupy real space and time and change how we experience ourselves in the world. As director of student teaching, Barbara found more and more of her day was spent in front of computer screens, looking at data points or developing rubrics that would be used to create data points, or at webinars that were calibrating her to give the "correct" data point in response to certain observations. It cannot be said forcefully enough how much this changes how we know ourselves and our students. We become technocrats by acting as technocrats—no matter what is in our hearts. That is not to say that we are engulfed completely and that we are not still finding spaces in which we enact our humanity, but those spaces are becoming smaller and smaller. It gets more difficult to discern the difference between our hope to protect our humanity and lying to ourselves about our complicity and alienation. The sense we have of ourselves as complicated, uncertain, loving, angry, provocative, creative, unknowing, confused, and connected human beings is pushed to the side to only manifest legitimately in the privacy of our homes.

When we marginalize our sense and questioning of what it means to be human, we narrow the possibilities for coming together in communion and solidarity to make our lives together. The shared discourse and experience becomes technocratic and impersonal; the experiences of the personal that we have in our classrooms and work spaces no longer get told but instead become private affairs. That which would bind us alienates us. In this way, hyperaccountability erases teaching and teacher education as the work of public intellectuals who wrestle with critical ideas about what it means to be human, why we educate, the relationship of schooling to democracy, the possibilities for the greater good, and so on. As well, these systems disconnect the personal from the political and pretend at a world where humans in relationship do not struggle with issues of power and justice and where poverty and racism are not relevant.

The Decoupling of Teacher Education from Institutions of Higher Education

The National Council for the Accreditation of Teacher Education blue-ribbon panel for teacher education includes recommendations for more closely aligned K–12 schools and teacher education and for student teachers to spend more time in the classroom. On its face, like many of the ideas being promulgated by neoliberal "reformers," these seem difficult to refute. Indeed, the argument for spending more time in the classroom is made across the political and ideological spectrum. But these recommendations must be examined closely and in context. The context of teacher education is one of narrowing what it means to know, simplifying the need for and the complexity of antiracist, anticolonial work, reducing teaching to techno-cratic work, reducing teachers to technocrats, and eliminating the idea and practice of teachers as public intellectuals and political actors. This context does not require schools of education in which students explore the his-tory of race and public education, the struggles to name and claim what it means to teach for and within a democracy, or the deep questions of mean-ing, purpose, and value that lie at the heart of all educational choices.

Praxis is theory in action. Praxis is action in theory. One informs the other, and both are necessary. To the degree that teacher education is decoupled from higher education it becomes disconnected from the pos-sibility of teacher education as theoretical work, of teaching as embedded in and emerging not only from research but also from theory and philoso-phy, from political economy and the humanities. Yet this is precisely what neoliberal reformers are pushing for. The Relay Graduate School of Educa-tion, started by the KIPP charter school network, grants teaching licenses in three states, without a university affiliation. The Growing Education Achievement Training Academies for Teachers and Principals Act, intro-duced to the US Congress in 2013, would allow for charter schools of edu-cation. And TFA continues to offer a high-profile pathway into teaching that bypasses university-based preparation and replaces it with five weeks of training. These are just three examples of recent attempts to decouple teacher education from universities. University-based teacher education programs are being squeezed by demands for efficient, behavior-focused, technocratic teacher training (Zeichner, 2012). This same disparagement of the work of teachers that paved the way for the attack on K–12 schools is now being used against teacher educators (Levine, 2006). Accessing old complaints about teacher education being "too theoretical" and not aligned enough with the "real world" of the classroom, people whose interests are privatization and not democratic education have been able to gain the dom-inant narrative. With the "shock doctrine" experience of reduced funding and the pressures to keep student enrollment up when other programs are cheaper and faster, schools of education have responded with more fast-track programs, more online courses, and compliance with the account-ability regime of state and federal mandates. In so doing we have allowed the core practice of our work to undergo profound changes (Aronson and Anderson, 2013; Sleeter, 2008).

The material realities of reduced resources and the adoption of market ideology within public universities can leave teacher educators with a nar-row perspective of their options. Our sense of how our programs are weak and could be stronger can leave us back on our heels when our practice is attacked. Teacher educators have been slow to identify the larger struggle of which we are a part in order to see the patterns of defunding, attacking, surveilling, and privatizing that have been used to undermine K–12 public education (Apple, 2001; Hill, 2007). Similarly, we have been too cautious about defending our work as critical, social justice work that requires time, resources, and a deep attention to praxis. Claiming our voices need not be a defense of the status quo (Zeichner, 2012). We need resistance that acknowledges how teacher education, like K–12 education, has always reproduced race and class inequality *and* resistance that boldly defends the work of critical social-justice education.

A JOURNEY TOWARD RESISTANCE

An essential aspect of our work as critical social justice teacher educators is to expose students of teaching to the historical and sociological structures that make public education a site of contestation. The texts, experiences, and conversations we explore in our teacher education classes are designed to unveil institutional power, the values and beliefs at the center of policies and practices, and the question of what it means to educate in and for democracy. For at least the last ten years, this has meant exposing the corporate actors behind the so-called reform movement in education; exposing the neoliberal ideology of individuality, competition, and marketization that allowed for corporate influence to be so pronounced; and encouraging students of teaching to look closely at how these impact classroom practice and how they might facilitate classroom experiences that rehumanize the classroom. In our courses we raised questions about the discourse of accountability, data-driven decision making, and standards. Our students, on the whole, appreciated the opportunity to engage these questions and tended toward a critical analysis that challenged neoliberal trends. They were becoming teachers, after all, in response to wishes to make a difference in the lives of young people—this difference being to spark curiosity, discover and use their writing voices, learn to investigate their world, and think through problems with clarity. Many were becoming teachers because they saw public education as a site from which to begin to right injustices. But they were practicing in classrooms where the floodwaters were already very deep.

Whereas, for the most part, our students wanted to embrace models of teaching and learning that were democratic and humane, they did not know how to do that in classrooms in which they were being monitored for objectives, pacing within the curriculum, and student performance in preparation for standardized assessments. Nor did they know how knowledge of poverty, homelessness, families disrupted by the need for multiple minimum wage jobs, poor health care, and the daily reality of racism fit into their practice of teaching within systems of hyperaccountability. Student teachers, under the tutelage of classroom teachers who are themselves struggling to negotiate increasingly narrow definitions of their practice, would tell us it was just not possible to engage the practices we discussed in the classroom. And, increasingly, we understood that our hope to help them find the possible inside such a system was becoming a kind of denial. We started to question the relationship between meaningful hope in lessons that maneuvered around the accountability regime and a pretense of critical pedagogy within a hidden (or not-so-hidden) curriculum of compliance and denial. We wondered, individually and together, what we were setting students of teaching up for if we led them to believe that we could swim around the mines when perhaps there were now too many mines. At the same time, we were aware that opting out of teaching was a privilege that denied the necessity of public education to our hopes for justice (Madeloni, forthcoming). It was in this context that Madeloni, who was directing a two-year teacher education pathway, took action.

Barbara's Experience

As the floodwaters of the corporate assault on public education were rising, I was trying to determine where and how to build some resistance. Like my K–12 colleagues, I hoped to be able to stay in schools and create spaces where the values of education as freedom were protected, where possibilities for liberation could be nourished. The question of any resistance movement is how much to work from within the system and how much to work outside it. As educators, the inside work of our classroom practice is our resistance. I entered teaching to develop activist imaginations in the classroom. This focus can, however, limit our attention to the larger social forces under which we labor until it is too late, until the floodwaters are seeping under the classroom door.

As I was trying to understand how to support teachers teaching in the midst of the flood, the waters began to lap at the feet of teacher educators—first through the accreditation process and next through the demand for a single national assessment of student teacher readiness, the edTPA. I began to experience the questions my students had been asking and continued to ask: Can I do the work of social justice education within a high-surveillance, standards-based, hyperaccountability system? Am I deluding myself that I am teaching for social justice when, in the end, I require students to comply with systems that are dehumanizing, push out the time for conversations and imagination about education as liberation, and impose a technocratic authoritarian vision of teaching?

Educators for justice have a commitment to working within what Foucault (1988) refers to as the capillaries of our daily lives. Classrooms are our sites, and we do our work within the context of individual relationships and the community of the classroom. As important as this work is, to the degree that it maintains an individualistic perspective on action toward change, it undermines our goals for justice. We cannot simply address the floodwaters in our contexts; we must investigate, name, and stem the tide at its source, and this requires shared understandings, risks, and actions. When I was told that Pearson Inc. would be leading a field test of a new national assessment of student teaching readiness and that our student teachers would be required to participate in it, I found myself at a cross-roads. How, I asked myself, could I continue to pretend to find the place where my words and actions were aligned when my actions increasingly constituted compliance? What were the real lessons of my teaching if my words were so far from my deeds?

In the spring of 2012, 67 of 68 student teachers in the secondary program at the University of Massachusetts–Amherst refused to participate in the field test of the Pearson-Stanford edTPA (Winerip, 2012). In this moment, the words we had spoken together in various courses coincided with our actions (Madeloni and Hoogstraten, 2013). We would not be party to the corporate assault on public education. We would join in solidarity to say no and claim our voices and our understandings of what teacher education could and should be. This action, which I supported and fought for, resulted in my receiving a letter of nonrenewal for my contract, but it led to much more. It opened the door to a national conversation about the edTPA, a conversation that was otherwise dominated by one voice (Madeloni and Gorlewski, 2013a, 2013b). It provided the students of teaching with an experience of solidarity in action and critical lessons about the possibilities of acting beyond the classroom to resist the corporate takeover of public education. But it taught me lessons as well and compelled me to rethink the role of activism in teacher education and the entire teacher education for social justice project.

WHAT IS NECESSARY MUST BE MADE POSSIBLE

As K–12 teachers and teacher educators attempt to survive the increasingly technocratic demands on our work, it becomes more difficult to embody the values and practices that originally brought us to education. Speaking out against these measures might lead to job loss, difficulty attaining grant funding, and marginalization in the workplace. Many of us try to maintain our livelihoods while not abandoning our values by working within the art of the possible, doing what we can where we can to maintain a space of active hope. This is necessary and important work, but it is not enough. To the degree that we allow our work to be limited in scope and possibility, we risk losing our foundational values. The discourse shifts, and soon we have forgotten how to imagine something bigger. Working within the narrow band of what seems possible is the work of individuals making sense within their classrooms. Organizing a resistance beyond that narrow band, claiming our voices and vision for education, and refusing to participate in policies that dehumanize and corporatize education is the work of educators acting together in solidarity with parents, students, and community members.

The narrow spaces we are allowed leave little space for antiracist work. They leave little space for the consideration of the democratic project—its hopes and failures—and the implications of these for the choices we make in the classroom. The art of the possible does not allow for deep appreciation of the necessity of taking our time to think, to talk, to listen, and to wonder before we act. It boxes us into the necessity of speaking as if we know all the answers rather than within an informed uncertainty. The art of the possible teaches us and our students to succumb to demands for compliance and to respond to fear with cowardice and protections. In time, teacher education within the straitjacket we are allowed becomes devoid of passion, imagination, active hope, curiosity, and dogged commitment to justice.

Our experiences have taught us that we must name what is necessary for education for liberation and social justice and insist that it be possible. We can no longer hope to find some small space in which to enact the core of our work while allowing data-driven technocrats to occupy the space of our classrooms and our imaginations. We must name and fight for what is most important, and we must be ready to accept the risks attendant to claiming our space. This requires solidarity. But this is the work of education for liberation under any system that works to silence and dehumanize us. If we claim this as our work, we must enact it in our practice and our programs.

Teacher educators must extend their knowledge, experience, and connections beyond the university and the K–12 school. We need to act from an understanding of ourselves as political agents, just as we ask of the students who are becoming teachers. This necessitates fully informing ourselves about the larger context of K–12 and higher education as well as the broad context of racial and economic injustice in its myriad manifestations. Beyond extending our knowledge, we need to enter the world as the political agents that we are. Just as we expect student teachers to know the communities in which they teach, to reach out to parents and community members, we must know and be a part of those same communities. If we want new teachers to imagine themselves as political actors, we need to be with them—acting, leading, listening, and participating in the political life of the community.

If we are committed to antiracist education, then we cannot hope to slip some version of it in during one or two class sessions. Nor can we let our fear of angry white students writing bad evaluations silence us. Teacher educators need to not only engage in antiracist education, but also demand it for their students and stake a claim for the time necessary to do this work (Nieto, 2000). This means refusing the watered-down versions of cultural competence that deny the ways social and institutional powers work to silence and marginalize (Sleeter, 2008). It means bringing the language of antiracist work into our program descriptions and policy statements, connecting the dots between high-stakes testing and the eugenics movement and doing this not only in our classrooms, but in the public sphere. It means speaking out loud about the ways that fast-track programs exacerbate internalized racism and deficit ideologies and demanding that teacher education be allotted more time. A commitment to antiracist practice cannot allow for the cutting of corners.

Similarly, if as teacher educators we are committed to teaching as a space of constantly coming to ask better questions and be steadier within uncertainty, we must actively reject all efforts to measure the complexity of teaching as a precisely knowable technique. This means challenging the constraints imposed by state and professional accrediting agencies that require data reports that undermine teaching as contested work. Every time we comply with the mandates of the neoliberal education regime we allow its narrative to hold. Even if our hearts are not in it, and even if we hold a critique, our complicity reinforces and strengthens the neoliberal narrative. We must build solidarity and organizations that support teacher educators in resisting these mandates. We must continue to design our own classroom practice to be more open, questioning, and uncertain.

Further, as educators for social justice, our courses should include the history of educational activism, of the nature and process of the struggles for social justice, and of the roles of community organizations, parents, students, teachers, and unions in that struggle. We should not limit the possibility of teaching for social justice to the classroom, where student teachers and novice teachers are most likely to find themselves isolated and overwhelmed, but we should teach and practice the power of organizing (Katsarou, Picower, & Stovall, 2010).

If we are truly committed to teacher education as the development of teachers who will enact liberatory practices, we must also critique and resist the oppressive and hierarchal nature of the institutions of which we are a part. This includes rejecting the hierarchies of knowledge and the limitations we accept about what it means to be an engaged scholar. We need to close the false divide between scholarship and activism, a divide that serves to protect privilege, and we need to engage as activists and intellectuals.

Social context reform recognizes that educational inequality is inextricably intertwined with other social inequalities (racism, poverty, class inequality, healthy care, wages, housing, and the criminal injustice system). Thus, our resistance must work at these intersections and be linked with struggles for broader social change. As the late Jean Anyon argued (2005), we must redefine what counts as education reform so it includes antipoverty measures such as improvements in job creation, health care, housing, and wages. Situating educational activism within broader social movement building not only reflects a more accurate analysis of the issues, but is also the most promising way to build the social movement necessary to fight back against the powerful corporate interests behind neoliberal education. Critical social justice teacher education is an essential part of the resistance to the neoliberal assault.

Each of these reimaginings requires that we claim a new vision for teacher education. Teacher educators can no longer sit back on our heels, hoping to gain favor and shyly suggesting other alternatives within the discourse of the corporatists. Nor can we limit ourselves to papers and presentations about social justice education that address like-minded colleagues. It is time to fully engage the struggle. The corporate assault on public education is not a passing fad nor just one more annoyance passed on from administrators. It emerges from and is linked to racism and growing economic injustice. We are in real danger of losing the possibility of our democratic project and our public schools. As social justice educators, we must, as Herbert Kohl (2010) reminds us, be outraged by this circumstance. We must commit to action.

REFERENCES

Anyon, J. (2005). *Radical possibilities*. New York: Routledge.

Apple, M. (2001). Markets, standards, teaching, and teacher education. *Journal of Teacher Education, 52*(3), 182–196.

Applebaum, B. (2004). Social justice education, moral agency, and the subject of resistance. *Educational Theory, 54*(1), 59–72.

Aronson, B., & Anderson, A. (2013). Critical teacher education and the politics of accreditation: Are we practicing what we preach? *Journal for Critical Education Policy Studies, 11*(3), 244–262.

Au, W. (2009). Teaching under the new Taylorism: High-stakes testing and the standardization of the 21st century curriculum. *Journal of Curriculum Studies, 43* (1), 25–45.

Baines, L. (2010). *The teachers we need vs. the teachers we have: The realities and the possibilities*. Lanham, MD: Rowman and Littlefield.

Berlak, A. (2010). Coming soon to your favorite credential program: National exit exams. *Rethinking Schools, 24*(4), 41–45.

Britzman, D. (2000). Teacher education in the confusion of our times. *Journal of Teacher Education, 51*(3), 200–205.

Council for the Accreditation of Educator Preparation. (2013). Standard 4: Program impact. Retrieved from http://caepnet.org/accreditation/final-standards/standard4/

Delandshere, G., & Pretosky, A. (2004). Political rationales and ideological stances of the standards-based reform of teacher education in the US. *Teaching and Teacher Education, 20,* 1–15.

Feistritzer, C. E. (2011). *Profile of teachers in the United States in 2011*. National Center for Educational Information. Retrieved from http://www.edweek.org/media/pot2011final-blog.pdf

Foucault, M.(1988) *Power/knowledge : Selected interviews and other writings, 1972–77*. (Colin Gordon, ed.) NewYork: Random House

Gay, G. (2010). Acting on beliefs in teacher education for cultural diversity. *Journal of Teacher Education, 61*(1–2), 143–152.

Harvey, D. (2005). *A brief history of neoliberalism*. New York: Oxford University Press.

Hill, D. (2007). Critical teacher education, new labour, and the global project of neoliberal capital. *Policy Futures in Education, 5*(2), 204–225.

hooks, b. (1994). *Teaching to transgress: Education as the practice of freedom*. New York: Routledge.

Katsarou, E., Picower, B., and Stovall, D. (2010). Acts of solidarity: Developing urban social justice educators in the struggle for quality education. *Teacher Education Quarterly, 37*(3), 137–153.

Kesson, K. (2004). Inhuman powers and terrible things: The theory and practice of alienated labor in urban schools. *Journal of Critical Policy Studies, 2*(10), 40–72.

Kohl, H. (2009). The educational panopticon. *Teachers College Record*, ID Number 15477. Retrieved from http://www.tcrecord.org,

Kohl, H. (2010). Teaching for social justice. In T. Burant, L. Christensen, & K. Dawson Salas (Eds.), *The new teacher book: Finding purpose, balance, and hope during your first years in the classroom* (pp. 35–38). Milwaukee, WI: Rethinking Schools.

Kornfeld, J., Grady, K., Marker, P., & Rapp Ruddell, M. (2007). Caught in the current: A self-study of state-mandated compliance in a teacher education program. *Teachers College Record, 109*(8), 1902–1930.

Labaree, D. (1992). Power, knowledge, and the rationalization of teaching: A genealogy of the movement to professionalize teaching. *Harvard Educational Review, 62*(2), 123–154.

Labaree, D. (2010). Teach for America and teacher ed: Heads they win, tales we lose. *Journal of Teacher Education, 61*(1–2), 48–55.

Ladson-Billings, G. (2000). Fighting for our lives: Preparing teachers to teach African American students. *Journal of Teacher Education, 51*(30), 206–214.

Lea, V. (2011). Concocting crisis to create consent. In P. Carr & B. Porfilio (Eds.), *The phenomenon of Obama and the agenda for education: Can hope audaciously trump neoliberalism?* (pp. 23–47). Charlotte, NC: Information Age.

Leahey, C. (2013). Catch-22 and the paradox of teaching in the 21st century. *Critical Education, 4*(6), 1–18.

Levine, A. (2006). *Educating School Teachers*. Retrieved from http://www.edschools.org/pdf/Educating_Teachers_Report.pdf

Lipman, P. (2004). *High stakes education: Inequality, globalization, and urban school reform*. New York: Routledge.

Liston, D. (1995). Work in teacher education: A current assessment of U.S. teacher education. In N. Shimahara & I. Holowinsky (Eds.), *Teacher education in industrialized nations* (pp. 87–123). New York: Garland.

Madeloni, B. (forthcoming). From a whisper to a scream: Ethics and resistance in the age of neo-liberalism. *Learning and Teaching: The International Journal of Higher Education in the Social Sciences.*

Madeloni, B., & Gorlewski, J. (2013a, June 21). Radical imagination, not standardization: Critical teacher education and the edTPA. *Teachers College Record*, ID Number 17163. Retrieved from http://www.tcrecord.org

Madeloni, B., & Gorlewski, J. (2013b). The wrong answer to the wrong question: Why we need critical teacher education, not standardization. *Rethinking Schools, 27*(4), 16–21.

Madeloni, B., & Hoogstraten, R. (2013). The other side of fear. *Schools: Studies in Education, 10*(1), 1–14.

Miner, B. (2010). Looking past the spin: Teach for America. *Rethinking Schools, 24*(3), 24–33..

National Council for the Accreditation of Teacher Education. *Transforming teacher education through clinical practice: A national strategy to prepare effective teachers*. Retrieved from http://www.ncate.org/LinkClick.aspx?fileticket=zzeiB1OoqPk%3D&tabid=715

Nieto, S. (2000). Placing diversity front and center: Some thoughts on transforming teacher education for the new century. *Journal of Teacher Education, 51*(3), 180–187.

Sleeter, C. (2008). Equity, democracy, and neoliberal assaults on teacher education. *Teaching and Teacher Education, 24*(8), 1947–1957.

Smagorinsky, P. (2010). The culture of learning to teach. *Teacher Education Quarterly, 37*(2), 19–32.

Taubman, P. (2009). *Teaching by numbers: Deconstructing the discourse of standards and accountability in education.* New York: Routledge.

Tuck, E. (2013). Neoliberalism as nihilism: A commentary on educational accountability, teacher education, and school reform. *Journal for Critical Education Policy Studies, 11*(2), 324–347.

Varenne, H. (2007). On NCATE standards and the culture at work: Conversations, hegemony and (dis-)abling consequences. *Anthropology and Education Quarterly, 38*(10), 16–23.

Winerip, M. (2012, May 6). Move to outsource teacher licensure draws protest. *New York Times.*

Zeichner, K. (2012). Two visions of teaching and teacher education for the twenty-first century. Colloquium Series, Education Leadership and Research Policy Studies Unit. Retrieved from http://www.umassd.edu/media/umassdartmouth/seppce/edleadership/Kenneth_Zeichner_Two_Visions_of_Teaching_and_Teacher_Education.pdf

Part II
School-Based Reform for Equity and Opportunity

5 Changing the Colonial Context to Address School Underperformance in Nunavut

Paul Berger[1]

> The government schools were basically "outpost" versions of southern schools. Their programs had nothing to do with our language, culture, or the adaptive challenges faced by our people. . . . Rather than making us stronger, they tended to undermine our confidence and identity.
>
> —Sheila Watt-Cloutier, "Honouring Our Past, Creating our Future: Education in Northern and Remote Communities"

INTRODUCTION

At first glance, the educational context in Nunavut, 1750 miles north of Washington, D.C., is nothing like the neoliberal disaster that is continuing to unfold across the U.S. and—in our Canadian habit of imitation—growing in some Canadian provinces. Nunavut has no charter schools and only a few standardized tests. Teachers are not under attack nor paid depending on how well their students do. There is significant work being done on creating locally relevant curricula and in trying to reinvent the school system to provide bilingual and bicultural education according to Inuit wishes (McGregor, 2013). But all is definitely not well.

In this chapter I explore what Inuit in one community say are barriers to school success and link them to major theories explaining school underachievement for minority and Indigenous youth. I argue that colonialism is a common thread and that neoliberal thinking provides a barrier to moving away from colonialism. Whereas "social and political forces" may be primarily responsible for school failure (Thomas, 2011a), I suggest things that schools might do to respond.

SCHOOLING IN NUNAVUT

Nunavut is a gigantic territory in northern Canada, about 12 times the size of Florida, with a population of 31,906, 85% of whom are Inuit (Statistics Canada, 2011). About 9,000 students attend schools in Nunavut's 27 isolated communities (Inuit Tapiriit Kanatami, 2008). Schools were built across the Canadian eastern Arctic 60 years ago as part of the Canadian government's plan to move Inuit from the coastlines into communities. Inuit were told that attendance was mandatory and that family allowance payments would be withheld from parents who did not send their children to school (Tester & Kulchyski, 1994). The schools imposed White ways of educating (Douglas, 1994), displacing Inuit ways (Nungak, 2004); the goal was assimilation and the creation of a workforce ready for an industrial economy (Brody, 1977; Chisholm, 1994). From their genesis, then, they were colonial intrusions with what would become a neoliberal goal—schooling for job readiness (Elmore, 2013).

Formal schooling began with English as the language of instruction, Euro-Canadian curriculum, and White teachers (Van Meenen, 1994). Students in many communities now start their schooling with Inuit teachers and instruction in an Inuit language, but they are soon pushed into all-English environments with southern Canadian teachers in the junior grades (McGregor, 2010). Euro-Canadian curriculum, structures, and values continue to dominate schooling in Nunavut and often conflict with deeply held Inuit values (Douglas, 1998). To complete their K–12 schooling, Inuit students must pass courses with curriculum from the western Canadian provinces and pass exams designed for students from western Canada (McGregor, 2010).

Despite much work by Inuit and non-Inuit, only 36% of Inuit students graduate from high school (Nunavut Bureau of Statistics, 2012), and almost none of them pursue university studies (Dorais & Sammons, 2002). To improve student achievement and increase student well-being, schooling in Nunavut must accelerate its move away from colonialism—"the centering of the experience, beliefs, values and way of life of the newcomers and the displacement of the indigenous group to the margins" (Tompkins, 2006, p. 36). With the newcomers' way of life shaped by consumer capitalism and the newcomers still largely in control, there is much work to be done. As Rasmussen (2000) wrote, Inuit culture is under attack by education and money.

WHY DO SCHOOLS FOR MINORITY AND INDIGENOUS STUDENTS UNDERPERFORM?

Different models compete to best explain school underperformance. The *cultural deficit* model explains that students from poor and minority backgrounds arrive at school unprepared for success due to deficiencies in their home cultures, specifically with respect to language, psychological, and social development (Jacob & Jordan, 1993, p. 5). The theory has been discredited, though teachers often think in deficit terms (Fuzessy, 2003) and the model fits well with the neoliberal tendency to blame people for structural factors outside of their control (Thomas, 2011a).

The *cultural difference* or *cultural discontinuity* model focuses on the communication, social, and learning style differences between Indigenous and minority students and the ways they are expected to learn in schools (Erickson, 1975; Philips, 1993). This explanation shifts blame from the child and his or her culture to the school's failure to respond to the learner. It remains popular today (Castagno & Brayboy, 2008), though it does not explain the ability of students from some minority groups to succeed in mainstream schools despite cultural incompatibility (Ogbu, 1993).

John Ogbu's (1993) *structural theory*, based largely on his work with African American communities, postulates that students' motivation is reduced by concerns about loss of culture through schooling and poor labor-market outcomes. Parents, Ogbu (1992) wrote, say they support schooling but may put less pressure on their children to succeed than Euro-American parents do. Structural theory may focus too much on historical oppression while ignoring racial bias in today's schools (Foster, 2005), putting too much emphasis on student and family responsibility and too little on what schools should do differently (Gibson, 2005).

Racism and *differential treatment* are explanations for school underperformance that have not yet had the focus they deserve (Castagno & Brayboy, 2008), though there is a growing scholarship on the connection between Whiteness and racism in educational contexts (Comeau, 2007). A literature review on racism in Indigenous schooling found many studies pointing to racism as having a major negative impact on First Nations students' school experiences (St. Denis & Hampton, 2002).

Community control of schooling is expected to increase Indigenous students' success (Cummins, 1986; Kirkness, 1998; Lipka, 1989); the lack of local control allows continuing "cognitive imperialism" (Battiste, 2000, p. 193). Self-determination or sovereignty in schooling is rarely discussed in the literature on culturally responsive schooling (Castagno & Brayboy, 2008).

How do these competing explanations for school failure look in the Arctic schooling context in Nunavut, and what can schools do to improve things? As part of my doctoral research (Berger, 2008), I set out to explore these questions.

METHODOLOGY

A White Euro-Canadian, I have been interested in contributing to decolonizing Inuit schooling since teaching grade 7 in Tuktulik (a pseudonym meaning "place of caribou") in the mid-1990s. This chapter draws on my master's degree work (Berger, 2001), ongoing collaborative work on increasing the number of Inuit teachers in Nunavut, and work with parents and students in the western Arctic, but it comes mostly from interviews with 74 Inuit adults for my dissertation (Berger, 2008).

In the community where I used to teach I received support from the mayor and the hamlet council, modified the research design to address the district education authority's concern that I might increase tension in the community (I removed planned workshops with teachers), and received approval from Lakehead University and the Nunavut Research Institute to proceed. I asked what people liked about schooling, what they thought should change, and what created barriers for Inuit student learning.

I strived to conduct the research respectfully and tried to be useful through volunteering while in the community (Smith, 1999; Steinhauer, 2002). Ideally, research with Indigenous people would be initiated by the community (Menzies, 2004). Although this study was researcher initiated, I approached the work in a "spirit of advocacy" (Kral & Idlout, 2006).

Tuktulik has about 1,300 residents, about 93% of whom are Inuit (Statistics Canada, 2006). Demographically, Tuktulik shares a number of characteristics with most small Nunavut communities. The majority of Qallunaat residents are from southern Canada and came to Nunavut for employment.[2] Many Inuit are not involved in the wage economy, and many pursue land activities, primarily hunting and fishing and their related technologies. Many are also involved in artistic endeavors, principally printmaking and soapstone carving, and there is high unemployment in Tuktulik.

The interview participants' ages, wage employment status, highest level of schooling, and participation in land activities all roughly mirrored Tuktulik and Nunavut demographics (City-Data, n.d.). This roughly representative sample increases the likelihood that what I heard would be easily recognizable by community members, though this work does not represent the views of all Inuit in Tuktulik and it remains my Qallunaat interpretation of what I heard and saw.

COLONIAL DISRUPTION, NOT CULTURAL DEFICIT

Teachers sometimes blame parents and students' home lives for difficulties in schooling (Aylward, 2009; Fuzessy, 2003), a cultural deficit model. Disruption in some students' homes is undoubtedly a significant barrier to learning, but this is colonial disruption, not cultural deficit.

Many participants cited drugs or alcohol as reasons they themselves left school, and addiction, gambling, violence, abuse, and other problems such as food insecurity as barriers to student learning. For example, one participant said, "Of course the number one thing is dope," and one Inuit teacher said, "As you know, there are many parents with drugs, alcohol, violence, and the students bring it to the school and take it out on other kids, teachers."

Addiction and violence are not unique to Nunavut, though they are often especially acute in the aftermath and in the midst of colonization. Colonial processes change how people make a living, destroy languages and spirituality, and assault family structure (Lane, Bopp, & Bopp, 2003), while paternalistic treatment grooms people for dependence (Watt-Cloutier, 2000). When Indigenous peoples repeatedly hear the colonizers' ideas and are subject to their attitudes and behaviors, self-destruction often results (Brody, 2000)—"the aimlessness, family violence, alcoholism, the monotony of despair that comes with colonialism and dispossession" (Kulchyski, 2005, p. 111). For Inuit, many stressors related to colonialism still exist (Nungak, 2004), including overcrowded housing, poor health, low median income and high unemployment (Nunavut Social Development Council, 1998; Statistics Canada, 2006; Tester, 2006).

Violence and substance abuse may go together. One participant said, "I've experienced violence, drugs and alcohol myself, and when people don't talk about violence then they'll tend to turn to substance abuse." Participants expressed concern about the lack of support for people in dealing with violence, alcoholism, and drug addiction; there is less help than can be found in southern Canadian settings.

Social problems—colonial disruptions—in Nunavut communities create obstacles for learning. The neoliberal tendency to place blame on teachers and schools (Thomas, 2011b) is hazardous; school reform must be paralleled by broader moves to address the poverty, unemployment, poor health, and housing problems that contribute to social problems (Thomas, 2011a), and local programs are needed to facilitate healing. Still, the schools cannot wait for this. They can respond by doing everything possible to create relevant and empowering programs (Watt-Cloutier, 2000), remembering that schools have played a key role in disrupting Inuit life (Tester & Kulchyski, 1994), and that addictive and harmful behaviors may in part be a response to the assimilation still demanded by the schools (Malaurie, 2007).

School staff may look to schools that are successful with students coming from difficult life circumstances (Nieto, 1994), the literature on teaching students with violent pasts (Horsman, 1999), and Nunavut examples (Berger, 2001; Tompkins, 1998, 2004). Creating safe and respectful environments, valuing students' home language and culture, believing that students deserve and are capable of learning, encouraging parental involvement, and holding high expectations are all needed (Nieto, 1994). A concrete example of one school addressing the social problem of food insecurity comes from the western Arctic, where a culinary arts program sees students making healthy snacks and meals that are sold inexpensively to students. The impact of this type of initiative should not be underestimated. As a man in his 30s said, "Can't do much work when you're really hungry, eh? I used to be like that."

CULTURAL DIFFERENCE AND NUNAVUT SCHOOLING'S LACKLUSTER RESPONSE

In Tuktulik there is ample evidence of cultural differences between Inuit students' lives inside and outside of schools, something stable over time (Douglas, 1994). Especially salient are differences in preferred learning style, language, and values. Whereas Inuit parents do want students to have success in typical academic subjects, basing schooling on others' pedagogy, language, and values is a sign of the continuing colonialism in Nunavut schooling, and it negatively affects student learning.

Incongruence in Learning Style

The most salient way that Inuit experience is different from typical Qallunaat school practice is in the area of learning style. I asked most participants what they liked to do in their free time and how they had learned to do it. Almost no one had learned to do nonschool things in the typical ways students are expected to learn in Qallunaat schools. A quote helps to illustrate this. Asked how she learned to carve, a female Elder said, "By watching. Nobody ever taught me how to do the shaping. I only did my own shaping by watching my father carve."

Historically, Inuit boys' play imitated their fathers' hunting and fishing gestures, and learning proceeded with no formal teaching and almost no questions asked (Balikci, 1970). This is consistent with participants' descriptions. Two recent grade 12 graduates said they had learned to hunt from their father. As one explained, "We would go out with him when we were growing up, just seeing how he's hunting, just by watching. Mostly from watching."

An Elder was especially clear that there was little direct teaching when he was young:

> By looking. We weren't taught. We watched our fathers; when we went out with them we watched our relatives. How they did things. They didn't try to say to us this is how anything. . . . Things like building an igloo, I learned how to do it by watching. . . . Like the cracks; the guy was building the igloo he had to fill the holes. You learn by looking at it.

He then connected the very different teaching methods he encountered in college to his inability to complete the program:

> I found it more difficult when I went to college. In a college environment you listen to the instructor talking away all day long, never writing anything on the board most of the day. I found that difficult, myself, because I wasn't too sure what is it that I was supposed to do.

Whereas it may be difficult to teach some things using Inuit learning preferences (Darnell & Hoem, 1996), explicit instruction on how to learn in other ways might make a significant difference. Unfortunately, Whiteness can often mean not noticing that how we do things can be culturally specific (Shore, 2003), and the neoliberal "standardization" mantra (Elmore, 2013) probably contributes to this.

Out-of-school learning across all ages was consistently described as happening through observation and doing, often autonomously. This Inuit learning style or preference may be closely connected to Inuit epistemology—how we come to know things or what we feel counts as knowledge (Arnakak, 2000)—which privileges personal experience (Briggs, 1970; Møller, 2005). Ignoring Inuit epistemology can be hazardous, as described by a participant: "A lot of young people die out there 'cause nobody teaches them. They tell them, they don't show them how."

It is clear that Inuit have learned, continue to learn, often prefer to learn, and value learning in ways that differ sharply from the abstract and textually mediated ways that are typically found in Qallunaat teachers' classrooms (Stairs, 1994). Whereas it would be damaging to only offer Inuit students hands-on tasks (Watt-Cloutier, 2000),[3] it is a disservice to teach primarily in ways that do not honor the way they have learned to learn (Nunavut Department of Education, 2005). Because there is no territory-wide orientation or professional development for new Qallunaat teachers who want to know how to best teach Inuit students (Berger & Epp, 2007), schools will need to take on this task themselves. It is not enough for White teachers, most of whom are late career recruits from southern Canada, to teach only in the ways they are used to.

Learning in the Wrong Language

Schools in Tuktulik use Inuktitut as the language of instruction in the primary grades before switching to English in grades 5 or 6. Inuit want more Inuktitut in the schools, primarily because of ongoing loss of language, but language was also named as a barrier to student learning, congruent with the *cultural difference* model (Philips, 1993).

Participants wanted English taught, but many spoke of difficulties created by its use as the language of instruction. They themselves struggled in school because teachers talked too fast, the vocabulary used was difficult, and things were not always explained clearly. One recent high school graduate said, "Hardest thing for me going to school was mostly the English part; like sometimes it was very difficult for me to understand some of the things that were being taught in school because of English." Another said:

> I've seen a lot of students growing up and dropping out because they don't know how to speak that good English, and so when someone's teaching you in a language that's not your own, you don't understand anything and then it really becomes discouraging for people.

The "early-exit" model of second-language schooling is academically hazardous (Martin, 2000), and especially so when most Qallunaat teachers have not had ESL training (Berger & Epp, 2007). English instruction makes learning more difficult, but it also erodes Inuktitut competence

(Dorais & Sammons, 2002) and threatens identity. A woman in her 50s said, "My children's Inuktitut is more English than anything else. They may be speaking in Inuktitut, but they're putting their words together in Qallunaatitut [like white people]." A man in his 20s said, "That little kid's pure Inuk. I would not believe that little kid was speaking English instead of our language."

An assault on language is a colonial assault (Brody, 2000). Nunavut needs a bilingual, bicultural education system (T. Berger, 2006), a system described in the *Nunavut Bilingual Education Strategy* (Nunavut Department of Education, 2004), but unrealized. Unfortunately the Canadian government response to Inuit wishes to reinvent the imposed colonial model of schooling was uninspiring. At the time of a large budget surplus, then Minister of Indian and Northern Affairs Jim Prentice denied funding, saying that more money was already spent on Nunavut students than any others in Canada (Windeyer, 2006). This discounted the real conditions of running schools in Nunavut with a neoliberal argument for efficiency (Gorlewski & Gorlewski, 2013). Nunavut is left with policy and aspirations for culturally and linguistically relevant schooling that is impossible to achieve.

Absent a system-wide push to change the early exit model to a bilingual one (which is actually now mandated by the Education Act; see McGregor, 2013), schools must do everything they can to raise the presence and status of Inuktitut (Tompkins, 1998).

Value Differences

In Qallunaat schools Inuit students face pedagogy that may be less than ideal in a language that may pose difficulties, but there may also be a clash in values between home and school that makes learning more difficult. Some of this may play out in pedagogy, as when Qallunaat teachers reprimand students for "speaking out of turn" (though they were following culturally acceptable speech patterns) and for "cheating" (though they were following culturally expected norms of helping each other) (Crago et al., 1997). In Tuktulik, the Inuit valuing of autonomy might mean that parental decisions are misinterpreted by teachers, to the detriment of students.

The valuing of autonomy was often shown subtly. When I asked a participant if she was confident that her children would do well in school, she said, "I'm confident. It's them having to want to. I hope they feel that they have to go to school every day." Another parent, who said it is the parents' responsibility that children are in school, added, "As well as the child has to want to do it. Or it'll be disrupting other kids in the school, you know." The Inuit belief in autonomy "is fundamental to the Inuit way of being in the world" (Brody, 2000, p. 31), but without parental intervention, some students may have poor punctuality and attendance.

Unfortunately I experienced rigidity in the high school about these issues. Qallunaat teachers expressed the need for Inuit to learn to come on time and were not open to Inuit ideas about the school's attendance policy. This removed the possibility of working together, ignored the Inuit cultural priority of autonomy, and ignored the context of the community—where many parents do not have regular wage labor that structures their day.

One of the most damaging potential consequences of Qallunaat teachers not understanding Inuit culture is that they may mistakenly believe that Inuit parents fail in their parenting (Brody, 2000). According to a participant, it could happen like this:

> Inuit are very patient, even though they don't really need to sometimes. But that's one of the biggest lifestyles we learn is patience, so I think that can be misinterpreted. . . . If I didn't know how to speak English and you were my daughter's teacher and if I ignored something because I didn't know, even though I had the best interest in my child . . . it would be seen that way, that I don't care at all. Even though it's not that way.

Marked value differences can lead to misunderstanding. Qallunaat schools still exist in the Arctic, with unilingual English-speaking teachers who lack the support to understand the cross-cultural English as a second language environment in which they teach. The broader structures here will not be changed by individual teachers or schools, but a school commitment to professional development, as described by Joanne Tompkins (1998), may lead to more student learning and less disruption. The focus should not be uncritically on helping students succeed in the Qallunaat school, but on how schools can respond to Inuit ways and values.

STRUCTURAL BASES FOR INUIT STUDENT STRUGGLES

Ogbu (1993) postulated that student motivation among "involuntary minorities" was reduced by concern that school success would mean loss of culture, and by poor prospects for employment in a labor market dominated by Whites. Minority parents, he wrote, may put less pressure on their children to do well in school than Euro-American parents (Ogbu, 1992). In Tuktulik the schools enjoy support primarily as the gateway to wage employment, currently a tenuous connection. Schools could generate more support by honoring Inuit culture—an anticolonial and anti-neoliberal agenda.

Graduating from grade 12 is seen as necessary for securing a job or at least dramatically improving a young person's chance. For example, one participant said, "You have to be a graduate today," and an Elder said, through an interpreter, "He hears that school, education counts a lot when it comes to finding jobs." Some were less optimistic. One said that you could see that graduates do not get jobs easily "because there's lots of graduates and they're just walking around."

Another said that graduates will not necessarily find a job, "because some people, when they graduate, they don't really have any experience about the job." This is commentary on schools that largely ignore Inuit ways of knowing (Briggs, 1970). One person said some jobs could be done without "paper qualifications," a reminder of the colonial imposition of a system of credentialing.

Historically, all government positions were filled by Qallunaat (Brody, 1977). Now, Inuit employment in the government of Nunavut is mandated to rise to representative levels (85%), but this is stalled because lower management positions are staffed by Inuit and there is a shortage of high school graduates pursuing postsecondary education (T. Berger, 2006). Grade 12 is no longer enough to guarantee a job, and support for the schools based on their utility in helping secure wage employment will likely diminish as more people graduate and cannot find work.

It is also possible that finding a job may be a more ambivalent proposition for some Inuit than might immediately be assumed (by White folks). Work within traditional Euro-Canadian structures might be very unappealing to many Inuit.[4] Euro-Canadian wage employment is often very rigid and in Inuit communities may clash with values such as hunting, autonomy, and what is considered mature behavior (Stern, 1999). The individual drive to accumulate wealth may be antithetical to some Inuit values (Rasmussen, 2000), a point also made by Taiaike Alfred (cited in Kulchyski, 2005, p. 270) with respect to Aboriginal values. Several people in Tuktulik said that full-time wage employment was not desirable, and one person said missing goose hunting was the most difficult part of his job.

In one case, a man in his 20s discussed his motivation for completing school:

> It was really expensive to have a snow machine [for hunting]. The only way to get a snow machine was to finish high school and get a job. That's how I felt. . . . When I was in school I always wanted to go out hunting. Do some shootings, animals. And I was planning to go out hunting more often after I finished high school, and that's what I did. I reached my goal.

Wage employment may be necessary to enable involvement in subsistence activities on the land (Kulchyski, 2005), making schooling more attractive. If, however, employment is seen as preventing an adequate level of participation in land activities, schooling as a means of getting a job may not be so motivating. The inevitability of rigidly structured wage employment should be seen as the product of a colonial an industrial mind-set. Several examples in which flexibility existed to meet local circumstances were in fact described by people in Tuktulik—for example, ways to deal with predictable exigencies like the babysitter not showing up[5]—but flexibility is not the norm in Eurocentric wage employment.

If we assume that young Inuit want wage labor, the many professional and upper management government positions that are available for Inuit (T. Berger, 2006) should provide a major incentive to excel in school. But at the time of my interviews the high school offered only general level courses, insufficient for university entrance; the nearest university was in Ottawa, and no participants could think of anyone who had gone away to university—and come back. If school success means losing culture, students might resist on those grounds (Ogbu, 1993); this is just one of several large hurdles.

To increase the likelihood of students seeing university as a possibility, Nunavut high schools need to provide advanced level courses, even if that means a creative program of enrichment or independent work on modules. Guidance, career information, and—where possible—job shadowing may be helpful. These things will not make Ottawa any closer or Eurocentric ways of working more palatable, but they may increase the possibility of students seeing university as an option.

Inuit parents overwhelmingly expressed support for schooling and their children's learning, though there may be some ambivalence about sending children to Qallunaat schools. More support could be generated if Inuit wishes for more Inuit culture in schools—something desired almost unanimously—were acted upon. Some see the schools as responsible for weakening Inuit culture; for example, an Elder said, "They learn Inuktitut first, the first three years of their life in school, and then they drop that and go to Qallunaaq school. They forget their Inuktitut.[6]"

Nunavut schools should work to embody Inuit wishes. In Tuktulik, this means offering curricula to prepare students for future studies—and incorporating Inuit language and culture much more than at present. Qallunaat teachers and principals are not currently well positioned to do this.

RACISM

A literature review on culturally responsive schooling found that students experience racism through paternalism, prejudice, "low expectations, stereotypes, violence and biased curricular materials" (Castangno & Brayboy, 2008, p. 950). These exist in Nunavut communities and schools as the effects of colonialism and as part of continuing colonialism.

Low expectations of Inuit students were mentioned by almost a third of participants, who said schools should have higher academic standards. For example, an Elder said, "I have a feeling; I always feel that our kids are being cheated out of that system. 'Cause they can't compete when they go to college or university down south." Several recent graduates said that schoolwork should be harder to make it more interesting and a number of people expressed concern about lack of homework.

Sheila Watt-Cloutier has written powerfully about the damage to Inuit students when teachers have low expectations. The school system, she notes, "challenges our youth so little that it undermines their intelligence. . . . The watering down of programs, the lowering of standards and expectations is a form of structural racism that we must make every effort to stop" (2000, p. 115). It is ironic that in the U.S. the political elite call for more rigor in schooling to further their neoliberal agenda of inequality (Thomas, 2011a), whereas in Nunavut the calls come from the community to redress inequality.

When I read Watt-Cloutier (2000) it made me think of some good work my grade 7 students did on measurement and model building, and a disastrous class where they were to measure and draw real buildings. I had not prepared them well enough, and chaos ensued. I did not revisit the lesson, feeling like relationships were more important than my original goals. Watt-Cloutier (2000) helped me understand the message this must have sent students: *I don't believe you can do this.*

Unintentional racism works against student achievement, as does the lack of curriculum and resources, especially in Inuktitut. One Inuit teacher said, "We have to make everything!" Although slow progress is being made, inadequate curriculum and resources is a persistent problem in Nunavut (Berger, Epp & Moeller, 2006; NWT LASCE, 1982). In high schools, curriculum from the western Canadian provinces is used. This may not be a calculated plan to assimilate by using standardized curricula, but the outcome is the same.

Ideally, high schools would mitigate the damage from using foreign curriculum by using local projects and contexts to fulfill curriculum requirements, and by critiquing curriculum with senior high school students. Unfortunately, most teachers from southern Canada have little knowledge of Inuit culture or communities, leave Nunavut after only a few years, are themselves immersed in Whiteness (Shore, 2003), and may not understand the need for Nunavut schools to be different. An Elder put it well: "When you don't understand the lifestyle and culture of students it's a problem."

Also problematic is that stereotypes, paternalism, and prejudice were observed and described by participants. Some prejudice was noted subtly, such as the widely expressed belief of White people that Elders should volunteer to teach Inuit culture in the schools. Whereas it is reasonable for a family member to help a class once in a while, expecting what should be an integral part of the school program to be delivered by volunteers devalues the program and is unfair. To ask Inuit to teach for free what Qallunaat set out to eradicate is the ultimate arrogance and devalues Inuit knowledge.

Some Qallunaat, who would certainly defend the right of Inuit to maintain their culture, still in various ways suggested that living and working like Qallunaat was inevitable. I saw this in the high school in teachers' beliefs that Inuit would "get used to" the structure of schools, with no interest shown in finding a "third way" (Stairs, 1994). This is not surprising or an individual weakness, but results from socialization into Whiteness

(McIntosh, 1995; Shore, 2003) and the relentless logic of globalization that makes alternatives difficult to imagine, even for people who have a critical perspective (O'Sullivan, 2012). Unexamined biases can thwart even those with good intentions (Aylward, 2009).

Without a belief in the possibility of doing things differently, assimilation results. The message conveyed is one of Inuit inferiority, with one consequence being self-blame (Skutnabb-Kangas, 1988). I heard this often from participants; for example, "I regret that I didn't graduate from school. I learned myself that I was not a very good student." It appears that the colonial school system marginalizes people and makes them believe that their marginalization is their own fault (Tompkins, 2004; Watt-Cloutier, 2000).

White schools are colonial tools (Lindberg, 2007), and I see no easy way to counter this narrative without largely replacing those in charge. Inuit leaders and teachers will have a better chance of creating something different—Inuit schools following Inuit wishes. While moving toward this ultimate goal, teachers from southern Canada should be screened for attitude. As former Nunavut principal Joanne Tompkins (1998) wrote, resistant southern teachers are almost impervious to professional development, whereas those who are open can make great strides. It may take a strong mentor like Tompkins, though, because White people may not even know that they are White (Carr & Lund, 2007).

Qallunaat attitudes would not matter as much if White people did not wield so much power. A number of participants mentioned control; one said, "We're so used to when White people come up they control. We don't want that anymore." And an Elder, speaking through an interpreter, said,

> She knows that Qallunaaqs have helped the Inuit a whole lot. She knows that for a fact. She's not against any Qallunaaqs. But . . . we Inuit among ourselves have abilities to do things, so it would be nice to see all Inuit doing things together . . . running the life of the community. Just Inuit.

In the first decades of the settlements, everything was set up to block local control (Brody, 1977). Whereas this has changed to some degree, in Tuktulik I saw both large and small instances of control still in the hands of Qallunaat institutions, including the schools (cf. Laugrand & Oosten, 2009). This lack of local control is an impediment to the success of minority students (Agbo, 2002; Cummins, 1986).

Racism, whether embodied by the continuing lack of resources in Inuktitut, the prejudicial assumptions of White teachers, low expectations, the lack of professional development for new teachers from the south, or Nunavut schools still under Qallunaat control, is inherited from a colonial past and is part of the colonial present in Nunavut. It provides a major barrier to Inuit student success and well-being. In its demand for sameness and its placing of blame on those who struggle, it looks much like the neoliberal logic 2,000 miles to the south (Elmore, 2013).

CONCLUSION

Inuit students face a myriad of obstacles predicted by major theories of school failure for Indigenous students. Whereas there is no cultural deficit (Jacob & Jordan, 1993), decade after decade of colonial relations have left their mark; some students struggle with addictions themselves, and social problems ranging from overcrowded housing to violence make it difficult to learn. The Canadian state underfunds education, housing, and social programs in Nunavut, encouraging the continuance of these problems. Schools must respond, but Canadians must push for changes in the underlying relations that lead to the social problems.

Currently, that seems like a distant hope. Canadian Prime Minister Stephen Harper visits the Arctic every year to assert its importance to Canada, but there has been no indication that the Inuit are important to him or his government. The Arctic, especially as it melts under the assault of global climate change, is strategically important and a major new arena for resource extraction (Flanagan, 2013). When Canada's Indigenous peoples are noticed at all by this government, it is usually in the context of getting them training (not education) to enable them to take part in resource extraction (Chase, 2013). Unfortunately, most Canadians seem politically disengaged from any sort of action that might push the government to treat the Inuit fairly, or to even suggest that it should.

As regards schooling, cultural difference (Philips, 1993) is everywhere, with the middle and high schools staffed in a way that virtually ensures that preferred Inuit learning styles and the Inuit mother tongue will not be used seriously after the early grades. Inuit values remain likewise unknown or undervalued, and Inuit students suffer the costs (Stairs, 1991). Inuit politicians, the Nunavut government, and many in the Department of Education want this to change, but it is a slow process. Federal government unwillingness to fund the reinvention is part of the problem, a shortage of Inuit educators to work on the changes plays a role (Heather McGregor, personal communication with the author), and White resistance to change sometimes blocks even small steps (Berger, 2009). White people have grown up marinated in Eurocentric thought (Battiste, 2005) and the global corporatism that is currently killing the planet (Hedges & Saco, 2012; Jensen, 2006); it will take a major shift to decolonize. Schools can start with professional development that helps teachers understand how to use Inuit learning preferences to improve instruction, a baby step that may not be too threatening.

Schooling receives broad support in Tuktulik because it is still seen as the best chance for entry into the labor market, though the connection has become tenuous. Parental support and student motivation could be increased if the labor market were decolonized, if there were more work available, and if Inuit wishes for more Inuit culture in the schools were realized. It is not inevitable that the structures of work and schooling are so rigidly Euro-Canadian.

Racism, through low expectations, subtle assumptions, open prejudice, or inappropriate schooling, erodes self-esteem and the ability to learn (St. Denis & Hampton, 2002). It is the embodiment of colonialism (Go, 2004), destructive in Nunavut and linked to the neoliberal education policy eroding education in other jurisdictions (Berry, 2007; Imbong, 2013; Shahjahan, 2011).

Nunavut schooling lacks the obvious markers of the neoliberal pressures on schools farther south, but it would be a mistake to believe that the ideology of colonialism and globalization are unrelated.

NOTES

1. The author would like to thank the Social Sciences and Humanities Research Council of Canada for funding that supported this research.
2. *Qallunaat* is the Inuit word for non-Inuit.
3. Paying attention to learning preferences should not lead to stereotyping and low expectations (Dehyle, 1995) or lead teachers to ignore differences between learners (Abdallah-Pretceille, 2006).
4. It is also unappealing to many Qallunaat, who have become so used to it that it seems natural and inevitable.
5. Tuktulik has a good day-care center, but it has far too little capacity for the need, so reliance on babysitters is high.
6. *Inuktitut* literally means "like an Inuk" (Brody, 2000), and this participant is likely referring to Inuit ways and not just the language.

REFERENCES

Abdallah-Pretceille, M. (2006). Interculturalism as a paradigm for thinking about diversity. *Intercultural Education, 17*(5), 475–483.

Agbo, S. A. (2002). Decentralization of First Nations education in Canada: Perspectives on ideals and realities of Indian control of Indian education. *Interchange, 33*(3), 281–302.

Arnakak, J. (2000, August 25). Commentary: What is Inuit Qaujimajatuqangit? Using family and kinship relationships to apply Inuit Qaujimajatuqangit. *Nunatsiaq News*. Retrieved from http://www. Nunatsiaq.com/archives/ Nunavut 000831/nvt20825_17.html

Aylward, M. L. (2009). Culturally relevant schooling in Nunavut: Views of secondary school educators. *Inuit Studies, 33*(1–2), 77–94.

Balikci, A. (1970). *The Netsilik Eskimo*. Garden City, NY: Natural History Press.

Battiste, M. (2000). Maintaining aboriginal identity, language, and culture in modern society. In M. Battiste (ed.), *Reclaiming indigenous voice and vision* (pp. 192–208). Vancouver: University of British Columbia Press.

Battiste, M. (2005). You can't be the global doctor if you're the colonial disease. In P. Tripp & L. Muzzin (Eds.), *Teaching as activism: Equity meets environmentalism* (pp. 121–133). Montreal: McGill–Queen's University Press.

Berger, P. (2001). *Adaptations of Euro-Canadian schools to Inuit culture in selected communities in Nunavut*. (Master's thesis, Lakehead University, Thunder Bay, Ontario, Canada.)

Berger, P. (2008). *Inuit visions for schooling in one Nunavut community* (Doctoral dissertation, Lakehead University, Thunder Bay, Ontario, Canada).

Berger, P. (2009). Eurocentric roadblocks to school change in Nunavut. *Inuit Studies, 33*(1–2), 55–76.

Berger, P., & Epp, J. (2007). "There's no book and there's no guide": The expressed needs of Qallunaat educators in Nunavut. *Brock Education, 16*(2), 44–56.

Berger, P., Epp, J., & Moeller, H. (2006). The predictable influences of colonialism, culture clash, and current practice on punctuality, attendance, and achievement in Nunavut schools. *Canadian Journal of Native Education, 29*(2), 182–205.

Berger, T. R. (2006). *"The Nunavut project": Conciliator's final report.* Retrieved from http://www.ainc-inac.gc.ca/pr/agr/nu/lca/nlc_e.pdf

Berry, K. (2007). Exposing the authority of whiteness: An auto-ethnographic journey. In P. R. Carr and D. E. Lund (Eds.), *The great white north? Exploring whiteness, privilege and identity in education* (pp. 19–32). Rotterdam, Netherlands: Sense.

Briggs, J. L. (1970). *Never in anger: Portrait of an Eskimo family.* Cambridge, MA: Harvard University Press.

Brody, H. (1977). *The people's land: Inuit, whites, and the eastern Arctic.* Toronto, ON, Canada: Douglas and McIntyre.

Brody, H. (2000). *The other side of Eden: Hunters, farmers, and the shaping of the world.* Toronto, ON, Canada: Douglas and McIntyre.

Carr, P. R., & Lund, D. E. (2007). Introduction: Scanning whiteness. In P. R. Carr and D. E. Lund (Eds.), *The great white north? Exploring whiteness, privilege and identity in education* (pp. 1–18). Rotterdam, Netherlands: Sense.

Castagno, A. E., & Brayboy, B.M.J. (2008). Culturally responsive schooling for indigenous youth: A review of the literature. *Review of Educational Research, 78*, 941–993.

Chase, S. (2013, August 20). Harper unveils northern mining grant in northern Canada. *Globe and Mail.* Retrieved from http://www.theglobeandmail.com/news/politics/harper-unveils-aboriginal-mining-grant-in-northern-canada/article13869277/

Chisholm, S. (1994). Assimilation and oppression: The northern experience. *Education Canada, 34*(4), 332–343.

City-Data. (n.d.). Nunavut cities and villages. Retrieved from http://www.city-data.com/canada/ Nunavut-Index.html

Comeau, L. (2007). The parents of Baywoods: Intersections between whiteness and Jewish ethnicity. In P. R. Carr and D. E. Lund (Eds.), *The great white north? Exploring whiteness, privilege and identity in education* (pp. 151–160). Rotterdam, Netherlands: Sense.

Crago, M. B., Eriks-Brophy, A., Pesco, D., & McAlpine, L. (1997). Culturally based miscommunication in classroom interaction. *Language, Speech, and Hearing Services in Schools, 28*(3), 245–254.

Cummins, J. (1986). Empowering minority students. *Harvard Educational Review, 56*(1), 18–36.

Darnell, F., & Hoem, A. (1996). *Taken to extremes: Education in the far north.* Oslo: Scandinavian University Press.

Dehyle, D. (1995). Navajo youth and Anglo racism: Cultural integrity and resistance. *Harvard Educational Review, 65*(3), 403–436.

Dorais, L., & Sammons, S. (2002). *Language in Inuit society: Discourse and identity in the Baffin Region.* Iqaluit, NU, Canada: Nunavut Arctic College.

Douglas, A. S. (1994). Recontextualizing schooling within an Inuit community. *Canadian Journal of Education, 19*(2), 154–164.

Douglas, A. S. (1998). *"There's life and then there's school": School and community as contradictory contexts for Inuit self/knowledge* (Doctoral dissertation, McGill University, Montreal, Quebec, Canada).

Elmore, J. M. (2013). Neoliberalism and teacher preparation: Systematic barriers to critical democratic education. In P. L. Thomas (Ed.), *Becoming and being a teacher: Confronting traditional norms to create new democratic realities* (pp. 107–118). New York: Lang.

Erickson, F. (1975). Gatekeeping and the melting pot: Interaction in counseling encounters. *Harvard Educational Review, 45*(1), 44–70.

Flanagan, T. (2013, August 21). Arctic symbolism, Harper stagecraft. *Globe and Mail.* Retrieved from http://www.theglobeandmail.com/commentary/arctic-symbolism-harperstagecraft/article13876049/

Foster, K. M. (2005). Narratives of the social scientist: Understanding the work of John Ogbu. *International Journal of Qualitative Studies in Education, 18*(5), 565–580.

Fuzessy, C. (2003). An investigation of teachers' role definitions in Nunavik. *Canadian Journal of Native Education, 27*(2), 195–204.

Gibson, M. A. (2005). Promoting academic engagement among minority youth: implications from John Ogbu's Shaker Heights ethnography. *International Journal of Qualitative Studies in Education, 18*(5), 581–603.

Go, J. (2004). "Racism" and colonialism: Meanings of difference and ruling practices in America's Pacific empire. *Qualitative* Sociology, *27*(1), 35–58.

Gorlewski, J. A., & Gorlewski, D. A. (2013). Too late for public education? Becoming a teacher in a neoliberal era. In P. L. Thomas (Ed.), *Becoming and being a teacher: Confronting traditional norms to create new democratic realities* (pp. 119–136). New York: Lang.

Hedges, C., & Saco, J. (2012). *Days of destruction, days of revolt.* New York: Knopf.

Horsman, J. (1999). *Too scared to learn: Women, violence and education.* Toronto, ON, Canada: McGilligan.

Imbong, R.A.D. (2013). Neoliberalism and the Filipino teacher: Shaking the system for a genuine democracy. In P. L. Thomas (Ed.), *Becoming and being a teacher: Confronting traditional norms to create new democratic realities* (pp. 215–226). New York: Lang.

Inuit Tapiriit Kanatami. (2008). *Report on the Inuit Tapariit Kanatami education initiative, April 15–17, 2008.* Ottawa: Author.

Jacob, E., & Jordan, C. (1993). Understanding minority education: Framing the issues. In E. Jacob & C. Jordan (Eds.), *Minority education: Anthropological perspectives* (pp. 3–14). Westport, CT: Ablex.

Jensen, D. (2006). *Endgame: Volume 1. The problem of civilization.* Toronto, ON, Canada: Seven Stories.

Kirkness, V. J. (1998). Our people's education: Cut the shackles; cut the crap; cut the mustard. *Canadian Journal of Native Education, 22*(1), 10–15.

Kral, M., & Idlout, L. (2006). Participatory anthropology in Nunavut. In P. Stern & L. Stevenson (Eds.), *Critical Inuit studies: An anthology of contemporary Arctic ethnography* (pp. 54–70). Lincoln: University of Nebraska Press.

Kulchyski, P. (2005). *Like the sound of a drum: Aboriginal and cultural politics in Denendeh and Nunavut.* Winnipeg: University of Manitoba Press.

Lane, P., Bopp, J., & Bopp, M. (2003). *Aboriginal domestic violence in Canada.* Ottawa, ON, Canada: Aboriginal Healing Foundation.

Laugrand, F., & Oosten, J. (2009). Education and transmission of Inuit knowledge in Canada. *Inuit Studies, 33*(1–2), 21–34.

Lindberg, T. (2007). On indigenous academia: The hermeneutics of indigenous Western institutional participation. In P. R. Carr and D. E. Lund (Eds.), *The great white north? Exploring whiteness, privilege and identity in education* (pp. 67–75). Rotterdam, Netherlands: Sense.

Lipka, J. (1989). A cautionary tale of curriculum development in Yup'ik Eskimo communities. *Anthropology and Education Quarterly, 20*(3), 216–231.

McIntosh, P. (1995). White privilege and male privilege: A personal account of coming to see correspondences through work in women's studies. In M. C. Anderson & P. H. Collins (Eds.), *Race, class, & gender: An anthology* (2nded.) (pp. 76–87). Toronto, ON, Canada: Wadsworth.

Malaurie, J. (2007). *Hummocks: Journeys and inquiries among the Canadian Inuit*. Montreal: McGill–Queen's University Press.

Martin, I. (2000). *Aajiiqatigiingniq: Language of instruction research paper*. Iqaluit, NU, Canada: Nunavut Department of Education/Culture, Language, Elders and Youth.

McGregor, H. E. (2010). *Inuit education and schools in the Eastern Arctic*. Vancouver: University of British Columbia Press.

McGregor, H. E. (2013). Situating Nunavut education with indigenous education in Canada. *Canadian Journal of Education, 36*(2), 87–118.

Menzies, C. R. (2004). Putting words into action: Negotiating collaborative research in Gitxaala. *Canadian Journal of Native Education, 28*(1–2), 15–32.

Møller, H. (2005). *A problem of the government? Colonization and the sociocultural experience of tuberculosis in Nunavut* (Master's thesis, University of Copenhagen).

Nieto, S. (1994). Lessons from students on creating a chance to dream. *Harvard Educational Review, 64*(4), 392–426.

NunavutBureauofStatistics.(2012).Nunavutsecondaryschoolgraduates1999–2011. Retrieved from http://www.google.ca/url?sa=t&rct=j&q=&esrc=s&source=web&cd=1&ved=0CCwQFjAA&url=http%3A%2F%2Fwww.stats.gov.nu.ca%2FPublications%2FHistorical%2FEducation%2FNunavut%2520Secondary%2520School%2520Graduates%2C%25201999%2520to%25202011%2520%282%2520tables%29.xls&ei=jp9cUsG8MajC2wXN3YDYDA&usg=AFQjCNFoi0pQgfgZNPGXjdlDxR_mW9RxFA&bvm=bv.53899372,d.b2I

Nunavut Department of Education. (2004). *Bilingual education strategy for Nunavut: 2004–2008*. Iqaluit, NU, Canada: Author.

Nunavut Department of Education. (2005). *Nunavut education act (K–12): 2005 public consultations*. Iqaluit, NU, Canada: Author.

Nunavut Social Development Council. (1998). *Report of the traditional knowledge conference, Igloolik, March 20–24, 1998*. Retrieved from http://www.pooka.nunanet.com/~research/docs/TK%20Conference.htm

Nungak, Z. (2004). Capping the Inuktitut formal education system. *Inuktitut, 94*, 14–16.

NWT LASCE (Northwest Territories Legislative Assembly Special Committee on Education). (1982). *Learning, tradition and change in the Northwest Territories*. Yellowknife, NWT, Canada: Northwest Territories Information.

Ogbu, J. U. (1992). Understanding cultural diversity and learning. *Educational Researcher, 21*(8), 5–14.

Ogbu, J. U. (1993). Variability in minority school performance: A problem in search of an explanation. In E. Jacob & C. Jordan (Eds.), *Minority education: Anthropological perspectives* (pp. 83–112). Westport, CT: Ablex.

O'Sullivan, M. (2012). Getting beyond flat-out bored: The challenges and possibilities of creating a democratic space for social justice education in publically funded schools. In P. R. Carr, D. Zyngier, and M. Pruyn (Eds.), *Can educators make a difference? Experimenting with, and experiencing, democracy in education* (pp. 109–134). Charlotte, NC: Information Age.

Philips, S. (1993). *The invisible culture: Communication in classroom and community on the Warm Springs Indian Reservation*. New York: Longman.

Rasmussen, D. (2000). Dissolving Inuit society through education and money: The myth of educating Inuit out of 'primitive childhood'and into economic adulthood. *INTERculture, 139*, 1–64.

Shahajan, R. A. (2011). Decolonizing the evidence-based education and policy movement: Revealing the colonial vestiges in educational policy, research, and neoliberal reform. *Journal of Education Policy, 26*(2), 181–206.

Shore, S. (2003). What's whiteness got to do with it? Exploring assumptions about cultural difference and everyday literacy practices. *Literacies, 2,* 19–25.

Skutnabb-Kangas, T. (1988). Resource power and autonomy through discourse in conflict—A Finnish migrant school strike in Sweden. In T. Skutnabb-Kangas & J. Cummins (Eds.), *Minority education: From shame to struggle* (pp. 251–277). Philadelphia: Multilingual Matters.

Smith, L. T. (1999). *Decolonizing methodologies.* London: Zed.

Stairs, A. (1991). Learning processes and teaching roles in Native education: Cultural base and cultural brokerage. *Canadian Modern Language Review, 47*(2), 280–294.

Stairs, A. (1994). Indigenous ways to go to school: Exploring many visions. *Journal of Multilingual and Multicultural Development, 15*(1), 63–76.

Statistics Canada. (2006). *Aboriginal population profile.* Retrieved from https://www12.statcan.gc.ca/census-recensement/2006/dp-pd/prof/92–594/search-recherche/lst/page.cfm?Lang=E&GeoCode=62

Statistics Canada. (2011). Focus on Geography series, 2011 census: Nunavut. Retrieved from http://www12.statcan.gc.ca/census-recensement/2011/as-sa/fogs-spg/Facts-pr-eng.cfm?Lang=eng&GK=PR&GC=62

St. Denis, V., & Hampton, E. (2002). *Literature review on racism and the effects on aboriginal education.* Ottawa, ON, Canada: Minister's National Working Group on Education, Indian and Northern Affairs Canada.

Steinhauer, E. (2002). Thoughts on an indigenous research methodology. *Canadian Journal of Native Education, 26*(2), 69–84.

Stern, P. (1999). Learning to be smart: An exploration of the culture of intelligence in a Canadian Inuit community. *American Anthropologist, 101*(3), 502–514.

Tester, F. J. (2006). *Iglutaq (in my room): The implications of homelessness for Inuit.* Vancouver: Author.

Tester, F. J., & Kulchyski, P. (1994). *Tammarniit (mistakes): Inuit relocation in the eastern Arctic 1939–63.* Vancouver: University of British Columbia Press.

Thomas, P. L. (2011a). Orwellian educational change under Obama: Crisis discourse, Utopian expectations, and accountability failures. *Journal of Inquiry and Action in Education, 4*(1), 68–92. Retrieved from http://digitalcommons.buffalostate.edu/cgi/viewcontent.cgi?article=1034 &context=jiae

Thomas, P. L. (2011b, December 30). Poverty matters! A Christmas miracle. Retrieved from http://truth-out.org/news/item/5808:poverty-matters-a-christmas-miracle

Tompkins, J. (1998). *Teaching in a cold and windy place: Change in an Inuit school.* Toronto: University of Toronto Press.

Tompkins, J. (2004). *Sivuniksamut Ilinniarniq "Learning for the Future": Student consultation report.* Iqaluit, NU, Canada: Nunavut Department of Education.

Tompkins, J. (2006). *Critical and shared: Conceptions of Inuit educational leadership* (Doctoral dissertation, University of Toronto).

Van Meenen, M. A. (1994). *Government policies on education for the native peoples of Siberia and the Northwest Territories 1900–1990: A historical examination.* Unpublished doctoral dissertation, Dalhousie University, Halifax, Nova Scotia, Canada.

Watt-Cloutier, S. (2000). Honouring our past, creating our future: Education in northern and remote communities. In M. B. Castellano, L. Davis, & L. Lahache (Eds.), *Aboriginal education: Fulfilling the promise* (pp. 114–128). Vancouver: University of British Columbia Press.

Windeyer, C. (2006, April 24). Minister promises talk on Berger report. *Nunavut News North,* p. 18.

6 An Injury to All?

The Haphazard Nature of Academic Freedom in America's Public Schools

Robert L. Dahlgren, Nancy C. Patterson, and Christopher J. Frey

INTRODUCTION

Public school teachers, once venerated for their service to their communities, are today portrayed as villains in the political drama surrounding neoliberal, corporatist school reform. Columnist David Brooks captured this sentiment succinctly in a much-discussed *Atlantic* magazine feature titled "Teachers Are Fair Game." In his article, Brooks railed against "union rules that protect bad and mediocre teachers, teacher contracts that prevent us from determining which educators are good and which need help, and state and federal laws that either impede reform or dump money into the *ancien régime*" (2010, p. 1). It is immediately striking in this statement that public school teachers, once thought to be selfless paragons of virtue who had made vows of near poverty in order to serve children, are now portrayed by Brooks and others as akin to bewigged bluebloods in the Court of Versailles. Within the well-heeled punditocracy that Brooks inhabits, those who work in public education represent an unaccountable government-funded aristocracy, fattened on years of inflated union contracts and tenure protection. Moreover, Brooks posits that the supposed institutional power of tenured teachers, and the organizations that protect them, act as a bulwark against the progress imagined by proponents of neoliberal educational reforms today.

Brooks is hardly alone in these sentiments; nor is he expressing novel notions of educational reform. Despite standards reformers' insistence that they represent a breath of fresh air within the education debate, neoliberal efforts to narrow the curriculum; punish schools, teachers, and students for perceived weaknesses; and ultimately to privatize one of the core public institutions in the U.S. have their roots in the *Nation at Risk* report that has just enjoyed its 30th anniversary (Commission on Excellence in Education, 1983). As Diane Ravitch, a reformed reformer, has noted, "The policies we are following today are unlikely to improve our schools. Indeed, much of what policymakers now demand will very likely make the schools less effective and may further degrade the intellectual capacity of our citizenry" (2010, p. 224). Despite the voluminous research to the contrary, the assumptions of the standards reform movement continue to have a stranglehold over educational policy in political circles. Moreover, as Steven J. Klees (2008) has shown, business-driven reforms, cuts in state funding, and privatization of public institutions are a global phenomenon and, as Henry A. Giroux (2013) suggests, contributed to the revolts that led to the Arab Spring.

One salient impact of the accountability movement has been to impinge upon the freedom of teachers to decide on academic and other curricular content. (Misco, Patterson, & Doppen, 2013; Patterson et al., 2013). As Kevin K. Kumashiro has noted, this campaign is at root an effort to measure the achievement levels of schools, teachers and students by the narrow metrics of the marketplace, not coincidentally profiting the corporate partners of reformers. He comments,

> There is also much profit to be earned from public education. The American educational system is a $500 to $600 billion enterprise, funded overwhelmingly by public dollars in services and products to be outsourced, and with political lobbying groups like the Democrats for Education Reform (DFER), financed by hedge-fund millionaires who are leading the push to further outsource. (2012, p. 61)

In this chapter, we present an argument that the accountability movement is placing teachers and the teaching profession in imminent danger. The argument begins with a focus on the importance of and threats to academic freedom in schools. *Academic Freedom and the Social Studies Teacher*, a National Council for the Social Studies position statement originally adopted in 1969 and revised most recently in 2007, calls us to remain aware of the impacts the accountability movement is having on social studies teachers:

> In some schools, the movement for accountability has led to the imposition of unhealthy pressure to cover content in a superficial manner, serving as a constraint on meaningful teaching and learning. While the goal of high standards for student achievement is worthy, we must remain aware that powerful and creative teaching requires a strong measure of academic freedom for teachers to serve as thoughtful curricular-instructional decision makers. (National Council for the Social Studies, 2007, section 4, para. 3)

This statement is particularly important in the wake of the trend toward mandated curricula across the disciplines, represented most critically by the Common Core, which compels qualified teachers to impart scripted, prefabricated, "teacher proof" curricula to students (Hacker & Dreifus, 2013)

Each generation must remain diligent about protecting academic freedom in schools through all avenues at our disposal, from local school board policies to district contract language to the court system. In the context of the accountability regime and courts increasingly unfavorable to teacher rights, this chapter focuses on the key avenue of employment contract language related to academic freedom in two states, Ohio and New York, both of which have deep traditions in trade unionism in public education. Here we will outline the history of "no excuses" standards reform and the social and political context of the current accountability regime, especially as it relates to the two states that provided the focus of our study. We seek to describe the scope and nature of contract language that protects academic freedom, and as a result of this analysis will argue for a policy shift based on the framework of "social context reform" that advocates for protection of academic freedom in this generation.

This chapter is based on a study of academic freedom language embedded in the employment contracts of K–12 public school teachers in Ohio and New York. We employed the methods of document analysis in order to review the contracts from 191 districts in 25 counties in two states that not only have strong union traditions but also receive funding through president Barack Obama's administration's policy Race to the Top. In this survey, we sought to uncover the protections, if any, that might allow teachers in these states to resist the current trends toward standardized curricula and high-stakes testing. In the following sections we trace the social and historical context of the standards reform movement, review the literature related to academic freedom, and detail the procedures of our study.

TEACHERS AT RISK IN *A NATION AT RISK*

The historic context for current attacks on the teaching profession is the seminal document—*A Nation at Risk*—that argued that the low academic standards among America's schoolchildren threatened the nation's very existence. Issued under the auspices of the administration of president Ronald Reagan and largely drafted by a team led by Reagan's first secretary of education, Terrell Bell, the report opened with words that chilled the hearts of policy makers and ordinary citizens alike: "Our Nation is at risk. Our once unchallenged preeminence in commerce, industry, science, and technological innovation is being overtaken by competitors throughout the world" (CEE, 1983, p. 1). This rhetoric of economic insecurity struck a chord with both blue-collar workers (often dubbed "Reagan Democrats" in the mainstream media), who were watching their jobs slowly shift down toward the *maquiladora* factory zone just below the U.S.-Mexico border, and with white-collar professionals who worried that their jobs might be the next ones slated for downsizing.

Instead of casting the blame on the economic imperatives of global capitalism in the late 20th century, *A Nation at Risk* focused its attention on the American public education system, the foundations of which, it argued, were "being eroded by a rising tide of mediocrity that threatens our very future as a Nation and a people." "If an unfriendly foreign power had attempted to impose on America the mediocre educational performance that exists today," the argument soared, "we might well have viewed it as an act of war" (CEE, 1983, p. 1). In stark terms, the hegemonic political discourse of the period, exemplified in the report, tied the perceived crisis in education to the national security agenda. The report also employed language meant to resonate with those who could remember previous security crises; for example, the authors cited the finding that "average achievement of high school students on most standardized tests is lower than 26 years ago when Sputnik was launched" (p. 2), referring ominously to the 1957 Soviet satellite probe launch that had produced furious hand-wringing in policy circles and led to the passage of the National Defense Education Act in September 1958.

Under a heading titled "Indicators of Risk," the report's authors listed a number of alarming statistical findings highlighting the shortcomings of the American public education system and the products of that schooling, including:

- Some 23 million American adults are functionally illiterate by the simplest tests of everyday reading, writing, and comprehension.
- The College Board's Scholastic Aptitude Tests demonstrate a virtually unbroken decline from 1963 to 1980. (CEE, 1983, pp. 2–3)

A Nation at Risk ended with a clarion call for the return to a "Learning Society," in which there is "the commitment to a set of values and to a system of education that affords all members the opportunity to stretch their minds to full capacity, from early childhood through adulthood" (p. 5). Anticipating the arguments of critics that the focus of educational reform be placed on underserved and disenfranchised school populations, *A Nation at Risk* cast its language in the framework of equality: "All, regardless of race or class or economic status, are entitled to a fair chance and to the tools for developing their individual powers of mind and spirit to the utmost" (p. 1). What rational person, after all, could resist this call to equality and fairness in schooling, this new civil rights movement? Thus was born the era of market-driven standards reform.

The origins and consequences of *A Nation at Risk* have been documented and debated for decades. For left-of-center educational policy makers, the intent of the report was the privatization of one of the nation's most hallowed public institutions and its results were both inevitable and damaging; for those on the right side of the educational policy spectrum, however, *A Nation at Risk* represented a genuine effort to reform an outdated and ossified bureaucracy and ushered in a period of unrivaled achievement. The historian William J. Reese summarized the report's effect:

By demanding a more academic curriculum and tougher standards for all pupils to beat the Japanese and other foreign competitors, *A Nation at Risk* spoke to fears generated by the ongoing cold war and realities of economic decline. It suited the conservatism of the age, which had been reacting against Johnsonian liberalism since the mid-1960s. (2005, p. 249)

David C. Berliner and Bruce J. Biddle (1995) provided a comprehensive response to the arguments contained in *A Nation at Risk*, arguing against its false comparisons with countries in Europe and Asia that track a large number of working-class and poor students out of formal education and into the workforce at an age at which American teenagers are still required to attend school and to complete the state-mandated assessments upon which much of the report's case was built. Berliner and Biddle contended that "most of these claims were said to reflect 'evidence,' although the 'evidence' in question either was not presented or appeared in the form of simplistic, misleading generalizations" (1995, p. 3). Thus, the neoliberal "no excuses" reform movement that came to dominate educational policy for the next 30 years was based largely on erroneous and deceptive premises.

The mainstream media focus on the daily partisan rancor on Capitol Hill notwithstanding, this tilt against America's public school teachers and their organizations has in the decades since *A Nation at Risk* achieved a bipartisan consensus within the Beltway. Throughout the decade, liberals and progressives critiqued No Child Left Behind (NCLB) for its hodgepodge of unfunded mandates, including narrowly ideological provisions prohibiting comprehensive sex education instruction and promoting "faith-based initiatives." Wayne Au and colleagues have argued,

By any measure, NCLB was a dismal failure in both raising academic performance and narrowing gaps in opportunity and outcomes. But by very publicly measuring the test results against benchmarks no real schools have ever met, NCLB did succeed in creating a narrative of failure that shaped a decade of attempts to "fix" schools while blaming those who work in them. (Au et al., 2013, p. 5)

Because of this very public failure, presidential candidate Barack Obama promised throughout his campaign in 2007 and 2008 to have scrapping NCLB at the top of his education agenda.

Despite these promises, in his first speech regarding education as president, Obama echoed the negative rhetoric of his predecessors about the alleged failures of America's schools, stating, "It's time to start rewarding good teachers, stop making excuses for bad ones" (2009, p. 1). Teachers must be held accountable by rewarding those whose students perform well with merit-based pay increases and firing those whose students perform poorly on standardized assessments, and any teachers or teachers' organizations or advocates that have the temerity to criticize this dominant paradigm are ironically attacked as supporters of a supposed status quo and as obstacles to reform, change, and progress in American education.

Even those conservatives who have been highly critical of the plurality of Barack Obama's foreign and domestic policies, such as former Florida governor Jeb Bush, have rallied to his cause in the arena of education (Boedeker, 2012). Amanda Ripley, for example, trumpeted the Obama administration's focus on attacking teachers' unions, stating that "a Democratic President is standing up to his party's most dysfunctional long-term romantic interest, the teachers' unions" (2010, p. 35). Responding to Obama's 2010 State of the Union address, the ranking Republican member of the House Education and Labor Committee, representative John Kline of Minnesota, commented that the president had "indicated a surprising willingness to take on education special interests" (Kline, quoted in Berman, 2010, p. 1).

As Henry A. Giroux and Kenneth Saltman (2010) note, much as Bill Clinton had his Sister Souljah moment and welfare reform policies that appeased his most vociferous Republican opponents, Barack Obama has had his charter school initiatives and jeremiads against American Federation of Teachers president Randy Weingarten. Indeed, Obama and his secretary of education Arne Duncan have been especially bullish on eliminating the traditional protections afforded unionized public school teachers, including collective bargaining, tenure, and due process in regard to termination of contract.

Duncan was appointed secretary of education in January 2009 after his tenure as CEO of the Chicago public school system, during which he supported a range of market-based educational initiatives. The choice was initially surprising to many education watchers as Obama's senior educational consultant during his campaign had been Linda Darling-Hammond, a Stanford University education professor who had expressed many misgivings about the dominant neoliberal agenda. Jitu Brown, Eric Gutstein, and Pauline Lipman sum up the Duncan record in Chicago:

> Although not the architect, Duncan has shown himself to be the central messenger, manager, and staunch defender of corporate involvement in, and privatization of, public schools, closing schools in low-income neighborhoods of color with little local input, limiting democratic control, undermining the teachers union, and promoting competitive merit pay for teachers. (2009, p. 12)

As a result of this neoliberal consensus in favor of standardized curriculum and instructional practices, the autonomy of K–12 public school teachers has been under threat.

THE WAR ON THE PUBLIC SECTOR IN OHIO AND NEW YORK

The two states under study here have common and unique features. New York is along the northeastern seaboard and the third most populous state, whereas Ohio is in the Midwest and is the seventh most populous state. New York has been carried by the Democratic Party candidate in the past four elections, and Ohio has been carried by each of the two dominant political parties twice in the last four elections.

Ohio and New York share similar current contexts that have been increasingly unfavorable to teachers. The current Ohio governor, Republican John Kasich (2011–present), has not had a favorable record with Ohio public school teachers, having stated prior to his gubernatorial campaign his intention to "break the back of organized labor in the schools" (State Impact Ohio, n.d., para. 5) At the 2010 Republican Governor's Association meeting, he was quoted as saying that only "unions that make things" are deserving of public support (Niquette, 2010, para. 2). Shortly after Kasich was elected and took office, the Republican-led legislature passed Senate Bill 5, which proposed significant scaling back of the power of public employee unions. Ohio labor unions placed the issue on the November 2011 ballot as a referendum, and 61% of Ohioans voted to repeal Senate Bill 5 (Gonzales & Walker, 2011). Kasich has since conceded that the Ohio public has spoken, and he has not raised the issue again.

Much as was Barack Obama's presidential victory in 2008, New York governor Andrew Cuomo's gubernatorial victory in November 2010 was greeted by many educators in New York with a sense of hope and great optimism for the future of social policy and especially considering education. The American Federation of Teachers' house organ, for example, vigorously endorsed Cuomo in its "Vote 2010" feature, referring to him as a "difference maker" (American Federation of Teachers, 2010, p. 8).

Cuomo, the oldest son of former New York governor Mario Cuomo, came to Albany with a reputation as a high-profile and effective attorney general. Given his liberal public stances on many social policy issues, such as his support for marriage equality, it was expected that Cuomo would carry on the liberal tradition of his father—such as Mario Cuomo's social policy positions against the death penalty and in favor of reproductive rights for women. This was also in stark contrast to his opponent, the Tea Party–endorsed Republican candidate Carl Paladino, who now heads the Buffalo City School District's school board.

However, much of this optimism overlooked Cuomo's neoliberal economic policies, including his pronouncements on education during the campaign. Following Obama's lead, Cuomo made numerous statements during his gubernatorial campaign endorsing the idea of expanding charter schools. In his first State of the State address on January 5, 2011, Cuomo announced his first major education policy initiative: replacing the traditional state grants to public schools with new performance-based incentive largely modeled on the Obama administration's Race to the Top program. In office, Cuomo has promoted the expansion of a draconian teacher evaluation system in which teacher performance is tied to student achievement on standardized tests. This inauthentic measure has had the inevitable result of narrowing the curriculum in critical areas to those topics and skills most likely to be assessed on state-mandated tests. Thus, in both Ohio and New York, two states led by governors from different parties and with seemingly different political outlooks, K–12 teachers' freedom to practice their craft in their areas of expertise, using their extensive training, has been seriously undermined.

TEACHERS AND ACADEMIC FREEDOM

The Importance of Protecting Academic Freedom

Most would affirm that "the freedom to teach and learn is basic" (Hahn, 1984), that this gives meaning to our profession, and that it provide us with the tools we need to promote democratic life through education. This long-standing tradition in American thought is reflected in John Dewey's famous quote, "Since freedom of mind and freedom of expression are the root of all freedom, to deny freedom in education is a crime against democracy" (1936, p. 136).

We likewise take for granted that these rights are guaranteed, in place, and protected when in fact they require the vigilant attention of each generation. Jack L. Nelson and Carole Hahn ask,

> Is the freedom to teach and learn so well entrenched in the United States that it is no longer a current issue? Should educators shift their concern to other problems, and show courage in other settings? On the contrary, there is considerable contemporary evidence that academic freedom is extremely fragile, highly vulnerable in times of social stress, and often forsaken by teachers and ignored by social educators. It is a time to renew our concerns and our courage. (2010, p. 298).

They proceed with an accounting of past and recent academic freedom challenges, noting that over the past decade, the American Library Association has recorded about 6,500 direct and formal challenges to books, magazines, speakers, topics, and classroom activities of teachers and librarians. Approximately 75 percent of these were school related (Nelson & Hahn, 2010).

The age of accountability appears to have heightened threats to academic freedom. In a recent, large-scale study of the state of social studies teaching in the U.S. (Patterson, et al., 2013), researchers compared freedom over teacher curricular choice across both testing and nontesting states and found that the traditional gatekeeping role of the social studies teachers in testing states was significantly less than among teachers in nontesting states. Teachers of secondary social studies in testing states reported a significantly different experience than did teachers of social studies in nontesting states, with less control over curricular emphasis, instruction, evaluation and grading, and textbook and material selection.

THE NEED FOR STRONG CONTRACT LANGUAGE

One should rest assured that with this state of affairs, the recourse that teachers have in our court system is a dependable support. In fact, case law reviews reveal declining protection of teacher academic freedoms over the past three decades (Patterson & Chandler, 2008; Schimmel, Stellman, & Fischer, 2011; Simpson, 2010). The U.S. Supreme Court has been ruling on academic freedom cases since 1952, but has "never squarely answered the question" (Simpson, 2010, p. 310) of what teachers should be allowed to teach and how. During the 1960s and '70s, many federal courts recognized expansive curricular freedoms for teachers, from speech to pedagogical to content selection, but since the 1980s, the courts have shifted, such that it is fair to say that "K–12 teachers have no constitutional right to decide what to teach or how to teach it" (Simpson, 2010, p. 310). In the last 30 years there have been over a hundred academic freedom cases and, with rare exceptions, teachers have not been successful (Simpson, 2010).

David Schimmel, one of the authors of *Teachers and the Law*, now in its eighth edition (2011), has argued that in the current context, teachers should use avenues other than the courts to protect academic freedoms, and do so as a preventive rather than a reactive measure. Michael Simpson, the current assistant general council for the National Education Association (NEA), has consistently made recommendations (1998, 2010) that teachers seek protections locally through school board policies and collective bargaining agreements (CBAs). He has cited examples of teachers winning academic freedom rights from districts based on strong academic freedom contract language, noting that CBA arbiters are "much more sympathetic to teachers' claims of academic freedom than state and federal courts" (2010, p. 313).

Simpson notes that 40 states have bargaining rights, and has provided sample model contract language that includes 10 distinct categories: academic freedom, classroom presentation and discussion, personal expression, nondiscrimination, personal life, censorship, alteration of grades, monitoring and observation of teachers, Internet usage, and teacher assessment (Simpson, 2010, p. 313). In the following study, we surveyed the employment contract language in two states—Ohio and New York—in order to investigate whether these contracts provide adequate support and protection of K–12 public school teachers seeking to express themselves creatively in the classroom and to practice their crafts on the basis of their extensive training and expertise.

RESEARCH METHODS

This study is a descriptive document analysis, which allows researchers to examine and interpret text and images without researcher intervention to elicit meaning, gain understanding, and develop empirical knowledge (Corbin & Strauss, 2008). For this study, we reviewed the employment contracts during the period 2006–2011 for K–12 school districts in two states with strong educational union traditions and *Race to the Top* (U.S. Department of Education, n.d.) grants. All of the documents are public records and were found through online database searches on district websites. The 17 counties in Ohio and eight counties in New York State were chosen because they constituted discrete regions roughly defined by *Race to the Top*—the northwest region in Ohio and western region in New York State. The 17 Ohio counties represented 95 districts, 25 of which (26.3%) included some type of academic freedom language in their employment contracts. The eight New York counties represented 96 districts, eight of which (12%) included some type of academic freedom language in their employment contracts.

We independently skimmed, thoroughly examined, and then interpreted each instance of academic language through content and thematic analysis (Bowen, 2009). We used the 10 elements of model contract language set forth by Simpson (2010) as the framework for analysis, coding each of the 33 statements on a scale of 1 to 10 for the presence or absence of each element. There was 33.9% agreement among our ratings, and agreement was reached on all statements after discussion. While the majority of elements were easy to identify as either present or absent in examined contract language (nondiscrimination, personal life, censorship, alteration of grades, monitoring and observation of teachers, Internet usage, and teacher assessment), the first three in Simpson's list (academic freedom, classroom presentation and discussion, and personal expression) required clarification. During discussions wherein we negotiated coding agreement, we clarified criteria for these three elements in the following ways:

First, in order for a statement to meet the first element of academic freedom, it had to directly state that academic freedom is guaranteed. We arrived at this conclusion after discussing several statements that employed weaker language, such as references to commitment to a democratic classroom environment or to the U.S. Constitution and Bill of Rights. We agreed that such commitments, although desirable and critical, did not ensure district commitment to teacher academic freedom specifically. One exemplar of strong language for this element is from a New York urban district in Erie County:

> Academic freedom shall be guaranteed to teachers and no special limitations shall be placed upon study, investigation, presenting and interpreting facts and ideas concerning man, human society, the physical and biological world, and other branches of learning, except those standards of professional educational responsibility applicable to elementary and secondary education.

Alternatively, a weaker statement from a New York suburban district in Cattaraugus County uses generic democratic environment language and the word "encouraged" as opposed to "guaranteed":

> The Association and Board seek to educate young people in the democratic tradition, to foster recognition of individual freedom and social responsibility, to inspire meaningful awareness of and respect for the Constitution and the Bill of Rights, and to instill appreciation of the values of individual personality. It is recognized that these democratic values can best be transmitted in an atmosphere in which academic freedom for teacher and student is encouraged.

Second, in order for a statement to meet the second element, classroom presentation and discussion, we agreed that a statement had to include language that teachers either would be "solely responsible for decisions regarding the methods and materials used for the instruction of students" (Simpson, 2010, p. 315), guaranteed the freedom to teach relevant controversial material, or both. Some statements include one, the other or both. The following, from a suburban district in Fulton County, Ohio, is a strong example of language that includes both. It defines academic freedom as

> 1. the right to teach and to learn about controversial issues appropriate to the age and maturity of students in relation to subjects taught in the curriculum guide and/or course of study. 2. the right to use materials and methods that meet the objectives of the course of study and which are professionally deemed appropriate to the levels of ability and maturity of the students. 3. the right to maintain a classroom environment, which is conducive to the free examination and exchange of ideas. 4. the right of teachers and students to debate and discuss divergent ideas,

keeping in mind and respecting the standards of the community and the policies of the Board.

Finally, in order for a statement to meet the third element, personal expression, we agreed that it had to include language that guaranteed protection of teacher expression of opinions in an objective manner. This element is exclusive of element 2 in that it refers specifically to rights of teacher personal expression as opposed to teacher choices of controversial materials or topics. For example, a statement such as the following, from a suburban district in Putnam County, Ohio, would receive a point for element 2: "Freedom of individual expression which exhibits the basic objectives of a democratic society will be encouraged. Each teacher must be mindful that his/her presentations be open-minded, fair, responsible, and respectful of differing opinions of others. "A statement such as the following, from Cattaraugus County, New York, would receive a point for element 3: "The teacher has the right to identify and express his/her own point of view in the classroom as long as he/she indicates clearly that it is his/her own."

One theme emerged from the analysis that initially confounded our individual coding. Two of us independently noted numerous caveats that weakened previously stated strong academic freedom language and complicated decisions about whether or not such language would pose barriers to academic freedom protections. We decided to return to the statements and designate each as containing or not containing "caveat" language, defined as language that posited the final decision for curriculum and pedagogy outside the individual teacher's classroom. Collaborative language about negotiating curricular and pedagogical decisions in communication with administration and community members was not considered caveat language but instead best practice in schools. An example of collaborative language that would likely show respect for and offer protection of teachers' academic freedoms is this, which comes from a rural district, Genesee County, New York: "The administration will be available to assist teachers who are in doubt regarding the appropriateness of discussing certain controversial issues."

Contract language from a rural district in Allegany County, New York, provides an example of strong caveat language that negates previously strongly stated academic freedom language in the final sentence (in italics):

The Board will attempt through its policies to employ capable teachers, supply them with the necessary teaching materials, and maintain an atmosphere of academic freedom in the schools. The teachers as individuals and through their councils, committees and departments, and through the Administration will be responsible for determining when and how to deal with controversial issues according to the maturity and needs of students and the policies of the Board of Education. C. *The provisions of this Article I—Section 2 shall not conflict with or limit the authority of the Board of Education to determine the District's educational program, curriculum, textbook selection and teaching materials.*

We agreed that, if a statement met criteria for at least two of the 10 elements but also included caveat language, it would still retain its rating. Language that included one or more caveats would receive zero points.

FINDINGS: THE GOOD NEWS AND THE BAD

Despite warnings of the need for specific language in employment contracts protecting teachers' academic freedom in the research reviewed above, the findings of this survey show that the concrete results of this understanding remain at a nascent level in Ohio and New York K–12 public school districts. Of the 191 school districts surveyed in Ohio and New York, a mere 25 districts (26.3%) in Ohio and eight districts (12%) in New York included any specific language related to teacher academic freedom embedded in employment contracts. Additionally, what language there was fell far short of what the NEA assistant general council considers strong contract language (see the Appendix). The findings are reported here from statements deemed the weakest (with the fewest points awarded) to the strongest (with the most points awarded), followed by a census of the frequency with which the various elements were addressed.

THE STRENGTH OF ACADEMIC FREEDOM LANGUAGE

We found that no school achieved more than four out of ten points, and that four of the 33 (8.25%) received no points at all (see Table 6.1).

Table 6.1 Ratings of School Districts

Points Total	*Number of Districts*
4/10 points	3
3/10 points	5
2/10 points	13
1/10 points	8
0/10 points	4

Of the 25 statements, 14 (or 56%) had some form of caveat language. The zero ratings were due to our assessment that the only language present was punitive caveat language, or that the language directly invalidated any protective language related to academic freedom. For example, language in one rural Ohio district in Putnam County stated strictly punitive language, with no other mention of the various academic freedoms:

> Before introducing materials, methods, and/or issues of a known controversial nature, the teacher shall consult with the principal as to the advisability of such materials and/or issues and together they will develop plans to minimize any possible negative reactions to the introduction and use of said controversial materials, methods, and/or issues.

In this case the contract language that firmly establishes the authority of the building principal nullifies any possibility for the autonomy of individual teachers over the choice of curricular materials, instructional methods, or topics for discussion. Thus, the contract does not begin to address even the first point in Simpson's guidelines—that "academic freedom shall be guaranteed to teachers" (2010, p. 315). A similar statement from the rural district in Putnam County that received zero points merely described in detail the complicated process by which a teacher must get approval to "introduce any materials, methods, and/or issues of a known or potentially controversial nature." The statement ended by asserting that committee decisions would not be subject to appeal.

One statement, from a suburban district in Erie County, New York, that received zero points included academic freedom language and a strong caveat all in one simple sentence:

> It will be the teacher's professional responsibility to choose the appropriate materials and time they should be presented in class in accordance with the powers and duties as stated in the Education Law for Boards of Education . . . and the Superintendent of Schools.

We awarded eight school districts one point out of 10. In four of these cases, this rating related to the first of Simpson's (2010) guidelines—the basic guarantee of academic freedom to teachers. For example, the employment contract for a large urban district in Erie County, New York, stated,

> Academic freedom shall be guaranteed to teachers, and no special limitations shall be placed upon study, investigation, presenting and interpreting facts and ideas concerning man, human society, the physical and biological world, and other branches of learning, except

those standards of professional educational responsibility applicable to elementary and secondary education.

In the case of 13 school districts in the sample, we rated the employment contract language two points out of 10. In three of these districts, we assigned points for elements 5 and 6. As detailed below, element 6 of the guidelines refers to protection of teachers against censorship. For example, the employment contract covering a suburban district in Sandusky County, Ohio, stated, "It is recognized that these democratic values can best be transmitted in an atmosphere which is free from censorship and artificial restraints upon free inquiry and learning, and in which academic freedom for teachers and students is encouraged." One suburban district in Lucas County, Ohio, included element 7 of Simpson's guidelines—freedom from alteration of grades. The contract stated, "Teachers shall enjoy academic freedom to the extent that they shall be free from unreasonable interference in the conduct of their classes including the grading of students."

Among the five statements that were rated three out of ten, three corresponded with the elements 2, 3, and 4. As was indicated above, these elements include the vital concerns of classroom presentation and discussion, personal expression, and nondiscrimination. For example, the employment contract covering one rural district in Fulton County, Ohio, included the following statement:

> It is the right of teachers to encourage freedom of discussion of controversial questions in the classroom and to develop in students a love of knowledge and a desire to search for truth. The teachers should keep in mind that academic freedom is not a guaranteed political right, but rather a necessary condition for the successful practice of the academic profession in a free society. However, the application of the principle of academic freedom at the elementary-secondary school level involves considerations that are not always present in a college or university setting. The teachers should take into account the relative immaturity of their students, and the need for guidance and help in studying the issues and arriving at balanced views.

While this statement makes a sharp distinction between the protections afforded tenured academics at the higher education level and those afforded tenured teachers working at the K–12 level, we found the initial statement strong enough to align with the core academic freedoms of curricular and pedagogical choices.

Finally, we assessed the employment contract language in three districts worthy of four points out of 10—the highest mark awarded in the analysis. In the case of one suburban district in Sandusky County, Ohio, the contract language included elements 3, 4, and 6. In addition, it included element 5 related to protections against intrusions in the personal lives of K–12 teachers, stating,

> A bargaining unit member has the right, without reprisals or recrimination, to become involved in any political or religious activity or organization of his/her choice outside regular working hours. The political or religious views expressed by a bargaining unit member outside of regular working hours are strictly the bargaining unit member's own and shall not be represented or construed as being the policies, opinions, or beliefs of the Board, administration, or teaching staff. Students shall not be solicited to promote a bargaining unit member's cause.

This language includes the important provisions assuring teachers' privacy in regard to their activities beyond working hours and marks an important distinction between the professional and private realms in teachers' lives. The employment contract covering teachers in one suburban district in Cattaraugus County, New York, included language related to element 8 in addition to elements 1, 2, and 3 discussed earlier. One important principle rarely discussed in employment contracts reviewed for this study involves the protection of teachers from abusive evaluation processes. This particular district's contract stated, "Under no circumstances will there be any classroom visitation by anyone other than administrative personnel without consent of the teacher and the administration," meaning that in 190 other districts reviewed, no specific language existed that protects teachers from unscheduled classroom visits by immediate supervisors. Among all 33 statements examined, this was the only one that referenced protection of these particular freedoms.

THE NATURE OF ACADEMIC FREEDOM LANGUAGE

Table 6.2 indicates the frequency of each of the elements in Simpson's (2010) framework that were in the 33 employment contract statements analyzed for this study. The most common element included in contract statements was element 1 of Simpson's framework—the basic guarantee of academic freedom for teachers, mentioned in 15 (45.5%) of the 33 statements. Thirteen (39.3%) employment contract statements included element 2, involving pedagogical freedom for teachers. Element 3, involving the freedom of personal expression for teachers, was mentioned in nine statements (27.2%). Freedom from censorship, element 6, was also mentioned in nine statements (27.2%). Element 4, involving nondiscrimination, was included in six statements (18.1%). Elements 5 (personal life), 7 (alteration of grades) and 8 (monitoring and observation of teachers) were mentioned on a mere handful of occasions in contract language. Finally, elements 9 and 10—related to Internet use and assessment, respectively—were not mentioned in any of the 33 statements analyzed.

Table 6.2 Frequency of Academic Freedom Elements

Academic Freedom Elements	Number of Districts
1—Academic freedom	15
2—Classroom presentation and discussion	13
3—Personal expression	9
4—Nondiscrimination	6
5—Personal life	3
6—Censorship	9
7—Alteration of grades	2
8—Monitoring and observation of teachers	1
9—Internet use	0
10—Teacher assessment	0

DISCUSSION: FALLING SHORT OF IMPORTANT PROTECTIONS

It should almost go without saying that, in our estimation, none of the employment contracts covering 191 school districts in Ohio and New York—states typically regarded as being among the vanguard in terms of unionization—contain adequate protection of teachers' rights as regards academic freedom. To begin with, in 158 cases (82.8%), there was no specific language related to academic freedom at all. Even in the 33 school districts that included a modicum of academic freedom protections in their employment contracts, none of these included even half of the points in Simpson's framework, falling far short of adequate protections.

Intriguingly, none of the employment contracts we reviewed discussed either elements 9 or 10 in Simpson's (2010) guidelines. As shown below, element 9 relates to the freedom of Internet use in planning and instruction. While it might be argued that these employment contracts covering the period 2006–2011 simply were not timely in keeping up with the contemporary trends in communications, the absence of this language may also be connected to administrators' fears of exposing students to supplementary materials beyond those approved by school boards, even when chosen by qualified teachers.

Even more profoundly, given the centrality of standardized testing practices within the parameters of the current reform movement, the final point not discussed in any employment contract was element 10, relating to the autonomy of teachers with regard to assessment measures. Simpson carefully and clearly delineated this concept in his framework:

> The Board and the Association recognize that the ability of pupils to progress and mature academically is a combined result of school, home,

economic and social environment and that teachers alone cannot be held accountable for aspects of the academic achievement of the pupil in the classroom. Test results of academic progress of students shall not be used in any way as evaluative of the quality of a teacher's service or fitness for retention. (2010, p. 315)

Rather than this fair and contextual language, many of the employment contracts contained ominous language about the ultimate authority of administrations and school boards in an era in which inauthentic assessment processes have become increasingly unpopular among students, parents, and teachers. For example, even one of the better employment contracts reviewed (rated 4/10) included a closing statement that undermines much of the language that preceded it:

Nothing herein shall interfere with the statutory authority of the Board and the administration to control, oversee and regulate the contents of course materials and instruction and other educational affairs within the expressed statutory control of the administration and/or the Board.

In the end, the academic freedom rights of K–12 public school teachers mean nothing if they merely can be invalidated by the whims of administrators and school board members. Teachers in unionized districts must be vigilant in negotiating their collective bargaining agreements as our best hope of ensuring academic freedoms in the context of the current accountability regime.

APPENDIX: SAMPLE ACADEMIC FREEDOM CONTRACT LANGUAGE (SIMPSON, 2010)

1. Academic Freedom

Academic freedom shall be guaranteed to teachers, and no special limitations shall be placed upon the study, investigation, presenting and interpreting facts and ideas concerning human society, the physical and biological world, and other branches of learning subject to accepted standards of professional responsibility. The right to academic freedom herein established shall include the right to support or oppose political causes and issues outside of the normal classroom activities.

2. Classroom Presentation and Discussion

As a vital component of academic freedom, teachers shall be solely responsible for decisions regarding the methods and materials used for the instruction of students. Accordingly, employees shall be guaranteed full freedom in classroom presentations and discussions and may introduce issues that have economic, political, scientific or social significance, or otherwise controversial material relevant to course content.

3. Personal Expression

No teacher shall be prevented from wearing pins or other identification or symbolism in expression of membership in the association, religious orders, political systems, or sympathy with social causes or traditions in or outside the classroom. In performing teaching functions, teachers shall have reasonable freedom to express their opinions on all matters relevant to the course content in an objective manner. A teacher, however, shall not utilize her/his position to indoctrinate students with her/his own personal, political and/or religious views.

4. Nondiscrimination

No teacher will be subject to discrimination or harassment in any terms or conditions of employment, because of her/his personal opinion or scholarly, literary or artistic endeavors.

5. Personal Life

The personal life of a teacher is not an appropriate concern of the Board for purposes of evaluation or disciplinary action, unless it prevents the teacher from performing her/his duties.

6. Censorship

Employees shall not be censored or restrained in the performance of their teaching functions solely on the ground that the material discussed and/or opinions expressed are distasteful or embarrassing to the school administration or to the school's public relations.

7. Alteration of Grades

Grades given a student by a teacher shall be final and not subject to alteration unless fraud, bad faith, incompetency or mistake can be shown on the part of said employee.

8. Monitoring and Observation of Teacher

All monitoring or observation of the work performance of a teacher shall be conducted openly and with full knowledge of the teacher. The use of eavesdropping, public address, audio systems, and similar surveillance devices shall be strictly prohibited. No mechanical or electronic device shall be installed in any classroom or brought in on a temporary basis that would allow a person to be able to listen or record the procedures in any class.

9. Internet Usage

Academic freedom, subject to accepted standards of professional responsibility, will be guaranteed to bargaining unit members, and no special limitations will be placed upon study, investigation, presentation and interpretation of facts and ideas, including email and Internet usage.

10. Teacher Assessment

The Board and the Association recognize that the ability of pupils to progress and mature academically is a combined result of school, home, economic and social environment, and that teachers alone cannot be held accountable for aspects of the academic achievement of the pupil in the classroom. Test results of academic progress of students shall not be used in any way as evaluative of the quality of a teacher's service or fitness for retention.

REFERENCES

American Federation of Teachers. (2010, October–November). Vote 2010. *American Teacher*, p. 8.

Au, W., Bigelow, B., Christensen, L., Gym, H., Levine, D., Karp, S., Miller, L., Peterson, B., Dawson-Salas, K., Sokolower, J., Tempel, M. B., & Walters, S. (2013). The trouble with the common core. *Rethinking Schools, 27*(4), 4–6.

Berliner, D. C., & Biddle, B. J. (1995). *The manufactured crisis: Myths, fraud, and the attack on America's public schools.* Reading, MA: Perseus.

Berman, R. (2010, January 28). On education, Obama gets a rare response: Praise. Retrieved from http://www.aolnews.com/2010/01/28/on-education-obama-gets-a-rare-response-gop-praise/

Boedeker, H. (2012, June 7). Jeb Bush praises Obama on education, worries the GOP is shortsighted. *Orlando Sentinel.* Retrieved from: http://blogs.orlandosentinel.com/entertainment_tv_tvblog/2012/06/jeb-bush-praises-obama-on-education-worries-that-gop-is-shortsighted.html

Bond, R. N., McInturff, B., & Bratty, A. (2009, August 2). A chance to say yes: The GOP and Obama can agree on school reform. *Washington Post*, A-14.

Bowen, G. A. (2009). Document analysis as a qualitative research method. *Qualitative Research Journal, 9*(2), 27–40.

Brooks, D. (2010, July–August). Teachers are fair game. *Atlantic.* Retrieved from http://www.theatlantic.com/magazine/archive/2010/06/teachers-are-fair-game/8155/

Brown, J., Gutstein, E., & Lipman, P. (2009). Arne Duncan and the Chicago success story. *Rethinking Schools, 23*(3), 10–14.

Bruce, M. (2010, January 29). Duncan: Katrina was the "best thing" for New Orleans school system. Retrieved from http://abcnews.go.com/blogs/politics/2010/01/duncan-katrina-was-the-best-thing-for-new-orleans-schools/

Carr, P. R., & Porfilio, B. J. (2011). Audaciously espousing hope within a torrent of hegemonic neoliberalism. In P. R. Carr and B. J. Porfilio (Eds.), *The phenomenon of Obama and the agenda for education: Can hope audaciously trump neoliberalism?* (pp. xxi–xlvi). Charlotte, NC: Information Age.

CEE (Commission for Excellence in Education). (1983). *A nation at risk.* Washington, D.C.: Author. Retrieved from http://www2.ed.gov/pubs/NatAtRisk/risk.html

Clinton, B. (1996). *Between hope and history: Meeting America's challenges for the 21st century.* New York: Times Books.

Corbin, J., & Strauss, A. (2008). *Basics of qualitative research: Techniques and procedures for developing grounded theory* (3rd ed.). Thousand Oaks, CA: Sage.

Cuomo, A. (2011, January 5). State of the State of New York Address to the New York Legislature. Retrieved from http://www.governor.ny.gov/sl2/stateofthestate2011transcript

Dewey, J. (1936). The social significance of academic freedom. *Social Frontier, 2,* 136.

Giroux, H. A. (2013). *Youth in revolt: Reclaiming a democratic future.* Boulder, CO: Paradigm.

Giroux, H. A., & Saltman, K. (2010). Obama's embrace of the corporate model of education. In H. A. Giroux (Ed.), *Politics after hope: Obama and the crisis of youth, race, and democracy* (pp. 137–143). Boulder, CO: Paradigm.

Gonzales, M., & Walker, T. (2011). Anti-worker law SB 5 repealed in Ohio. *NEA Today.* Retrieved from http://neatoday.org/2011/11/08/anti-worker-law-sb5-repealed-in-ohio/

Gutek, G. (2000). *American education, 1945–2000.* New York: Waveland.

Hacker, A., & Dreifus, C. (2013, June 8). Who's minding the schools? *New York Times,* A-36.

Hahn, C. (1984). The freedom to teach and learn is basic. *Georgia Social Science Journal, 15,* 1–7.

Kaestle, C. F. (1983). *Pillars of the republic: Common schools and American society, 1780–1860.* New York: Hill and Wang.

Klees, S. J. (2008). A quarter century of neoliberal thinking in education: misleading analyses and failed policies. Globalisation, Societies and Education, 6 (4), 311–348.

Klein, N. (2007). *The shock doctrine: The rise of disaster capitalism.* New York: Metropolitan.

Kumashiro, K. K. (2012). *Bad teacher: How distorting teachers distorts the bigger picture.* New York: Teachers College Press.

Misco, T., Patterson, N., & Doppen, F. (2011). Policy in the way of practice: How assessment legislation is impacting social studies curriculum and instruction in Ohio. *International Journal of Education Policy and Leadership, 6*(7), 1–13.

National Council for the Social Studies. (2007). Position statement on academic freedom and the social studies teacher. *Social Education, 71*(5), 282–283.

Nelson, J. L., & Hahn, C. (2010). The need for courage in American Schools: Cases and Causes. *Social Education, 74*(6), 298–303.

Nelson, J. L., Palonsky, S., & McCarthy, M. R. (2006). *Critical issues in education: Dialogues and dialectics.* New York: McGraw-Hill.

Niquette, M. (2010). "Unions that make things" will get chance to help. *Columbus Dispatch.* Retrieved from http://www.dispatch.com/content/stories/local/2010/11/23/unions-that-make-things-will-get-chance-to-help.html

Obama, B. (2009, March 10). Obama: "We've let our grades slip.". Retrieved from http://www.msnbc.msn.com/id/29612995/ns/politics/white_house/t/obama-weve-let-our-grades-slip/

Patterson, N. & Chandler, P. (2008). Free speech in the balance: What we know about the rights of public school teachers. *Social Studies Research and Practice, 3(2)*, 90–102.

Patterson, N., Horner, S., Dahlgren, R., & Chandler, P. (2013). Who is at the Gate? An examination of secondary social studies teacher support and curricular control in testing and non-testing states. In J. Passe & P. Fitchett (Eds.) *The status of social studies: Views from the field* (pp. 289–300). Charlotte, NC: Information Age.

Reese, W. J. (2005). *America's public schools: From the common school to "No Child Left Behind."* Baltimore: Johns Hopkins University Press.

Ravitch, D. (2010). *The death and life of the great American school system: How testing and choice are ruining education.* New York: Basic Books.

Reich, R. (1993, July 20). Workers of the world, get smart. *New York Times.* Retrieved from http://www.nytimes.com/1993/07/20/opinion/workers-of-the-world-get-smart.html?pagewanted=all&src=pm

Ripley, A. (2010, September 20). A call to action for public schools. *Time*, 32–42.

Rury, J. L. (2009). *Education and social change: Contours in the history of American schooling* (3rd ed.). New York: Routledge.

Schimmel. D., Stellman, L. R., & Fischer, L. (2011). *Teachers and the Law* (8th ed.). Upper Saddle River, NJ: Pearson.

Simpson, M. (1998, November). Academic freedom takes a hit. *NEA Today*, 1–3.

Simpson, M. D. (2010). Defending academic freedom: Advice for teachers. *Social Education, 74(6)*, 310–315.

State Impact Ohio. (n.d.). *Get to know governor John Kasich.* Retrieved from http://stateimpact.npr.org/ohio/tag/john-kasich/.

Tyack, D. B. (1974). *The one best system: A history of American urban education.* Cambridge, MA: Harvard University Press.

U.S. Department of Education. (n.d.). Race to the Top Fund. Retrieved from http://www2.ed.gov/programs/racetothetop/index.html

Zezima, K. (2010, February 25). A jumble of strong feelings after vote on troubled school. *New York Times*, A14.

7 Educating, Not Criminalizing, Youth of Color

Challenging Neoliberal Agendas and Penal Populism

Mary Christianakis and Richard Mora

INTRODUCTION

He who opens a school door closes a prison.

—Victor Hugo

The United States, which accounts for 5% of the planet's population, confines nearly 25% of the world's prison population (Hawkins, 2010), even though crime has been decreasing nationwide for decades and the increased use of imprisonment accounted for no more than 10% of the decline in crime during the 1990s (Western, 2006). At the end of 2011, local jails and state and federal prisons held 2,239,800 individuals (Glaze & Parks, 2012). An additional 4,814,200 individuals were on probation or parole in 2011, bringing the total number of individuals overseen by the criminal justice system to 6.98 million, or approximately one in every 34 adults (Glaze & Parks, 2012). In the case of juveniles, the U.S. incarcerated approximately 336 for every 100,000 youth, whereas Japan incarcerates 0.1, Finland 3.6, Sweden 4.1, the United Kingdom 46.8, and South Africa 69.0 (Hazel, 2008). High incarceration rates throughout the U.S. are accompanied by simultaneous growth in, and support of, private prisons in both state legislation and judicial practices (ACLU, 2011). Imprisonment, thus, marks a societal commitment to invest in the penal system rather than preventative and restorative measures.

A closer look at incarceration rates shows that racial disparity continues to be a long-standing trend. The vast majority of incarcerated adults are "people of color, people with mental health issues and drug addiction, people with low levels of educational attainment, and people with a history of unemployment or underemployment" (NAACP, 2011, p. 1). In the case of juveniles—that is, individuals under the age of 18—local municipalities' reports indicate that most of the 61,423 juveniles incarcerated in 2011 (Office of Juvenile Justice and Delinquency Prevention, 2011a) were disproportionately from ethnic and racial minority groups—68% minority (40% black; 23% Hispanic; 2% American Indian; 1% Asian), compared to 32% white (Office of Juvenile Justice and Delinquency Prevention, 2011b).

In fact, youth of color, especially African Americans and Latinos, are over-represented at every juncture within the juvenile courts system and receive differential treatment along the way (Hartney & Silva, 2007). Due to the racial composition of those behind bars, mass incarceration in the U.S. has been described as a racial caste system (Alexander, 2010).

As the prison population has grown in the U.S. over the past few decades, spending on incarceration has surpassed spending on education (NAACP, 2011). The investment decisions that many states are currently making are clear—prisons before public schools. California, for example, spends approximately $50,000 per inmate each year and $8,852 per pupil each year (Fensterwald, 2011). Additionally, between 1987 and 2007, state-level spending on prisons increased by 127%, a rate six times that of state spending on higher education (Fensterwald, 2011). Contrary to Victor Hugo's declaration in the epigraph above, our society has opted to support a "*grotesque* prison boom" that has resulted in less financing of public education (Jones, 2010, p. 395, emphasis in the original; Mauer, 2006).

In some cities across the U.S., there are "million-dollar blocks," areas where states have spent millions to incarcerate residents rather than educate them (Hawkins, 2010). These areas typically have low-performing schools. A NAACP report (2011) found, for example, that in Los Angeles, 69 of the 90 low-performing schools (67%) are in neighborhoods with the highest incarceration rates, and that $16.6 million is spent yearly to incarcerate residents from one New York City zip code with a 50% graduation rate and an unemployment rate of 53%. The result is that a disproportionate number of urban working-class black and Latino children attend "drop out factories" (Balfanz & Letgers, 2004, p. 5), or low-performing schools with high dropout rates, which partly explains why 17.6% of Hispanics and 9.3% of blacks between 16 and 24 years of age have dropped out, compared to the national average of 8.1% (Chapman et al., 2011).

With the implementation of zero-tolerance policies in schools, particularly after the highly publicized Columbine High School murder-suicides in Littleton, Colorado, many under-resourced schools resemble detention facilities. They staff school resource officers (Justice Policy Institute, 2011), and require students to pass through metal detectors, undergo random searches, and be subjected to surveillance from security cameras and guards (Devine, 1996; Rios, 2009). Additionally, public school students are also now more likely to be suspended. The Civil Rights Project at the University of California–Los Angeles estimates that over two million students were suspended during the 2009–2010 year alone (Losen & Martinez, 2013). Like the prison population, the suspension and expulsion rates are racialized and gendered. The National Center for Educational Statistics (2010) reports that black, Hispanic, and multiracial male students are suspended at significantly and disproportionately higher rates than Asian, Native American, and white students. Therefore, schools have become punishing institutions for many black and brown male students.

In this chapter we argue that the increase in prisons and the policing of schools is rooted in the convergence of neoliberalism, conservatism, and "penal populism" (Pratt, 2007). The convergence criminalizes minority youth and reinforces the school-to-prison pipeline, or the "policies and practices that systemically push at-risk youth out of mainstream public schools and into the juvenile or criminal justice systems" (Kim, 2009–2010, p. 956). As we discuss below, politicians and public servants criminalize minority youth by espousing media-driven, tough-on-crime rhetoric for political gain. Law enforcement and school officials compound the effect by implementing zero-tolerance policies in the name of public safety. Minority youth who have been suspended, expelled, and/or adjudicated in the juvenile justice system typically reside in neighborhoods with under-resourced schools that have a bureaucratic incentive to remove underperforming students in order to meet the performance outcomes stipulated by President Barack Obama's educational policies, particularly the competitive Race to the Top initiative. Consequently, there is a great likelihood that youth of color, in general, will be fed into the school-to-prison-pipeline and experience further exclusion from our neoliberal society. However, it need not be this way, and as a result, youth organizations, advocates, and educators throughout the country are organizing and fighting to dismantle the infrastructure that supports the school-to-prison pipeline.

NEOLIBERALISM AND PENAL POPULISM

Neoliberalism

As Loïc Wacquant points out, neoliberalism has turned the U.S. into a *"centaur state,"* a nation with small government accountability for those at the top and paternalistic control of those at the bottom (2009, p. 43, emphasis in the original). Control of the working class, poor, and marginalized has shifted from the dispensing of public services to the use of prisons. The expansion of the prison system and the defunding of the welfare state "are *two sides of the same political coin,*" such that "[t]he generosity of the latter is in direct proportion to the stinginess of the former, and it expands to the degree that both are driven by moral behaviourism" (Wacquant, 2009, p. 292–293, emphasis in original). The shift away from social services is justified with the argument that citizens must take personal responsibility for the problems they encounter in schools and in other social contexts. Hence, despite being the victims of structural inequalities and neoliberal policies, the working poor have become scapegoats, embodiments of social ills.

Prisons affirm the authority of the state and maintain social control. They serve to placate those in the growing working class that are dissatisfied with the greater inequalities and employment insecurities, and to warehouse both those who reject the labor market and those deemed disruptive elements (Wacquant, 2001). The low caste status ascribed to poor African Americans, for example, makes them the unfortunate beneficiaries of a perverse "de facto policy of *carceral affirmative action,*" resulting in over-representation in prisons, jails, and detention facilities (Wacquant, 2001, p. 403, emphasis in the original). Consequently, the burgeoning prison system is now a central institution in the U.S.

The expansion of the prison system in the U.S. has made incarceration a profitable business, with billions of dollars spent each year to incarcerate people (ACLU, 2011). In 2011, Correction Corporation of America, the largest private detention company in the country, reported total revenues of $1.7 billion; the Geo Group, Inc., the second largest private detention company, reported total revenues of $1.6 billion (Lee, 2012). These companies, which continue to operate despite accounts of prisoner maltreatment and abuse at their facilities (Lee, 2012), are indicative of how profit trumps morality in neoliberal economies.

Over the last couple of decades, new prisons have been built in depressed rural communities hit hard by deindustrialization and other economic changes. Many of these communities eagerly supported the construction of prison facilities, going as far as to provide tax breaks to the private detention companies to bring employment opportunities to their residents. The prisons, however, have proved not to be economic boons. Private prisons built in rural counties between 1997 and 2004 did not increase job opportunities for locals, and in the case of prisons in states with rapid prison privatization, employment growth in the hosting counties was impeded (Genter, Hooks, & Mosher, 2013). As a result, communities desperate for jobs did not gain economically from the mass incarceration of predominantly low-income and minority individuals and now have facilities that likely decreased residential property values.

The privatization of detention facilities resulted in a corruption case dubbed "kids for cash," which received worldwide attention (Ecenbarger, 2012). In 2011, two Pennsylvania judges, Mark Ciavarella and Michael Conahan, were found guilty of sending children as young as 11 years of age to two for-profit juvenile detention facilities in exchange for millions of dollars from the developer of the facilities (Ecenbarger, 2012.). The evidence showed that from 2003 to 2008, juveniles who came before the two judges received harsher penalties and were sent to the private detention facilities, which received thousands from the state for each juvenile they housed (Ecenbarger, 2012). The two judges were able to violate the constitutional rights of thousands of juveniles for personal gain, in part, because in the U.S. the detention of juveniles is not a measure of last resort.

Along with an expansion of the prison system in the U.S., neoliberalism has given rise to a new punitive common sense, which normalizes the economic competitiveness of the neoliberal economy, the insecurities in the wage-and-labor market, and the criminalization of poverty (Wacquant, 2009). The punitive thinking is driven in part by the ideas put forth by neoconservative think tanks such as the American Enterprise Institute, the Heritage Foundation, and the Manhattan Institute, since Ronald Reagan's first presidential term. Wacquant (2009) documents that policy entrepreneurs—such as Rudy Giuliani, who served as mayor of New York City (1994–2001), and William Bratton, who served as police commissioner of New York City (1994–1996)—also promulgated intrusive tough-on-crime policies. In New York City, Giuliani and Bratton trumpeted and enacted zero-tolerance policies that enforced misdemeanor ordinances to curtail crimes deemed detrimental to the quality of life (e.g., public intoxication and panhandling) and used stop-and-frisks as so-called crime-fighting tools.

Although Giuliani and Bratton are no longer public servants, zero-tolerance policing continued in New York City under the leadership of mayor Michael Bloomberg and police commissioner Ray Kelly. In the first nine months of 2009, the New York Police Department (NYPD) stopped approximately 450,000 people—84% of whom were black or Latino—and the majority were frisked (Herbert, 2010). These startling statistics are even more troubling considering that the data also indicate that only 6% of the total stops ended in an arrest; 1.5% of Hispanics, 1.6% of blacks, and 2.2% of whites were found with drugs; weapons were found on 1.1% of blacks, 1.4% of Hispanics, and 1.7% of whites (Herbert, 2010). In spite of such obvious inequities, the stop-and-frisk program was supported and trumpeted by Bloomberg and Kelly.

In 2012, a decade after the NYPD began stop-and-frisks, the rate of stops reached 532,911, a 448% increase since 2002; however, fewer than 10% of stops resulted in an arrest or citation (NYCLU, 2013). Blacks and Latinos, who experienced approximately 87% of all stops, were less likely to be found with guns than were whites (Ibid.). Black and Latino young men between the ages of 14 and 24 accounted for 40.6% of stops (133,119) in 2012 despite accounting for only 4.7 percent (158,406) of New York City's population (NYCLU, 2013). All these disgraceful statistics have led New York Civil Liberties Union executive director Donna Lieberman to state,

> With a 90-percent failure rate, the NYPD's stop-and-frisk program remains a tremendous waste of resources, sows mistrust between police and the communities of color and routinely violates fundamental rights. The city's next mayor must make a clean break from the Bloomberg administration's ineffective and abusive stop-and-frisk regime (NYCLU, 2013).

Despite such calls for change, a federal court ruling finding the stop-and-frisk program discriminatory, and statistical evidence showing that youth of color are less likely to be found with guns and drugs than their white peers, Bloomberg and Kelly continued to defend the racial profiling and criminalization of these youth. They argued that stop-and-frisks in communities of color ensure public safety.

Zero-tolerance policies, which date back to president Richard Nixon's war on drugs in the early 1970s (Newburn, 2010), are now regularly used to control working-class and poor youth throughout our neoliberal society. Numerous studies document the aggressive policing—unwarranted stops, questioning, and frisking—of urban minority youth (Brunson & Miller, 2006; Brunson & Weitzer, 2009; Carr, Napolitano, & Keating, 2007; Rios, 2009; Sanchez & Adams, 2011; Solis, Portillos, & Brunson, 2009). Such racialized policing tactics in the name of "safety" currently serve to hypercriminalize young people of color (Rios, 2009).

Penal Populism

Penal populism, or the populist response to crime (Pratt, 2007), criminalizes urban youth of color. Consider, for example, the alarmist media narratives that are part and parcel of penal populism. A *Time* magazine feature in September 2001 called Latina/o gangs in Los Angeles "a nightmare" and stated that these "[g]angs, it turns out, can take more beatings and lockdown time than any humane society is prepared to deal out" (quoted in Bender, 2003, p. 63). Such discourse of savagery (Macek, 2006) is not only dehumanizing but also in effect justifies "the social and physical deaths of young Latino men" (Cacho, 2007, p. 182). Like other media, film also stereotypically depicts youth of color as criminal elements. Research shows that films regularly portray urban youth, mostly blacks and Latinos, as threats to the social order (Mora, 2011; Mora & Christianakis, 2012). The representation of minority youth as criminals in the media and popular culture has become part of the public imagination through what Collins (1999) terms "controlling images"—stereotypical images used to justify the subordination of a segment of the population.

In the U.S., penal populism is promulgated by the very policy entrepreneurs who propagate "controlling images" of youth of color. Note that in the early 1990s, a number of conservative think tank fellows erroneously argued that the impending increase in the youth demographic, driven in part by high birthrates among nonwhites, would result in a new generation of young criminals they dubbed "superpredators" (see, e.g., DiIulio, 1995). The media and law enforcement then popularized the notion of superpredators and created a moral panic (Pizarro, Chermak, & Gruenewald, 2007) that resulted in anti-youth policies.

This superpredators discourse resulted in the passage of various laws targeting youth. In 1996, the U.S. Congress passed the Violent Youth Predator Act, which established mandatory minimum sentences for youth convicted of violent crimes and lowered the minimum age for trying juveniles as adults from 16 to 14 years of age. Four years later, having succumbed to the hysteria about youth crime, California voters passed

Proposition 21, the Gang Violence and Juvenile Crime Prevention Act of 1998, with 62% of the vote. Like other tough-on-crime legislation being urged by penal populism, Proposition 21 did not focus on rehabilitative or preventative interventions but instead on punishing juvenile offenders with increased sanctions, especially for crimes deemed to be gang-related, and giving prosecutors more discretionary power to try juveniles as adults (Taylor, 2002). Presently, more than 30 states have stiffened penalties against youth for various crimes, including nonviolent offenses, and nearly all states have made it easier to transfer juveniles to adult criminal courts (Wald & Losen, 2003). Juvenile courts now focus mostly on punishing youth rather than on protecting their well-being, which was the central aim of the nation's first juvenile court, established in 1899 (Fionda, 1998; Grisso & Schwartz, 2000; Muncie, 2005, 2008; Schaffner, 2002). The call for punishment is driven not by crime rates, which have been decreasing for decades, but by penal populist rhetoric espoused by neoliberals and conservatives alike.

Politicians promote, and are responsive to, penal populism (Pratt, 2007). We see this, for example, in the campaign for Proposition 21. Pete Wilson, the governor of California at the time, repeatedly invoked the Mexican Mafia, a violent Mexican American prison gang, to garner support for the ballot initiative (Rios, 2008). The construction of Mexican American youth as criminals was meant to resonate primarily with white voters who perceived Latino youth (and gang members) as dangerous beings encroaching on their children's safety and privileges (Rios 2008, p. 109). By collapsing the "controlling image" (Collins, 1999) of the prison gang member with the urban Mexican youth, Wilson drew on the superpredator script, which has been shown to increase whites' desire for harsher crime policies by 11% (Gilliam & Iyengar, 1998).

When president Barack Obama was elected in 2008, many hoped that his administration would counter penal populism and take up the issue of racial disparity within both the criminal justice system and the juvenile justice systems. In September 2013, U.S. attorney general Eric Holder did institute a new policy so that nonviolent drug offenders are not charged with federal mandatory minimum sentences, which are disproportionately given to offenders of color. However, President Obama took five years to appoint a permanent administrator to oversee the Juvenile Justice and Delinquency Prevention Act (JJDPA), which provides federal funds to states that: do not detain status offenders; do not place juvenile and adult offenders in same facilities, with some exceptions; and address the disproportionate minority contact in the juvenile justice system (Children's Defense Fund, n.d.). The JJDPA needs to be reauthorized by Congress, and it is not clear whether President Obama will expend political capital to secure the authorization before the end of his second term.

What is more, during Obama's presidency, the children of many undocumented immigrants have been contending with their parents' criminalization.

The number of inmates sentenced to more than a year for immigration violations has risen, with an increase of nearly 10% between 2010 and 2011. In fact, immigrants are now the third most incarcerated group, at 11%, accounting for more than 60% of federal convictions (U.S. Department of Justice, 2012). During a two-year span between 2010 and 2012, nearly 23 percent of removals—or, 204,810 deportations—were of undocumented individuals with U.S. born children (Wessler, 2012). Regardless of their citizenship, the children of incarcerated and/or deported immigrants have their lives and schooling disrupted when their parents are taken away.

Racialized fear mongering of the sort described herein stigmatizes and negatively impacts the lives of poor youth of color in the U.S. In neighborhoods with police-identified street gangs, the police not only regularly stop and search youth but also regularly classify many of them as gang members, associates, or affiliates, even when they have absolutely no gang ties. As Marjorie S. Zatz points out, the subjective "gang label (and the police perceptions and stereotypes consistent with this label) . . . [then] operate[s] as a 'master status' or contingency that influences the workings of the legal process and rates of movement through it" (1985, p. 15). Youth who are classified as gang involved by law enforcement face greater scrutiny when stopped, arrested, and tried. In California, for example, they may be wiretapped and face longer sentences if convicted of particular crimes. Consequently, throughout the country, many poor youth of color "find themselves trapped in a closed circuit of perpetual marginality, circulating between ghetto and prison" (Alexander, 2010, p. 191). Such marginalization negatively impacts entire communities, particularly the "million-dollar blocks," where residents have to contend with incarcerated family and friends as well as health issues, unemployment, lack of adequate housing, educational needs, and, in some cases, disenfranchisement (NAACP, 2010).

CRIME-CONTROL MODELS IN SCHOOLS

Schools throughout the country, especially urban public schools, use a crime-control model to manage students (Casella, 2001, 2006; Hirschfield, 2008; Kupchik & Monahan, 2006; Losen & Skiba, 2010; Simon, 2007; Skiba, 2000). Over 90% of public schools have implemented conservative disciplinary policies based on zero-tolerance frameworks (Kaufman et al., 2001). As a result, school suspensions and expulsions are now common punishments (Hirschfield 2008; Simon 2007; Skiba 2000). A nationwide study, for example, found that during the 2009–2010 academic year, there were over two million suspensions, with one out of nine secondary school students suspended at least once (Losen & Martinez, 2013). A closer look at the data shows that "6,957 of the nation's secondary schools that had at least 50 members of a racial subgroup, English learners, or students with disabilities met or exceeded a suspension rate of 25% for at least one of these subgroups" (Losen & Martinez, 2013, p. 3). Whereas proponents of conservative and neoliberal crime-control policies argue that zero-tolerance policies are necessary to curtail school violence, research clearly shows that punishment is meted out mostly for minor transgressions, such as the disruption of school activities and defiance of school authorities (Losen, 2011; Losen & Martinez, 2013; Simon, 2007; UCLA-IDEA, 2006).

School suspensions are commonly used to, in effect, exclude urban students who cannot be "responsibilized" (Muncie, 2006, p. 786). According to Paul J. Hirschfield,

> a troubled domestic economy, the mass unemployment and incarceration of disadvantaged minorities, and resulting fiscal crises in urban public education have shifted school disciplinary policies and practices and staff perceptions of poor students of color in a manner that promotes greater punishment and exclusion of students perceived to be on a criminal justice 'track.'" (2008, p. 79)

Criminalization for questionably "inappropriate" behavior reiterates the educational inequities to which poor youth of color without access to private schools are exposed.

Minority students, particularly those with disabilities, are overrepresented in school suspension and expulsion rates (Losen, 2011; Losen & Skiba, 2010; Noguera, 2003; Wald & Losen, 2003), likely because of "racial profiling in schools" (Wald & Losen 2003, p. 13). Nationally, during the 2009–2010 academic year, black female middle and high schoolers had a suspension rate of 18.3%, and 36% of all black male middle and high schoolers with disabilities were suspended at least once (Losen & Martinez, 2013). The behavior of minority children with disabilities is typically constructed as defiant or criminal rather than as an expression of their special needs, requiring the attention of skilled educators (Kim, Losen, & Hewitt, 2010). That may partly explain why minority students are more likely to be suspended for behavior viewed as threatening or disrespectful, whereas white students are typically suspended for carrying weapons or drug infractions (Skiba, 2000; Skiba et al., 2002).

The racial dimension of school suspension is evident when we compare suspension rates of secondary schools by racial group over time. During the 1972–1973 academic year, the national suspension rates were as follows: 11.8% of black students, 6.1% of Latino students, 6.0% of white students, 5.6% of American Indian students, and 2.4% of Asian/Pacific Islander students (Losen & Martinez, 2013). The national suspension rates by race during the 2009–2010 academic year show that black and Latino students are now twice as likely to be suspended: 24.3% of black students, 12.0% of Latino students, 7.1% of white students, 8.4% of American Indian students, and 2.3% of Asian/Pacific Islander students (Losen & Martinez, 2013). So, in the era of zero-tolerance policies, we have "an excluded student body whose makeup echoes the racial disparities seen in the US prison population" (Goddard & Myers, 2011, p. 659), with minority youth accounting for approximately two-thirds of the juveniles in detention facilities and nearly all the youth are tried as adults in some states (Muncie, 2005). The exclusion of minority youth from schooling initiates the process of "carceral affirmative action" (Wacquant, 2001, p. 5), which results in the removal of youth of color from their families, the labor market, and the welfare state.

The widespread use of zero-tolerance policies is startling given that compelling research indicates that such policies do not improve students' behavior, do not make schools safer, are unfair (e.g., they are uniform and leave no room for a discretionary consideration of the circumstances surrounding rule violations), and disproportionately impact minority students (American Psychological Association Zero Tolerance Task Force, 2008; Curwin & Mendler 1999; Losen & Skiba, 2010; Skiba & Peterson, 1999; Skiba & Rausch, 2006; Verdugo, 2000, 2002). Zero-tolerance policies create a false sense of security and serve only to reiterate the neoliberal and conservative discourse of personal responsibility and accountability.

Due to the expansion of zero-tolerance policies, there is now a visible police presence at many schools, particularly at those in urban neighborhoods (Ayers et al., 2001; Hutchinson & Pullman, 2007; Muncie, 2006; Sanchez & Adams, 2011; Wald & Losen, 2003). In many jurisdictions, the police are summoned for infractions (e.g., food fights) that in the past were handled by school officials (Sanchez & Adams, 2011; Wald & Losen, 2003), thus "extending the arm of policing from the neighborhood to the school setting" (Sanchez & Adams, 2011, p. 327). Some schools are even legally required to report students who fail to abide by particular disciplinary rules to the police (Browne, 2005; Wald & Losen, 2003). The result is that black and Latino students are exposed to racialized policing, and so they are more likely to be arrested than white peers, even when accused of the very same school code violations (Kim, 2009–2010, p. 957). Consequently, rather than being nurturing community institutions, many schools contribute to African American and Latino students' hypercriminalization (Sanchez & Adams, 2011) and reiterate the authority and legitimacy of the *centaur state* (Wacquant, 2009).

THE EXCLUSION OF MINORITY YOUTH FROM PUBLIC SCHOOLING

Youth who seek to reenter school after leaving detention facilities face a number of challenges. The juvenile justice system may not provide the paperwork students need to reenroll, and schools may not accept educational credits earned while in detention (Feierman, Levick, & Mody, 2009–2010). What is more, schools are often reluctant to support youth who were detained (Feierman et al., 2009–2010; Wald & Losen, 2003), in part because schools prefer to exclude those who may not do well on standardized exams mandated by No Child Left Behind (Darling-Hammond, 2007; Ryan, 2004), resulting in high dropout rates among these students (Feierman et al., 2009–2010; Wald & Losen, 2003). In other words, the neoliberal reforms that aim to make schools more competitive and accountable actually create systems of exclusion wherein students who need the most support are denied participation. The end result is that "the effects of the school-to-prison pipeline" are magnified and "heighten the likelihood that children will find themselves returning to the justice system they just exited" (Feierman et al., 2009–2010, p. 1115). Hence, the school-to-prison pipeline creates a feedback loop that brings many of the same children back into the system time and time again.

It seems that a good education and access to support services at school are particularly vital for the life opportunities of minority youth who may find themselves criminalized by police and schools upon returning from juvenile detention facilities. Most incarcerated youth struggle academically in school, do not read at grade level, do not attend school regularly, and have been suspended at least once (Balfanz et al., 2003; Vacca, 2008). Additionally, at least close to half of incarcerated youth have at least one learning disability (Morris & Morris, 2006; Quinn et al., 2005). Unfortunately, however, minority students are more likely to both attend schools with fewer resources and to have less access to qualified teachers than their white counterparts (Darling-Hammond, 2004, 2006; Oakes, 2004; Orfield, 2001). These inequalities contribute not just to the present "disparate achievement by race and class" (Darling-Hammond, 2006, p. 13), but also feed "the 'school-to-prison pipeline' that is increasingly well oiled in many states" (Darling-Hammond, 2006, p. 14). Nevertheless, rather than providing social and educational services for students, many states are cutting back school budgets.

Neoliberal and conservative policies that depict public education as an economic drain linked to an unsustainable welfare state (see Burchell, 1996) are defunding and privatizing public education; these are two reforms that do not bode well for low-income students of color, including those who reside in areas with high incarceration rates. Consider the neoliberal expansion of charter schools into urban communities, which President Obama's educational policies are now furthering (see Christianakis & Mora, 2011; Mora & Christianakis, 2011). Research indicates that charter school students, most of whom are children of color, are not faring any better than their peers at comparable traditional schools (Center for Research on Education Outcomes, 2009; Gwynne & De la Torre, 2009; Robelen, 2008; Zimmer et al., 2008). A recent U.S. Government Accountability Office (2012) report confirms that, as previous studies have found (Estes, 2006; Fierros & Blomberg, 2005; Grant, 2005; Howe & Welner, 2002; Rhim & McLaughlin, 2007), charter schools enroll students with special needs at rates below those of public schools, in part because these students are counseled out by charter schools.

In addition, researchers find that many charter schools underserve English language learners and students with special needs (Advocates for Children, 2002; Betts et al., 2006; Buckley & Schneider, 2007; Kane et al., 2009;). Charter schools typically employ unqualified and less experienced teachers (Brown, Gutstein, & Lipman, 2009; Fuller et al., 2003), who "are less likely to be knowledgeable about the Individuals with Disabilities Education Act (IDEA), the Least Restrictive Environment (LRE), and Free and Appropriate Education (FAE) requirements of the law" (Grant, 2005, p. 71), and have unqualified teachers teach English language learners (Fuller et al., 2003). Teachers who are less experienced and not credentialed are more likely to teach minority students and more likely to refer them for special education services, where students of color are overrepresented (Cartledge, 2005). Given how reluctant many charter schools are to serve students with learning needs, there is no reason to believe that charter schools will opt to serve underperforming students who have had contact with the juvenile justice system and may do poorly on the standardized tests.

CONCLUSION

The convergence of neoliberalism, conservatism, and penal populism has shifted the fiscal priorities in the U.S. away from social programs and education to the funding of prison expansion. It has also reified zero-tolerance policies that criminalize minority youth in and out of schools. As a result, youth of color are particularly vulnerable to the "policies and practices that systemically push at-risk youth out of mainstream public schools and into the juvenile or criminal justice systems" (Kim, 2009–2010, p. 956). The high suspension and expulsion rates and the political influence of penal populism allow neoliberals and conservatives to justify both prison spending and the policing of schools as necessary safety measures. In this way, the shift in fiscal priorities, along with policies criminalizing low-income youth, normalize the transfer of brown and black bodies from school classrooms to prison cells—all to the financial benefit of private detention facilities.

Children's lives are on the line. We must not accept the criminalization of our youth. We must bring an end to the discourses of penal populism that stigmatize low-income youth of color, perpetuate a racial caste system in the U.S. (Alexander, 2010), and threaten the future of democracy in the U.S. (Giroux, 2003). We concur with Barry Goldson and John Muncie, who—based on their studies of juvenile justice systems in the U.S. and Western Europe—argue that we need "youth justice with integrity" that transgresses "crude moralization, media sensationalism and the politics of intolerance" (2006, p. 102). For us to bring about such justice, it is imperative that we actively counter the conservative and neoliberal policies that are punishing rather than rehabilitating offenders, dismantling the welfare state, and wreaking havoc on economically depressed and socially marginalized communities.

Across the U.S., action is being taken so that our children are not fed into the school-to-prison pipeline. During the summer of 2013, the organization Communities United for Police Reform, the New York Civil Liberties Union, and local politicians successfully lobbied for the New York City Council to overturn Mayor Bloomberg's veto of the newly introduced Community Safety Act, which bans racial profiling practices and assigns an inspector general to oversee the NYPD (NYCLU, 2013; Reynolds, 2013). These efforts surely influenced Mayor de Blasio to ban the racial profiling practices in place under his predecessor. Also in 2013, students, parents, teachers, and concerned residents of Los Angeles convinced the Los Angeles Unified School District School Board to end suspensions for failing to follow directives and policies, that is, for acts of "willful defiance," such as wearing baggy attire, the use of cell phones, and public displays of affection (National Public Radio, 2013; Rott, 2013). Instead of suspending students for refusing to comply, Los Angeles public schools are now required to implement alternative disciplinary practices that have reduced suspensions in other public school systems, such as conflict resolution and positive behavior incentives (Watanabe, 2013). Moreover, a bill banning "willful defiance" suspensions is making its way through the California Senate. As Susan Frey (2013) details,

> Under [Assembly Bill] 420, elementary school students (in grades K–5) could not be suspended for willful defiance. Middle and high school students could only be suspended for a third offense—and only if alternative means of discipline had been tried the first and second times.

The bill represents the efforts of politicians, organizations, and citizens who find it unacceptable that the zero-tolerance policy accounted for 700,000 suspensions—half of all suspensions issued in the state in 2011–2012 (Watanabe, 2013).

Other efforts that challenge the pipeline are also currently underway. Act 4 Juvenile Justice, a nationwide coalition of organizations, is advocating for the reauthorization of the Juvenile Justice and Delinquency Prevention Act and for the federal funding of prevention, diversion, and intervention programs and services. In California, the Alliance for Boys and Men of Color, a group of individuals and organizations throughout the state, is working to bring about societal changes that will benefit California's boys and men of color. Among other efforts, the alliance is mobilizing support for legislative bills that limit school expulsions, prevent the involuntary school transfer of homeless youth, provide mental health services for students who experienced trauma due to violence, and require that parents be notified when a child is added to the CalGang database. These efforts need to be replicated across the nation in order to help keep children out of both the juvenile and criminal justice systems. If we truly want to have a pluralistic, democratic, and just society in the U.S., we must take action so that our children, particularly poor children of color, are no longer fed into the school-to-prison pipeline.

We cannot be silent, nor can we be complacent. Unfortunately, other countries, particularly in western Europe, seem to be experiencing the same convergence of political ideologies and penal populism that exists in the U.S. In Europe, as throughout the U.S., "punitive values associated with retribution, incapacitation, individual responsibility and offender account-ability have achieved a political legitimacy to the detriment of traditional principles of juvenile protection and support"; this shift away from protect-ing and supporting youth is resulting in the disproportionate incarceration of ethnic and immigrant youth in Europe (Muncie, 2008, p. 110). Thus, our efforts to educate and not incarcerate youth of color in the U.S. are part of a larger, global struggle for juvenile justice.

REFERENCES

ACLU (American Civil Liberties Union). (2011, November 2). *Banking on bond-age: Private prisons and mass incarceration.* New York: Author. Retrieved from https://www.aclu.org/prisoners-rights/banking-bondage-private-prisons-and-mass-incarceration

Advocates for Children. (2002). *Pushing out at-risk students: An analysis of high school discharge figures—A joint report by AFC and the Public Advocate.* Retrieved from http://www.advoatesforchildren.org/pubs/pushouts-11–20–02.html

Alexander, M. (2010). *The new Jim Crow: Mass incarceration in the age of color-blindness.* New York: New Press.

American Psychological Association Zero Tolerance Task Force. (2008). Are zero tolerance policies effective in the schools? An evidentiary review and recommen-dations. *American Psychologist, 63,* 852–862.

Ayers, W., Ayers, R., Dohrn, B., & Jackson, J. L. (2001). *Zero tolerance: Resisting the drive for punishment.* New York: New Press.

Balfanz, R., & Letgers, N. (2004). *Locating the dropout crisis: Which high schools produce the nation's dropouts? Where are they located? Who attends them?* Baltimore: John Hopkins University.

Balfanz, R., Spiridakis, K., Neild, R. C., & Legters, N. (2003). High poverty sec-ondary schools and the juvenile justice system. In J. Wald & D. J. Losen (Eds.), *Deconstructing the school to prison pipeline* (pp. 77–78). San Francisco, CA: Jossey-Bass.

Bender, S. W. (2003). *Greasers and gringos: Latinos, law, and the American imag-ination.* New York: New York University Press.

Betts, J., Rice, L., Zau, A., Tang, Y., & Koedel, C. (2006). *Does school choice work? Effects on student integration and achievement.* San Francisco, CA. Pub-lic Policy Institute of California.

Brown, J., Gutstein, E. R., & Lipman, P. (2009). Arne Duncan and the Chicago success story: Myth or reality? *Rethinking Schools Online, 23*(3). Retrieved from http://www.rethinkingschools.org/archive/23_03/arne233.shtml

Browne, J. A. (2005). *Education on lockdown: The schoolhouse to jailhouse track.* Retrieved from http://www.advancementproject.org/reports/FINALEOLrep. pdf

Brunson, R. K., & Miller, J. (2006). Race and urban policing: The experience of African American youth. *Gender & Society, 20,* 531–552.

Brunson, R. K. & Weitzer, R. (2009). Strategic responses to the police among inner-city youth. *Sociological Quarterly, 50*(2), 235–256.

Buckley, J., & Schneider, M. (2007). *Charter schools: Hope or hype.* Princeton, NJ: Princeton University Press.

Burchell, G. (1996). Liberal government and the techniques of the self. In A. Barry, T. Osbourne, & N. Rose (Eds.), *Foucault and political reason: Liberalism, neoliberalism, and rationalities of government* (pp. 19–37). Chicago: University of Chicago Press.

Cacho, L. M. (2007). "You just don't know how much he meant": Deviancy, death, and devaluation. *Latino Studies, 5,* 182–208.

Carr, P., Napolitano, L., & Keating, J. (2007). We never call the cops and here's why: A qualitative examination of legal cynicism in three Philadelphia neighborhoods. *Criminology, 45,* 445–480.

Carson, E.A., & Sabol, W. J. (2012, December). *Prisoners in 2011* (NCJ 239808). Washington DC: U.S. Department of Justice, Bureau of Justice Statistics. Retrieved from http://www.bjs.gov/content/pub/pdf/p11.pdf

Cartledge, G. (2005). Restrictiveness and race in special education: The failure to prevent or return. *Learning Disabilities: A Contemporary Journal, 3*(1), 27–32.

Casella, R. (2001). *At zero tolerance: Punishment, prevention, and school violence.* New York: Lang.

Casella, R. (2006). *Selling us the fortress: The promotion of techno-security equipment for schools.* New York: Routledge.

Center for Research on Education Outcomes. (2009). *Multiple choice: Charter school performance in 16 states.* Stanford, CA: Stanford University.

Chapman, C., Laird, J., Ifill, N., and KewalRamani, A. (2011). *Trends in high school dropout and completion rates in the United States: 1972–2009* (NCES 2012–006). Washington, DC: National Center for Education Statistics. Retrieved from http://nces.ed.gov/pubsearch

Children's Defense Fund. (n.d.). *Policy priorities: Juvenile justice.* Washington, DC: Author. Retrieved from http://www.childrensdefense.org/policy-priorities/juvenile-justice/

Christianakis, M., & Mora, R. (2011). Charting a new course for public education through charter schools: Where is Obama taking us? In P. R. Carr & B. J. Porfilio (Eds.), *The phenomenon of Obama and the agenda for education: Can hope audaciously trump neoliberalism?* (pp. 97–119). Charlotte, NC: Information Age.

Collins, P. H. (1999). Mammies, matriarchs, and other controlling images. In J. Kournay, J. Sterba, & R. Tong (Eds.), *Feminist philosophies* (2nd ed.) (pp. 142–152). Upper Saddle River, NJ: Prentice-Hall.

Curwin, R. L., & Mendler, A. N. (1999, January). Zero tolerance for zero tolerance. *Phi Delta Kappan,* 119–120. Retrieved from http://www.pdkintl.org/Kappan/kcur0010.htm

Darling-Hammond, L. (2004). The color line in American education: Race, resources, and student achievement. *W.E.B. Du Bois Review: Social Science Research on Race, 1*(2), 213–246.

Darling-Hammond, L. (2006). Securing the right to learn: Policy and practice for powerful teaching and learning. *Educational Researcher, 35*(7), 13–24.

Darling-Hammond, L. (2007). Race, inequality, and educational accountability: The irony of No Child Left Behind. *Race, Ethnicity, and Education, 10*(3), 245–260.

Devine, J. (1996). *Maximum security: The culture of violence in inner-city schools.* Chicago: University of Chicago Press.

DiIulio, J. J. (1995, November 27). The coming of the super-predators. *Weekly Standard,* 23–28.

Ecenbarger, W. (2012). *Kids for cash: Two judges, thousands of children, and a $2.8 million kickback scheme.* New York: New Press.

Estes, M. B. (2006). Charter schools: Do they work for troubled students? *Preventing School Failure, 51*(1), 55–61.

Feierman, J., Levick, M., & Mody, A. (2009–2010). The school-to-prison pipeline . . . and back: Obstacles and remedies for the re-enrollment of adjudicated youth. *New York Law School Review, 54,* 1115–1129.

Fensterwald, J. (2011). Now 43rd in per-student spending: California 30th in Ed Week's state rankings. Retrieved from http://toped.svefoundation. org/2011/01/12/now-43rd-in-per-student-spending/

Fierros, E. G., & Blomberg, N. A. (2005). Restrictiveness and race in special education placements in for-profit and non-profit charter schools in California. *Learning Disabilities: A Contemporary Journal, 3*(1), 1–16.

Fionda, J. (1998). The age of innocence? The concept of childhood in the punishment of young offenders. *Child and Family Law Quarterly, 10*(1), 77–87.

Frey, S. (2013, April 17). Bill restricting "willful defiance" for suspending students moves ahead. Retrieved from http://www.edsource.org/today/2013/bill-restricting-willful-defiance-for-suspending-students-moves-ahead/30522#. UfiU-W2DkfQ

Fuller, B., Gawlik, M., Gonzales, E., & Park, S. with Gibbons, G. (2003). Charter schools and inequality: National disparities in funding, teacher quality, and student support. Working Paper Series 03-2. Berkeley, CA: Policy Analysis for California Education.

Genter, S., Hooks, G., & Mosher, C. (2013). Prisons, jobs and privatization: The impact of prisons on employment growth in rural US counties, 1997–2004. *Social Science Research, 42*(3): 596–610.

Gilliam, F. D., Jr., & Iyengar, S. (1998). The superpredator script. *Nieman Reports,* 45–46.

Giroux, H. A. (2003). Racial injustice and disposable youth in the age of zero tolerance. *Qualitative Studies in Education, 16*(4): 553–565.

Glaze, L. E., & Parks, E. (2012). *Correctional populations in the United States, 2011.* Washington, DC: Bureau of Justice Statistics, U.S. Department of Justice.

Goddard, T., & Myers, R. (2011). Democracy and demonstration in the grey area of neo-liberalism: A case study of Free Los Angeles High School. *British Journal of Criminology, 51,* 652–670.

Goldson, B., & Muncie, J. (2006). Rethinking youth justice: Comparative analysis, international human rights and research evidence. *Youth Justice, 6*(2): 91–106.

Grant, P. A. (2005). Restrictiveness and race in special education: Educating all learners. *Learning Disabilities: A Contemporary Journal, 3*(1), 70–74.

Grisso, T., & Schwartz, R. G. (Eds.). (2000). *Youth on trial.* Chicago: University of Chicago Press.

Gwynne, J., & De la Torre, M. (2009). *When schools close: Effects on displaced students in Chicago public schools.* Chicago: Consortium on Chicago School Research. Retrieved from http://ccsr.uchicago.edu/publications/CCSRSchool-Closings-Final.pdf.

Hagan, J., Shedd, C., & Payne, M. (2005). Race, ethnicity, and perceptions of criminal injustice. *American Sociological Review, 70,* 381–407.

Hartney, C., & Silva, F. (2007). *And justice for some: Differential treatment of youth of color in the justice system.* Oakland, CA: National Council on Crime and Delinquency. Retrieved from http://www.nccdglobal.org/sites/default/files/publication_pdf/justice-for-some.pdf

Hawkins, S. (2010). Education vs. incarceration. *American Prospect.* Retrieved from http://prospect.org/article/education-vs-incarceration

Hazel, N. (2008). *Cross-national comparison of youth justice.* London: Youth Justice Board.

Herbert, B. (2010, February 1). Jim Crow policing. *New York Times.* Retrieved from http://www.nytimes.com/2010/02/02/opinion/02herbert.html

Hirschfield, P. (2008). Preparing for prison? The criminalization of school discipline in the USA. *Theoretical Criminology, 12,* 79–101.

Howe, K., & Welner, K. (2002). School choice and the pressure to perform: Déjà vu for children with disabilities. *Journal of Remedial and Special Education, 23*(4), 212–221.

Hutchinson, L., & Pullman, W. E. (2007). Socialization or prisonization? Utilizing Sykes' 'pains of imprisonment' to examine deprivations in America's public schools. *Critical Criminology, 15,* 171–84.

Jones, M. (2010). "Impedimenta state": Anatomies of neoliberal penality. *Criminology and Criminal Justice, 10*(4), 393–404.

Justice Policy Institute. (2011). *Education under arrest: The case against police in schools.* Retrieved from http://www.justicepolicy.org/uploads/justicepolicy/documents/educationunderarrest_fullreport.pdf

Kane, T., Abdulkadiroglu, A., Angrist, J., Cohodes, S., Dynarski, S., Fullerton, J., & Pathak, P. (2009). *Informing the debate: Comparing Boston's charter, pilot, and traditional schools.* Boston, MA: Boston Foundation. Retrieved from http://www.gse.harvard.edu/%7Epfpie/pdf/InformingTheDebate_Final.pdf

Kaufman, P., Chen, X., Choy, S. P., Peter, K., Ruddy, S. A., Miller, A. K., et al. (2001). *Indicators of school crime and safety: 2001* (NCES 2002–113/NCJ-190075). Washington, DC: U.S. Departments of Education and Justice.

Kim, C. Y. (2009–2010). Procedures for public law remediation in school-to-prison pipeline litigation: Lessons learned from Antoine v. Winner School District. *New York Law School Review, 54,* 956–974.

Kim, C. Y., Losen, D. J., & Hewitt, D. T. (2010). *The school-to-prison pipeline: Structuring legal reform.* New York: New York University Press.

Kupchik, A., & Monahan, T. (2006). The new American school: Preparation for post-industrial discipline. *British Journal of Sociology of Education, 27,* 617–31.

Lee, S. (2012, June 20). By the numbers: The U.S.'s growing for-profit detention industry. Retrieved from http://www.propublica.org/article/by-the-numbers-the-u.s.s-growing-for-profit-detention-industry

Losen, D. J. (2011). *Discipline policies, successful schools, and racial justice.* Bolder, CO: National Educational Policy Center.

Losen, D. J., & Martinez, T. E. (2013). *Out of school and off track: The overuse of suspensions in American middle and high schools.* Los Angeles: UCLA Civil Rights Project.

Losen, D. J., & Skiba, R.J. (2010). *Suspended education: Urban middle schools in crisis.* Los Angeles: UCLA Civil Rights Project. Retrieved from http://civilrightsproject.ucla.edu/research/k-12-education/school-discipline/suspended-education-urban-middle-schools-in-crisis/Suspended-Education_FINAL-2.pdf

Macek, S. (2006). *Urban nightmares: The media, the Right, and the moral panic over the city.* Minneapolis: University of Minnesota Press.

Mauer, M. (2006). *Race to incarcerate* (2nd ed.). New York: New Press.

Mora, R. (2011). Abjection and the cinematic cholo: The Chicano gang stereotype in sociohistoric context. *THYMOS: Journal of Boyhood Studies, 5*(2), 124–137.

Mora, R., & Christianakis, M. (2011). Charter schools, market capitalism, and Obama's neoliberal agenda. *Journal of Inquiry and Action in Education, 4*(1): 93–111.

Mora, R., & Christianakis, M. (2012). "No free rides, no excuses": Film stereotypes of urban working class students. In M. K. Booker (Ed.), *Blue collar pop culture in film* (pp. 167–180). Santa Barbara, CA: Praeger.

Morris, K. A., & Morris, R. J. (2006). Disability and juvenile delinquency: Issues and trends. *Disability and Society, 21*(6), 613–627.

Muncie, J. (2005). The globalization of crime control—The case of youth and juvenile justice: Neo-liberalism, policy convergence and international conventions. *Theoretical Criminology, 9*(1), 35–64.

Muncie, J. (2006). Governing young people: Coherence and contradiction in contemporary youth justice. *Critical Social Policy, 26*, 770–93.

Muncie, J. (2008). The "punitive turn" in juvenile justice: Cultures of control and rights compliance in western Europe and the USA. *Youth Justice: An International Journal, 8*(2), 107–121.

NAACP (National Association for the Advancement of Colored People). (2011). *Misplaced priorities: Over incarcerate, under educate.* Retrieved from http://naacp.3cdn.net/01d6f368edbe135234_bq0m68x5h.pdf

National Center for Educational Statistics. (2010). *Status trends in the education of racial and ethnic minorities.* Retrieved from http://nces.ed.gov/pubs2010/2010015/tables/table_17b.asp

National Public Radio. (2013, June 2). Why some schools want to expel suspensions. Retrieved from http://www.npr.org/2013/06/02/188125079/why-some-schools-want-to-expel-suspensions

Newburn, T. (2010). Diffusion, differentiation and resistance in comparative penality. *Criminology and Criminal Justice, 10*(4), 341–352.

NYCLU (New York Civil Liberties Union). (2013, May 22). Analysis finds racial disparities, ineffectiveness in NYPD stop-and-frisk program. Retrieved from http://www.nyclu.org/news/analysis-finds-racial-disparities-ineffectiveness-nypd-stop-and-frisk-program-links-tactic-soar

Noguera, P. A. (2003). Schools, prisons, and social implications of punishment: Rethinking disciplinary practices. *Theory into Practice, 42*, 341–350.

Oakes, J. (2004). Investigating the claims in Williams v. State of California: An unconstitutional denial of education's basic tools? *Teachers College Record, 106*(10), 1889–1906.

Office of Juvenile Justice and Delinquency Prevention. (2011a). Juveniles in corrections: Custody data. In *OJJDP Statistical Briefing Book.* Retrieved from http://www.ojjdp.gov/ojstatbb/corrections/qa08201.asp?qaDate=2011

Office of Juvenile Justice and Delinquency Prevention. (2011b). Juveniles in corrections: Custody data. In *OJJDP statistical briefing book.* Retrieved from http://www.ojjdp.gov/ojstatbb/corrections/qa08205.asp?qaDate=2011&text=

Orfield, G. (2001). Schools more separate: Consequences of a decade of resegregation. Los Angeles: UCLA Civil Rights Project.

Pew Center on the States. (2009). *One in 31: The long reach of American corrections.* Washington, DC: Author. Retrieved from http://www.pewcenteronthestates.org/uploadedFiles/PSPP_1in31_report_FINAL_WEB_3-26-09.pdf.

Pizarro, J. M., Chermak, S. M., & Gruenewald, J. A. (2007). Juvenile "superpredators" in the news: A comparison of adult and juvenile homicides. *Journal of Criminal Justice and Popular Culture, 14*(1), 84–111.

Pratt, J. (2007). *Penal populism.* New York: Taylor and Francis.

Quinn, M. M., Rutherford, R. B., Leone, P. E., Osher, D. M., & Poirier, J. M. (2005). Youth with disabilities in juvenile corrections: A national survey. *Exceptional Children, 71*(3), 339–345.

Reynolds, F. (2013, August 22). New York City Council overrides Bloomberg's veto of the Community Safety Act. *The Nation.* Retrieved from http://www.thenation.com/blog/175874/new-york-city-council-overrides-bloombergs-veto-community-safety-act#

Rhim, L. M., & McLaughlin, M. J. (2007) Students with disabilities in charter schools: What we now know. *Focus on Exceptional Children, 39*(5), 1–13.

Rios, V. M. (2008). The racial politics of youth crime. *Latino Studies, 6,* 97–115.

Rios, V. M. (2009). The consequences of the criminal justice pipeline on Black and Latino masculinity. *Annals of the American Academy of Political and Social Science, 623,* 150–162.

Robelen, E. W. (2008). NAEP gap continuing for charters: Sector's scores lag in three out of four main categories. *Education Week, 27*(38), 1–14.

Rott, N. (2013, May 15). LA schools throw out suspensions for "willful defiance," Retrieved from http://m.npr.org/news/U.S./184195877

Ryan, J. E. (2004). The perverse incentives of the No Child Left Behind Act. *New York University Law Review, 3,* 365–395.

Sanchez, C. G., & Adams, E. B. (2011). Sacrificed on the altar of public safety: The policing of Latino and African American youth. *Journal of Contemporary Criminal Justice, 27*(3), 322–341.

Schaffner, L. (2002). An age of reason: Paradoxes in the US legal construction of adulthood. *International Journal of Children's Rights, 10,* 201–232.

Simon, J. (2007). *Governing through crime.* New York: Oxford University Press.

Skiba, R. J. (2000). *Zero tolerance, zero evidence: A critical analysis of school disciplinary practice.* Bloomington: Indiana University Press.

Skiba, R. J., Michael, R. S., Nardo, A. C., & Peterson, R. L. (2002). The color of discipline: Sources of racial and gender disproportionality in school punishment. *Urban Review, 34,* 317–342.

Skiba, R. J., & Peterson, R. (1999). The dark side of zero tolerance: Can punishment lead to safe schools? *Phi Delta Kappan, 80,* 372–382.

Skiba, R. J. & Rausch, M. K. (2006). Zero tolerance, suspension, and expulsion: Questions of equity and effectiveness. In C. M. Evertson & C. S. Weinstein (Eds.), *Handbook for classroom management: Research, practice, and contemporary issues* (pp. 1063–1089). Mahwah, NJ: Erlbaum.

Solis, C., Portillos, E. L., & Brunson, R. K. (2009). Latino youths; experiences with and perceptions of involuntary police encounters. *Annals of the American Academy of Political and Social Science, 623,* 39–51.

Taylor, J. (2002). California's proposition 21: A case of juvenile injustice. *Southern California Law Review, 75,* 983–1019.

UCLA/IDEA (UCLA Institute for Democracy, Education, and Access). (2006). *Suspension and expulsion at-a-glance.* Los Angeles: Author.

U.S. Government Accountability Office. (2012, June). *Charter schools: Additional federal attention needed to help protect access for students with disabilities.* Washington, DC: Author.

Vacca, J. S. (2008). Crime can be prevented if schools teach juvenile offenders to read. *Children and Youth Services Review, 30*(9), 1055–1062.

Verdugo, R. R. (2000). *Zero tolerance policies: A critical review.* Washington, DC: National Education Association.

Verdugo, R. R. (2002). Race-ethnicity, social class, and zero-tolerance policies: The cultural and structural wars. *Education and Urban Society, 35*(1), 50–75.

Wacquant, L. (2001). The penalization of poverty and the rise of neo-liberalism. *European Journal on Criminal Policy and Research, 9,* 401–412.

Wacquant, L. (2009). *Punishing the poor: The neoliberal government of social insecurity.* Durham, NC: Duke University Press.

Wald, J., & Losen, D. J. (2003). Defining and redirecting a school-to-prison pipeline. *New Directions for Youth Development, 99*, 9–15.

Watanabe, T. (2013, May 15). L.A. Unified bans suspension for "willful defiance." *Los Angeles Times.* Retrieved from: http://articles.latimes.com/2013/may/14/local/la-me-lausd-suspension-20130515

Wessler, S.F. (2012, December 17). Nearly 205K deportations of parents of U.S. citizens in just over two years. *Colorlines.* Retrieved from: http://colorlines.com/archives/2012/12/us_deports_more_than_200k_parents.html

Western, B. (2006). *Punishment and inequality in America.* New York: Russell Sage Foundation.

Zatz, M. S. (1985). Los cholos: Legal processing of Chicano gang members. *Social Problems, 33*(1), 13–30.

Zimmer, R., Blanc, S., Gill, B. P., & Christman, J. B. (2008). *Evaluating the performance of Philadelphia's charter schools.* Santa Monica, CA: RAND Education.

Part III

Classroom-Based Reform
for Equity and Opportunity

8 Pedagogies of Equity and Opportunity
Critical Literacy, Not Standards

P. L. Thomas

As I approach the 30-year mark in teaching writing to students from high school through graduate school, I find that nearly all writers need feedback addressing the *claims* they make, the *evidence* they provide for those claims, and the *elaborations* used to give their writing authority and credibility. Public discourse often exhibits the kinds of issues teachers of writing confront in student writing, and the public discourse surrounding education reform includes disturbing and powerful examples of the failure to move beyond making unsupported claims in the rush to offer new policies for public education. For example, advocates for charter schools and Teach for America routinely present their advocacy without acknowledging the research base that contradicts their commitments. What messages do these pervasive arguments in the public domain teach students about clear and evidence-based writing?

This volume confronts the tension between "no excuses" reform (NER) and Social Context Reform (SCR), the former committed to in-school-only policies and the latter calling for social and educational reform that addresses equity and opportunity (Thomas, 2011). The volume sections addressing in-school and classroom reform focusing on equity center on discrediting claims that SCR embraces a fatalistic view that schools and teachers do not matter; but the arguments here are grounded in two claims: in-school and classroom reform must be couched in larger social reform, and these reforms must first address equity of opportunity. Thus, the essential flaw with NER includes advocates failing to present their reform proposals by identifying first, with evidence, the educational problems being addressed and the appropriateness of their reforms. Many of the NER commitments—such as increasing charter schools, linking teacher evaluations to student test scores, adopting and implementing Common Core curricula, and investing a tremendous amount of money in next generation high-stakes testing—either lack evidence of their effectiveness or have created additional problems in schools.

NER CLAIMS AS FLAWED POLICIES

To embrace the claims and policies of NER requires ignoring a tremendous amount of research on poverty and inequity in the U.S. That NER narrative goes something like this: education is the one true way to overcome all of society's ills, but because our schools are failing, we must reduce the standards-and-testing accountability reform model from 50 separate state policies to one national model. Let's briefly consider these claims against research on inequity before turning to an examination of pedagogies of equity and opportunity in classrooms addressing literacy.

First, is education a more powerful force than social status? Matt Bruenig (2013) asks, "What's more important: a college degree or being born rich?" to address the NER claim about education's ameliorative potential, and his discussion details the overwhelming evidence that social class is strongly static in the U.S., especially for the bottom and top fifths (see Fig. 8.1).

The U.S., it seems, is not the meritocracy many claim, and social mobility is increasingly an American myth (Pew Charitable Trusts, 2012). But possibly the most damning data are the ones that support the conclusion Bruenig (2013) reaches to answer his opening question:

> So, you are 2.5x more likely to be a rich adult if you were born rich and never bothered to go to college than if you were born poor and,

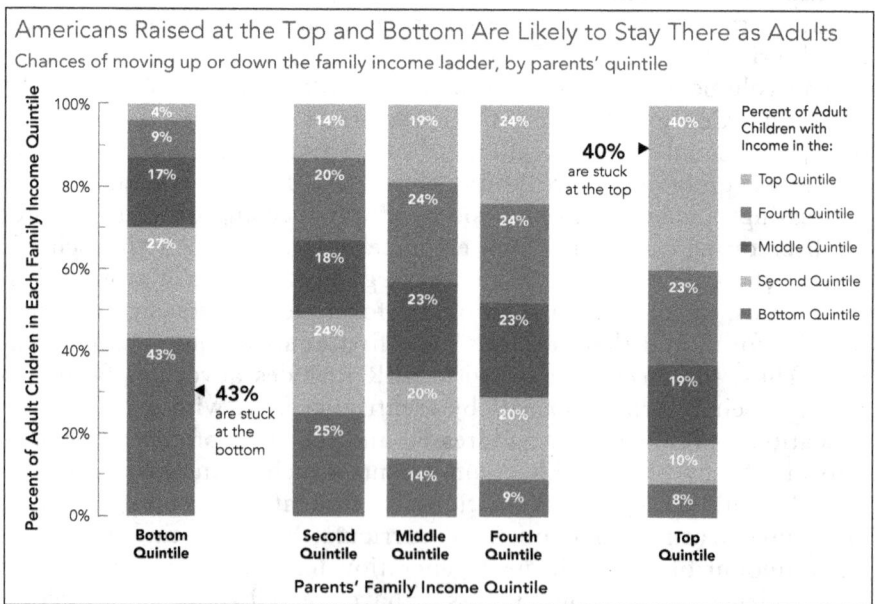

Figure 8.1 The static nature of class in the U.S.
Source: Bruenig, 2013, Figure 3.

against all odds, went to college and graduated. The disparity in the outcomes of rich and poor kids persists, not only when you control for college attainment, but even when you compare non-degreed rich kids to degreed poor kids!

Therefore, the answer to the question in the title is that you are better off being born rich *regardless of whether you go to college* than if you are born poor and do go to college.

In short, *education alone* is not the key to social reform or individual equity. Bruenig's conclusions also sit within a body of research that shows out-of-school factors overwhelm the ability of schools or teachers to overcome social inequity (Berliner, 2009). As Di Carlo (2010) comments,

> But in the big picture, roughly 60 percent of achievement outcomes is explained by student and family background characteristics (most are unobserved, but likely pertain to income/poverty). Observable and unobservable schooling factors explain roughly 20 percent, most of this (10–15 percent) being teacher effects. The rest of the variation (about 20 percent) is unexplained (error). In other words, though precise estimates vary, the preponderance of evidence shows that achievement differences between students are overwhelmingly attributable to factors outside of schools and classrooms.

The rest of the NER narrative embracing accountability proves just as baseless considering that over the past 30 years the U.S. has experienced 50 separate experiments with high-stakes standards and testing accountability that have resulted in a universal claim among all states that public schools are *still* failing (Hout & Elliott, 2011); most of those experiments have included multiple versions during those decades. Just as one representative example of how the accountability model has failed, Valerie Strauss (2013) notes,

> Consider this: On the National Assessment of Educational Progress, the test that is commonly referred to as "the nation's report card," Massachusetts students performed so well that the state ranked No. 1 in the nation.
>
> Sounds good, right? Then consider this:
>
> Massachusetts ranks in the bottom tier of states in progress toward closing the achievement gap for black, Hispanic, and low-income students, and, in fact, has some of the widest gaps in the nation between white and Hispanic students.

Dan French, Lisa Guisbond, and Alain Jehlen (2013) have examined the most recent 20 years of reform in Massachusetts, unmasking how the second part of the NER reform narrative also lacks credibility:

> The evidence we have gathered strongly suggests that two of the three major "reforms" launched in the wake of the 1993 law—high-stakes testing and Commonwealth charter schools—have failed to deliver on their promises.
>
> On the other hand, the third major component of the law, providing an influx of more than $2 billion in state funding for our schools, had a powerfully positive impact on our classrooms. But we will show that, after two decades, the formula designed to augment and equalize education funding is no longer up to the task. (p. 4)

Using data, then, as a basis for rethinking reform, the report argues that authentic reformers ought to increase school funding; stop high-stakes testing; reform charter schools; educate the whole child and close the opportunity gap; reject top-down, business-oriented reforms; and tackle poverty. The recommendations following decades of accountability-style reform, then, align with arguments made by SCR, not policies endorsed by NER.

With the broader claims of NER debunked, the first step to realizing classroom practices committed to equity of opportunity is to confront the failure of traditional and progressive methods in order to embrace critical methods—in other words, rejecting education done *to* and *for* students, and then fostering education done *with* students.

EDUCATION DONE TO, FOR, OR WITH STUDENTS?

Teachers caution student writers to avoid clichés like the plague, but many clichés harbor enduring truths. "Rearranging the deck chairs on the *Titanic*" is an accurate characterization of the rush to adopt and implement Common Core and next-generation assessments—particularly if the conditions of teaching and learning are ignored. *What* happens in the classroom and *which* populations of students have rich learning opportunities are essential factors contributing to student academic growth, regardless of the prescribed standards, new or not (Mathis, 2010), and regardless of which generation spawns the tests.

Because many current education reformers base their claims about a failing U.S. public school system on international comparisons of test scores, Finnish educator and scholar Pasi Sahlberg emphasizes that simply relying on in-school reform is misguided, as Bill Dow (2013) explains:

> While Dr. Sahlberg is quick to note the importance of adequate training for teachers, he condemns the notion that "poverty is only an excuse not to insist that all schools should reach higher standards." In his mind, children should be elevated out of poverty by public

policy, and "teachers alone, regardless of how effective they are, will not be able to overcome the challenges that poor children bring with them to school everyday."

However, the conditions of teaching and learning often reflect and perpetuate inequities related to race, class, gender, and sexuality found in society; thus, in-school reforms are necessary within larger social reform. One way to consider the conditions of teaching and learning in the classroom—and what reforms are needed—is to examine the *prepositions* of teaching: (1) education done *to* students, (2) education done *for* students, and (3) education done *with* students.

Education Done To Students

Traditional approaches to teaching and learning, as well as the more recent NER model for schooling, are driven by paternalistic assumptions (Whitman, 2008): Learning is reduced to a prescribed body of knowledge imparted by the teacher and deposited in the student (Paulo Freire [1993] labeled this the "banking" concept). School becomes a place, then, where teaching is done *to* students. Traditionally, education done to students has been common for the youngest students, couched inside an assumption that new learning is acquired best analytically (although about 80% of people are global, not analytical thinkers) and through prescriptive linear/sequential instruction.

Direct and isolated grammar and phonics instruction, for example, represents well *education done to students* as a traditional practice. More recently, during the rise of NER, younger students and students confronting new learning continue to receive an education done *to* them. Concurrently, high-poverty and minority students have been targeted in NER schools that tend to serve these populations by reducing schooling to highly structured test preparation: work sheets, programmatic textbooks, computer-based diagnostic testing, and benchmark testing. For example, a number of "no excuses" charter schools ground their entire curriculum around test-based commitments (such as to the ACT), and students are essentially taught throughout their schooling to succeed on one targeted exam (again, the ACT).

Increasingly, standards- and test-based accountability has driven education toward static and reduced curriculum, treating teachers as mere agents of dispensing that fixed curriculum and students as passive recipients of *what is tested is what is taught* (Bracey, 2006). In essence, *education done to students* fails everyone with respect to democratic goals of equity and opportunity because the agency of the learner is supplanted by the authority of the teacher as a compliant agent of mandated standards.

Education Done For Students

The progressive yin to the traditional yang above is education done *for* students.[1] Whereas the practices that characterize education done *for* students may be rooted in a kind of maternalism, those practices remain distorted by similar goals found in teaching done *to* students. A key example of the rise of teaching done for students is the work of Wiggins and McTighe (2006), marketed as understanding by design. Central to this concept are some compelling ideas, such as teachers being transparent with students about what learning outcomes are expected. Consequently, that transparency lends credibility to the rubric as a mechanism for guiding student work and promoting the appearance of greater validity and reliability to assigning grades to a wide range of assessments (particularly created responses, performances, and authentic products).

With the end *chosen by the teacher* in mind (the assessment), lesson planning remains focused on what the students must acquire in order to perform. Rubric-driven instruction and assessment do avoid the "gotcha" problem inherent in traditional teaching, but the rubric fails authentic learning because it—again—reduces learning to compliance (Kohn, 2006; Wilson, 2006, 2007). Within a culture of teaching done for students, teachers are encouraged to take great care, for example, in designing highly detailed and structured writing prompts and rubrics, with the argument that a well-crafted prompt and carefully constructed rubric ensure that students will write the essays teachers have identified for the students. In that context, however, student agency is ignored and student voice is reduced to observable and identified (*for* the student) criteria on the scoring rubric. In effect, whether or not a student incorporates three supporting details in a prompted essay becomes the goal instead of the far less predictable or manageable outcome of students learning to be independent and purposeful writers.

Whereas teaching done *for* students disproportionately affects young and new learners, impoverished students, English language learners, and minority students (in other words, those students most often marginalized by society and schools), a stark example of the failure of teaching done for students lies among the so-called top students, identified as the "good student trap" by Adele Scheele:

> We come to college with the unspoken anticipation of all that will be done for us. We expect to be made acceptable, valuable, knowledgeable, and finally professional and employable. By graduation, we presume everything will be dazzlingly clear: We will find our calling, brilliantly catapulting us to a guaranteed successful career. This wish, seldom even conscious, lies deep in our hearts. Yet we believe it will happen. . . .
>
> Most of us learned as early as junior high that we would pass, even excel if we did the work assigned to us by our teachers. We learned

to ask whether the test covered all of chapter five or only a part of it, whether the assigned paper should be ten pages long or thirty, whether "extra credit" was two book reports on two books by the same author or two books written in the same period. Remember?

We were learning the Formula.

- Find out what's expected.
- Do it.
- Wait for a response.

And it worked. We always made the grade. Here's what that process means: You took tests and wrote papers, got passing grades, and then were automatically promoted from one year to the next. That is not only in elementary, junior, and senior high school, but even in undergraduate and graduate school. You never had to compete for promotions, write résumés, or rehearse yourself or even know anyone for this promotion. It happened automatically. And we got used to it. . . .

So what's the problem? The problem is the danger. The danger lies in thinking about life as a test that we'll pass or fail, one or the other, tested and branded by an Authority. So, we slide into feeling afraid we'll fail even before we do-if we do. Mostly we don't even fail; we're just mortally afraid that we're going to. We get used to labeling ourselves failures even when we're not failing. If we don't do as well as we wish, we don't get a second chance to improve ourselves, or raise our grades. If we do perform well, we think that we got away with something this time. But wait until next time, we think; then they'll find out what frauds we are. We let this fear ruin our lives. And it does. When we're afraid, we lose our curiosity and originality, our spirit and our talent-our life. (Scheele, 2004)

In the end, both *education done to students* and *education done for students* fail students and society because such pedagogies ignore the agency of learners (and teachers) and allow arbitrary and symbolic outcomes to replace authentic demonstrations of understanding grounded in the wants and needs of the learner.

Education Done With Students

Historically and currently, what remains rare—especially with impoverished, African American, and Latino/a students—is education done *with* students in a teaching and learning environment for the teacher-student to guide and support the student-teacher (Freire, 1993). Education done with students is couched within democratic and liberatory goals, but also is well supported by decades of educational research, theory, and philosophy (Kincheloe, 2004). Education done with students shifts the teaching and learning focus away from outcomes (tests), standards, content, and the teacher by honoring each learner as the essential source for teaching and learning.

Briefly, the diverse and student-based research base on best practice (Zemelman, Daniels, & Hyde, 2012) shows that education done with students proves to be effective, but incredibly complex, resisting prepackaged programs and highly efficient testing formats. In fact, stating that best practice, broadly, means that teachers must be expert at adapting instruction to the demonstrated needs of each student sounds simple, if not simplistic. A clear example of the power of teaching done with students as well as the essentially complex nature of best practice is to examine the charts provided by Steven Zemelman, Harvey Daniels, and Arthur Hyde at the end of each content-based chapter. Significantly, best practice tends not to discount entirely or solely endorse any practice (the charts contain two columns, headed "increase" and "decrease"); instead, best practice is *collaboration* between teacher and student in which the teacher seeks those strategies that the student has demonstrated a need, and desire, to acquire.

Another powerful aspect of best practice that highlights the need for teaching done with students is the gradual release of responsibility, as Zemelman and colleagues explain: "The idea of gradual release is quite simple: in the most effective lessons, there is a stepwise transfer of responsibility from the teacher to the student" (2012, p. 39). In other words, there is nothing whimsical (letting students do whatever they want, whenever) or haphazard about teaching done with students. In fact, it is quite purposeful, simple in its essence, and incredibly complex, messy, and unpredictable in its application (and thus it remains rare in the classroom).

In the late 1970s and early 1980s, just as the current accountability era consumed public education, *education done with students* gained momentum through the rise of the National Writing Project and workshop-based writing instruction, made popular by Nancie Atwell and others. Atwell's workshop approach was controversial then and remains rare in classrooms today. But the essence of the workshop (which Atwell [1998] attributed to Mary Ellen Giacobbe)—time, ownership, and response—redefined the roles and agency of the teacher and the students, the nature of the curriculum (student choice within teacher guidance), and what assessments were honored (increased focus on authentic projects, such as original essays by students and letters by students to peers and their teacher about their chosen reading).

For all its promise, however, many of those initial commitments to best practice have been co-opted and consumed by traditional (teaching done to students) and progressive (teaching done for students) practices as education remains heavily focused on raising test scores as accountability mechanisms for mandated standards. The rush to adopt new standards (Common Core)—endorsed as a process to unify a diversity of standards quality among states—and the hyperbole about next-generation assessments are analogous to rearranging the deck chairs on the *Titanic*. Once again, our gaze is poised on the wrong things: standards and test quality. That myopic and trivial concern for moving around the same old furniture disregards the people involved or the iceberg (poverty and social inequity) right there before us. As long as reform is misplaced, however, and labeled as "excuses" by NER, we are certain to hear yet more cries of crisis.

PEDAGOGIES OF EQUITY AND OPPORTUNITY: CRITICAL LITERACY FOR ALL STUDENTS

NER's exclusive focus on in-school reform represents commitments to commanding control (Foucault, 1984) and fits within a model of maintaining a state of perpetual crisis, requiring reform (Deleuze, 1992). SCR, however, acknowledges the need for social reform and then in-school reform that embraces critical pedagogy and critical literacy (Freire 1993, 1998; Kincheloe, 2004) and creates a culture of noncooperation (Ramanathan, 2006) instead of compliance. Below, then, education done with students is outlined as pedagogies of equity and opportunity.

Pedagogies of equity and opportunity focus on the conditions of learning and teaching, not on the outcomes—and in particular, not solely on measurable, quantifiable outcomes. Those conditions of learning and teaching must remain transparent (as an alternative to the traditional accountability paradigm) and be evaluated against the equity of learning opportunities afforded all students regardless of any status or identified category related to race, class, gender, sexuality, or academic designation. Whereas NER has reinforced traditional commitments to measurement and prescription associated with learning and teaching, pedagogies of equity and opportunity exist within some broad guiding concepts—collaboration and choice, reimagining content, de-testing and de-grading schools—that honor the agency and autonomy of students and teachers.

The Power of Collaboration and Choice

In education done to students, collaboration is essentially absent, often marginalized as cheating; in education done for students, collaboration exists among students within contexts prescribed by the teachers. Both conditions of learning and teaching essentially devalue the full power of collaboration and choice because some authoritarian agent determines what is to be learned and how—often some bureaucratic agent and/or the teacher. Education done with students embraces an articulated collaboration among teachers and students, recognizing that teachers are authoritative (Freire, 1993, 1998) and that bureaucratic mandates govern almost all public schooling. Collaboration and choice within pedagogies of equity and opportunity are driven by a teacher-student and student-teacher dynamic (Freire, 1993).

As a brief example, a critical shift in my pedagogy while teaching advanced placement (AP) literature represents well how to implement pedagogies of equity and opportunity that honor collaboration and choice within real-world limitations and expectations found in U.S. public schools—notably, expectations connected to high-stakes testing. During my eighteen years teaching high school English in the rural South, I taught AP literature in a school that did not gate-keep and allowed many students to enroll in AP who would have been denied access in schools conforming to the College Board's recommendations for using test scores as entrance requirements for AP (a process predicated on a goal of increasing the likelihood of more students achieving scores of 3 or better on the exams). That policy also was supported by the administration's recognition that our students' scores on the AP test would often be lower than those of students at selective schools (many of our students scored 2's, but we felt the advanced curriculum and rich learning opportunities prepared them well for college even if they didn't gain college credit with their exam scores).

Because my AP courses were *not* high-stakes in terms of administrative expectations, I had the rare luxury of being trusted with my curriculum, pedagogy, and assessment, and only lightly monitored in how I conducted the classes. As a result, I implemented a *tethered choice* curriculum in my AP literature class, a decision that recognized that students would be taking the AP test at the end of the year but offered students targeted choices of their reading for the year (Thomas, 2003). The revised approach to curriculum shifted away from assigning whole-class texts (such as all students reading, discussing, and being assessed on William Faulkner's *As I Lay Dying* during the same instructional time) and toward workshop blocks of time in which students chose which texts to read and study within a broad guiding unit focus that would support whole-class discussions. For example, one learning unit was African American literature, and students were asked to choose a major novel by an African American author or that addressed the African American experience. Before students chose, however, we examined recommended works from the College Board and discussed which African American authors had gained access to the canon as a framework for their decisions.

Most class sessions were workshop oriented. Students read, talked with other students, conducted research on and read critical analyses of their novels or plays, held conferences with me, or joined in with small group discussions when several students chose the same text. Whole-class discussion allowed students to express and share both commonalities and differences among the texts as they explored literature by and about African Americans. These discussions were grounded in confrontations about power and cultural norms—in the setting of the works, the historical period of the authors, and our contemporary times. I also taught, supported, and challenged students with a wide range of literary analysis lenses, from Marxist and feminist (nearly unacknowledged by the College Board) to New Criticism (the implicit lens endorsed by the College Board).

This approach to curriculum and pedagogy honored the expertise of me as a teacher and scholar while also honoring the interests and needs (such as performing well on the AP test) of the students. Whereas a choice-based workshop learning and teaching environment is far more challenging for the students and the teacher, the outcomes are richer and more authentic than in traditional classes. The sheer number and variety of texts read and discussed in these AP classes in one year outnumbered the works explored in all the traditional years preceding it. And although student AP scores were low that year (Thomas, 2003), surveys of students revealed that students read more and were more engaged than in their reading experiences in previous years.

A key point to this example, however, is that SCR seeks this sort of experience for all students, not just AP students. *Learning and teaching environments that incorporate and honor collaboration and choice must be those all students experience.* In a pedagogy of equity and opportunity, teachers have a responsibility to make students aware of norms and conventional expectations, but that awareness must be the foundation for critical confrontations by students as they navigate their own views of those norms—which to embrace and which to reject or to try to change. The experiences provided in an AP class honoring choice and collaboration neither ignored nor blindly conformed to the limitations of the AP tests and the College Board's suggested (and thus canonized) texts and authors.

Collaboration and choice are foundational commitments in pedagogies of equity and opportunity—student and teacher moves that contribute to education done with students.

Reimagining Content

Just as the roles of teachers and students must be reimagined as part of pedagogies of equity and opportunity by honoring collaboration and choice, the role of content must also be shifted. In education done to and for students, content is often prescribed, static, and the goal of learning (demonstrating acquisition of discipline-specific content represents learning, in other words). For example, the curriculum identifies that all students must read Nathaniel Hawthorne's *The Scarlet Letter* and the summative assessment focuses on gathering evidence that the students have gained essential knowledge about that text, such as identifying Hester as a protagonist or analyzing how the use of color imagery throughout the novel supports a major theme.

As Ann M. Johns (2008) explains, *awareness* should supplant *acquisition* within pedagogies of equity and opportunity, a classroom in which education is done with students. For example, in my first years of teaching, I sought to offer my students a more authentic education in their literacy development, an aspect of education I believed was traditionally misserved, notably in teaching poetry. Because I was a practicing and published poet, I saw my role as bringing a rich and authentic view of poetry to the classroom, one in which we didn't simply use poetry to mine the text for literary terms: for example, *Find the use of figurative language in Emily Dickinson's "Because I Could Not Stop for Death."*

However, though I had moved beyond *education done to students*, my first attempts were trapped at *education done for students*—providing for them the characteristics of poetry I deemed worthy (just as I taught writing by providing for them templates of writing). Whereas the four broad characteristics of poetry I taught my students were grounded in both my expertise as a literary critic and reader as well as my work as a poet, these template-driven practices failed miserably. Students often wrote mechanical, lifeless, and simply bad essays trying to show the four characteristics through a poem I allowed them to choose. The failure, of course, was that the students' own agency was being ignored. Moreover, I was denying those students the opportunity to discover an understanding of poetry I had myself experienced (and thus, the corrosive influence of efficiency as a goal).

Consistent with the idea of education done *with* students, my approach to text became genre based, discovery oriented, and driven by essential questions instead of prescribed content. That meant that my poetry unit became a nine-week examination of many poems and some song lyrics revolving around a guiding question: What makes poetry poetry? Simultaneously, the poetry unit became much more simple and much more complex. The unit was more simple because the basic patterns of choosing, reading, and discussing poems were now shared by my students and me; the unit was more complex because we were all continually in the discovery mode, and what we discovered about poetry through the open-ended guiding question revealed that almost no fixed definition of poetry exists—except that poetry tended to be text written in purposeful lines and stanzas. Ultimately, this content shift for exploring poetry helped reinforce some of the best writing pedagogy I have ever taught because it emphasized the purposeful creation of texts.

As with collaboration and choice, reimagining content allowed students to identify conventions and norms in order to determine what agents drove those norms and in what ways students wished to conform to or reject those conventions. Content, then, became a *means* to learning and not the *goal* of learning—awareness, not acquisition (Johns, 2008).

De-Testing and De-Grading for Equity and Opportunity

In the past thirty years, pedagogy and curriculum have been subordinated to the pursuit of outcomes: high-stakes test scores. In pedagogies of equity and opportunity, when education is done with students, de-testing and de-grading the classroom become central elements of how to reform teaching and learning (Bower & Thomas, 2013). Traditional schooling and NER, whether education done to or for students, incorporate tests and grades as mechanisms for labeling, ranking, and sorting students as a microcosm of the larger New Jim Crow era of mass incarceration (Thomas, 2013). Testing and grading work in ways that are parallel to surveillance, arrests, and imprisonment in that all disproportionately target negatively African American, Latino/a, and impoverished students and people. Inequity is inherent in grading and testing because test scores and grades remain significantly correlated with affluence, race, and gender.

Feedback that supports learning replaces grades and tests in pedagogies of equity and opportunity in order to reject labeling and sorting with practices that respect the dignity and potential of all children. Teacher and peer feedback also reinforces the need to de-emphasize summative assessment by honoring ongoing revision of authentic artifacts that demonstrate not only students' understanding at any moment but also the journey those students have taken to understand. Shifting to feedback instead of tests and grades also supports the roles of teacher-student and student-teacher because it reinforces the authoritative feedback of the teacher as a model for the learning the student is exploring and honors peers as credible partners in any student's learning experiences.

In pedagogies of equity and opportunity, the goals of assessment also include students being supported as credible evaluators of their own work. As Miller (2008) explains:

> Young adults often feel disenfranchised from society because of their lack of power based on their age, ethnicity, appearance, sexual orientation, national origin, ability, and social class. Similarly, youth often feel disempowered in the school system because of the power structure of teacher over student. Desiring students to be part of the assessment process can act as an invitation into their brooding awareness as a person of power. (p. 161)

Education done with students incorporates teacher feedback instead of tests and grades in order to model for students their own emerging paradigms for evaluating their work against conventions, norms, and their own developing standards and expectations for themselves. Ultimately, Miller envisions,

> As we shift our beliefs to reconsider student work as an offering that provides insight about learning as a "byproduct of cultural schemata," then perhaps we may ease the reins on what materials and how we deem materials should be assessed; and then can begin to foster a shift with our students that enables the body and the mind to work synchronistically towards liberatory assessment. As we make this shift from the "I learn for you," to the existential "I learn for me; I am responsible for my own acts; I can make a difference," we support the activation

of both the body and mind of the learner and empower them to help transform assessment practices. (p. 170)

Traditional approaches to grading can and should be replaced by more authentic opportunities for students to demonstrate learning. Practices such as teacher and peer feedback, as well as developing students as their own evaluators of their work contribute to authentic goals (such as fostering student autonomy), whereas traditional practices tend to work against those goals. As a brief example of shifting assessment norms, and as a unifying example of all the foundational commitments to collaboration, choice, and reimagining content discussed above, let's consider assessment focusing on students exploring literature in a high school American literature course.

In education done to and for students, texts are assigned, such as whole-class units around Nathanial Hawthorne's *The Scarlet Letter*. Whereas whole-class-assigned texts do not work within the parameters of pedagogies of equity and opportunity, let's consider how to change the testing paradigm in this traditional setting in order to honor SCR goals. Typically, students would be tested by a selected-response test, addressing mostly knowledge recall of facts from the novel and some analysis of the novel (assessing, however, that the students can choose the interpretations verified by some authorities, but not the student), or through a prompted essay requiring students to perform within a New Criticism approach to analyzing the novel.

Even if the conditions of learning and teaching mandate a whole-class study of *The Scarlet Letter*, the assessment principles do not have to fail the students as well. After reading the text, students can be asked to create their own demonstrations of learning about the novel, allowing them—in conjunction with the guidance of the teacher—to become agents of their own evaluation. As well, assessments of student learning should not be based on the text of *The Scarlet Letter* because that honors the acquisition of the text as the goal, and not learning goals grounded in critical literacy, such as students confronting the complex messages encompassed in the setting of the novel, the time period of Hawthorne as writer, and the students' own time-bound cultural assumptions. For example, students could be presented with different texts by Hawthorne and asked to confront those texts in ways that show their understanding of his work, his culture, the critical response to Hawthorne, and a wide range of historical and contemporary responses to the themes and topics raised by Hawthorne and other writers.

NO LONGER FOREIGNERS: TEACHERS AND STUDENTS

NER remains trapped within social norms, committed to schooling that conforms children to those norms; it is thus ill equipped to confront inequity of opportunity plaguing the lives and learning of children, especially children in poverty. Commitments to education done to and for students render both teachers and students as "others," and as mechanisms for conforming both to the agendas of those in power. Instead, pedagogies of equity and opportunity are necessarily acts of noncooperation. As Vaidehi Ramanathan (2006) notes,

> Gandhi's views on enhancing the vernaculars . . . so that Indians are "not foreigners in their own land" are directly tied to his opinions on developing communities (for "the poorest of the poor") and making community service an integral part of any education. (pp. 235–236)

The conditions of learning and teaching must be transformed to replicate in school the conditions of noncooperation highlighted by Ramanathan:

> As is evident, the take on "education" presented here is not the usual one—of teaching and learning in formal contexts of classrooms and institutions—but one that is intended to move us toward becoming collectively open to realizing that very valuable "education" often goes on outside the constraints of classrooms. . . . Indeed, "education" in both these institutions is civic and community education that seems to assume Gandhian ideals of "Non-Cooperation" (and nonformal education) and that is aimed at primarily effecting changes in the community, sometimes before addressing issues relevant to formal education. (p. 230)

SCR calls for a radical reconsideration of the norms of society that benefit the affluent and marginalize and silence the impoverished. But it also calls for a radical reconsideration of in-school practices, ones that seek education done with students as the most equitable path to agency and autonomy for both teachers and students. Ultimately, NER claims about the failures of education and the reforms embraced by NER advocates have proven to be baseless and ineffective. SCR calls for reconsidering and expanding education reform by placing school reform within a wider social reform commitment. Both social and educational reform, then, must remain focused on achieving equity and opportunity as well as rejecting the need to honor outcomes and embracing the importance of the conditions of living, learning, and teaching that are the most powerful influences on those outcomes.

NOTES

1. Yin and yang are complimentary, not opposites; thus, I use this comparison to support my argument that traditional and progressive approaches to education are essentially the same flawed ideology because they remain trapped inside a single mechanistic paradigm; progressive education appears a bit more child-centered, a bit more kindhearted, but it isn't.

REFERENCES

Atwell, N. (1998). *In the middle: New understanding about writing, reading, and learning* (2nd ed.). Portsmouth, NH: Heinemann.

Berliner, D. C. (2009). *Poverty and potential: Out-of-school factors and school success.* Boulder, CO and Tempe, AZ: Education and the Public Interest Center/Education Policy Research Unit. Retrieved from http://epicpolicy.org/publication/poverty-and-potential

Bower, J., & Thomas, P. L. (eds.). (2013). *De-testing and de-grading schools: Authentic alternatives to accountability and standardization.* New York: Lang.

Bracey, G. W. (2006). *Reading educational research: How to avoid getting statistically snookered.* Portsmouth, NH: Heinemann.

Bruenig, M. (2013, June 13). What's more important: A college degree or being born rich? Retrieved from http://mattbruenig.com/2013/06/13/whats-more-important-a-college-degree-or-being-born-rich/

Deleuze, G. (1992). Postscript on the societies of control. *October, 59,* 3–7. Retrieved from https://files.nyu.edu/dnm232/public/deleuze_postcript.pdf

Di Carlo, M. (2010, July 14). Teachers matter, but so do words. Retrieved from http://shankerblog.org/?p=74

Dow, B. (2013, June 11). Maybe it isn't just the teachers in Finland. . . . Retrieved from http://washingtonpolicywatch.org/2013/06/11/maybe-it-isnt-just-the-teachers-in-finland/

Foucault, M. (1984). *The Foucault reader.* (P. Rabinow, Ed.) New York: Pantheon.

Freire, P. (1993). *Pedagogy of the oppressed.* (M. Bergman Ramos, Trans.) New York: Continuum.

Freire, P. (1998). *Pedagogy of freedom: Ethics, democracy, and civic courage.* (P. Clarke, Trans.) New York: Rowman and Littlefield.

French, D., Guisband, L., & Jehlen, A. (2013, June). *Twenty years after education reform: Choosing a path forward to equity and excellence for all.* Boston: Citizens for Public Schools. Retrieved from http://www.citizensforpublicschools.org/wp-content/uploads/2013/06/CPS-20th-Anniversary-of-ERA-Report-Executive-Summary-Online-6–10–13.pdf

Hout, M., & Elliott, S. W. (2011). *Incentives and test-based accountability in education.* Washington, DC: National Academies Press. Retrieved from http://www.nap.edu/catalog.php?record_id=12521

Johns, A. M. (2008). Genre awareness for the novice academic student: An ongoing quest. *Language Teaching, 41*(2), 237–252.

Kincheloe, J. (2004). *Critical pedagogy primer.* New York: Lang.

Kohn, A. (2006). The trouble with rubrics. *English Journal, 95*(4), 12–15.

Mathis, W. J. (2010). The "Common Core" standards initiative: An effective reform tool? Boulder, CO, and Tempe, AZ: Education and the Public Interest Center/Education Policy Research Unit. Retrieved from http://epicpolicy.org/publication/common-core-standards

Miller, sj. (2008). Liberating grades/liberatory assessment. *International Journal of Critical Pedagogy, 1*(2), 160–171.

Pew Charitable Trusts, Economic Mobility Project. (2012, July). Pursuing the American dream: Economic mobility across generations. Philadelphia, PA. Retrieved from http://www.pewstates.org/uploadedFiles/PCS_Assets/2012/Pursuing_American_Dream.pdf

Ramanathan, V. (2006). Gandhi, non-cooperation, and socio-civic education in Gujarat, India: Harnessing the vernaculars. *Journal of Language, Identity, and Education, 5*(3), 229–250.

Scheele, A. (2004, May 6). The good student trap. *Washington Post.* Retrieved from http://www.washingtonpost.com/wp-dyn/articles/A50758-2003May13.html

Strauss, V. (2013, June 13). How test scores can be deceiving. *Washington Post*. Retrieved from http://www.washingtonpost.com/blogs/answer-sheet/wp/2013/06/13/how-test-scores-can-be-deceiving/

Thomas, P. L. (2003, July). When choice failed—Or did it? *English Journal, 92*(6), 17–19.

Thomas, P. L. (2011, December 30). Poverty matters! A Christmas miracle. Retrieved from http://truth-out.org/news/item/5808:poverty-matters-a-christmas-miracle

Thomas, P. L. (2013, May 17). Education reform in the New Jim Crow era. Retrieved from http://truth-out.org/opinion/item/16406-education-reform-in-the-new-jim-crow-era

Thompson, J. (2013, June 19). The end might be near for Common Core. Retrieved from http://atthechalkface.com/2013/06/19/the-end-might-be-near-for-common-core-2/

Whitehurst, G. J. (2009, October). *Don't forget curriculum*. Retrieved from http://www.brookings.edu/research/papers/2009/10/14-curriculum-whitehurst

Whitman, D. (2008, Fall). An appeal to authority. *Education Next, 8*(4). Retrieved from http://educationnext.org/an-appeal-to-authority/

Wiggins, G., & McTighe, J. (2006). *Understanding by design* (2nd ed.). New York: Pearson.

Wilson, M. (2007). Why I won't be using rubrics to respond to students' writing. *English Journal, 96*(4), 62–66.

Wilson, M. (2006). *Rethinking rubrics in writing assessment*. Portsmouth, NH: Heinemann.

Zemelman, S., Daniels, H., & Hyde, A. (2012). *Best Practice: Bringing standards to life in America's classrooms* (4th ed.). Portsmouth, NH: Heinemann.

9 YouTube University

How an Educational Foundations Professor Uses Critical Media in His Classroom

Nicholas D. Hartlep

INTRODUCTION

At 29, I am the youngest assistant professor in Illinois State University's Educational Administration and Foundations Department,[1] where I teach, conduct research, and advise both undergraduate and educational foundations doctoral students. Being the youngest in my department, however, has not been exclusively a limitation. In fact, from my perspective, it has been mostly advantageous—for me and for my students. For instance, there is the obvious generational advantage: a noticeable strength of being young is one's ability to relate to young students. I am necessarily able to relate to my undergraduate students in certain ways that my older colleagues are unable to given the divergent frames of reference. With technology advancing so quickly and social media transforming the cultural landscape at a record pace, generational gaps that used to be measured in decades are now measured in years or even months. If I am occasionally confounded by students in their late teen and early 20s, I can only imagine the relational challenges they pose to teachers in their 40s or 50s. In addition to these noticeable generational gaps, there are also enormous disparities between those who have access to high technology and the Internet and those who do not, something referred to as the "digital divide" (Brown & Gibbons, 2011; U.S. Department of Commerce, 1999). This divide is real and exists across the globe. The majority of my university students are privileged to have such access, and as a professor I certainly am too.

In making this observation, it is not my intent to be ageist, nor to get into a tit-for-tat debate over ideal teaching age ("My age is better because I have more experience!" "No, my age is better because my experience is more relevant to the students!") I merely wish to highlight the fact that I am also member of the "YouTube generation."[2] Sixty-five percent of the YouTube generation is under the age of 35, and individuals in this group are unique "because they are highly engaged, making purposeful decisions about the way they choose to live their lives" ("Meet Gen C," 2013, p. 2). Younger professors have this one particular advantage: by benefit of being closer to the generational gap, they do not have as far to reach in bridging it.

THE PURPOSE OF THIS CHAPTER

This chapter presents how I, a young, tenure-track assistant professor of educational foundations, have used YouTube in my college classroom in order to cultivate critical literacy—what Paulo Freire and Donaldo Macedo (1987) identify as "reading the word and the world"—into the teaching praxis of my students (all of whom are preservice teachers). I share specific and detailed examples of how I have successfully used video clips from YouTube to (1) teach about Vincent Chin, (2) demystify the model minority stereotype of Asian Americans, and (3) teach the critical race theoretical concepts of *white interest convergence* and *false empathy.*

This topic is relevant and timely because YouTube may influence how—many, but not all—professors teach as well as how college students learn. Moreover, college students are becoming increasingly capable of learning through social media, which necessitates reforming the pedagogical approaches that higher education faculty use when delivering college content to students. Whereas university students may be able to navigate social media quite easily, in some ways, college students have little to no understanding about the social nature of computing technology, such as analyzing which groups benefit by using technology and which groups are harmed by the proliferation of technology.

This chapter is structured in the following way: First I provide a brief history of YouTube. I then discuss Freire and Macedo's (1987) idea of *reading the word and the world.* Subsequently, I trace how I have used YouTube in the college classroom to foster critical media literacy skills. I close with three short example lessons—ones that I have actually used and that I have found to be successful—followed by a few concluding remarks.

THE PARTICIPATORY CULTURE OF YOUTUBE

In 2005, three college students created YouTube. The brainchild of Chad Hurley (Indiana University of Pennsylvania), Steve Chen (University of Illinois at Urbana-Champaign), and Jawed Karim (University of Illinois at Urbana-Champaign), YouTube had by the following year become one of the fastest-growing websites on the World Wide Web (O'malley, 2006). Because of its immediate success, in 2006 Google purchased YouTube for $1.65 billion (Sorkin & Peters, 2006)—just one year after its debut.

To contextualize what has already been said about the YouTube generation, let me note that I graduated with an undergraduate degree in elementary teaching in December 2006. It is because of Hurley, Chen, and Karim that I have grown up with YouTube on the screens of my computers, smartphones, and iPads. They are the reason that I am able to peruse streaming media regularly on YouTube.

What Is It?

YouTube is generally considered to be a video-sharing platform; however, I view it as much more. It has also become a social space and educational vehicle because its users can not only share and watch videos on a variety of topics but also gain access to knowledge that was located in inconvenient spaces (e.g., libraries, books, historical museums). The fact that YouTube is instantaneous—users can view videos immediately—is one reason it has become so popular; it is also useful because it is a one-stop shop for many diverse and eclectic topics. For instance, by viewing YouTube videos, I have educated myself on a variety of topics, including statistics, cooking Korean food, and how to format my dissertation, among others. In fact, I believe it is quite possible that do-it yourself (DIY) books will soon be replaced by DIY YouTube videos.

Notably, the first ever video posted on the media-sharing giant's website was *Me at the Zoo*. The video, showing cofounder Jawed Karim at the San Diego Zoo, was uploaded on April 23, 2005, and can still be viewed on the site today. When I watched *Me at the Zoo* it had already been viewed 11,385,346 times. To place the original video's popularity in context, Psy's globally ubiquitous music video *Gangnam Style* was added to YouTube on July 15, 2012 and quickly became the first YouTube video to receive over a billion views, on December 21, 2012 (Cellan, 2012). *Me at the Zoo* may never be in the running for most-popular video, but it certainly blazed paths for the success that YouTube enjoys today. Indeed, it may join the ranks of historic technological artifacts along with the first Edison sound recordings or the first silent films.

Critical Literacy: Reading the Word and the World

Freire and Macedo (1987) describe a concept of critical literacy in their book *Literacy: Reading the Word and the World*. In a 1985 interview, Freire, using a literacy metaphor, describes what *reading the word and the world* means to him:

> If we think of education as an act of knowing, then *reading* has to do with knowing. The act of *reading* cannot be explained as merely *reading words* since every act of *reading words* implies a previous *reading of the world* and a subsequent *rereading of the world*. There is a permanent movement back and forth between *"reading"* reality and *reading words*—the spoken word too is our *reading of the world*. We can go further, however, and say that *reading the word* is not only preceded by *reading the world*, but also by a certain form of writing it or rewriting it. In other words, of transforming it by means of conscious practical action. For me, this dynamic movement is central to *literacy*. (Freire, 1985b, p. 18, emphasis added)

The ability to *read the word and the world* is a central skill that I attempt to equip my students with in my Social Foundations of Education course. Because many of my students were born in the 1990s and are members of the YouTube generation, I intentionally use YouTube regularly in my classroom. Knowledge of my students in terms of their life experiences is incredibly important. This is especially true because, according to Freire, "Our tendency as teachers is to start from the point at which we are and not from the point at which the students are" (Freire, 1985b, p. 15).

I am convinced that Freire and Macedo's (1987) notion of critical literacy as the ability to *read the word and the world* lends itself nicely to the social foundations of education and critical media studies. I actively teach my students that being critically media literate is important for all educators, irrespective of the grade level they teach or the content area they study. For one thing, as Malcolm X once asserted, "If you're not careful, the newspapers will have you hating the people who are being oppressed, and loving the people who are doing the oppressing."

Accordingly, in order to become critically literate, I deconstruct, reconstruct, and scaffold my course materials for my students in simple, albeit important, ways. For example, I begin where my students are when I attempt to bridge the chasm they perceive between *theory* and *practice* (see, e.g., Goodman, 2000; Thomas, 2007). I also use a diagram (see Fig. 9.1) in my Social Foundations of Education course to illustrate Freire's (2005) conception of praxis.

According to John Dewey (1962), it is difficult to describe the relationship of theory to practice. According to Phelps and Ryan, "'Praxis'—derived from the Greek verb meaning 'to do'—is 'the systematic and concerted synthesis of theory and practice'" (1995, p. 122).

I believe *praxis* is the connection between *theory* and *practice*. Freire defines *praxis* as "reflection and action upon the world in order to *transform* it" (2005, p. 51, emphasis added). He also notes that when one reaches critical consciousness one cannot accept "theory without practice" or "thinking without transforming action in the world" (1985a, p. 104). Why is reflection so important in teacher education? I believe the answer is tied to the fact that most college professors can *make the simple complicated*, whereas fewer professors can *make the*

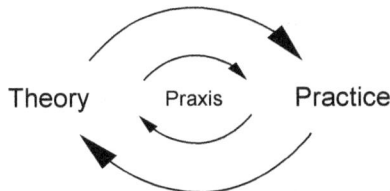

Theory   Praxis   Practice

Figure 9.1 A conceptual diagram of the theory/practice relationship.

complicated simple. What does that mean? In part it means that teacher educators must be self-reflective in order to understand what enhances student learning. Professors have a vast amount of theoretical and conceptual knowledge that their students may not have. Teacher educators need to be reflective when teaching about and assisting preservice teachers to understand critical concepts and theories. Albert Einstein said it best: "If you can't explain it simply, you don't understand it well enough."

Indeed, it was reflection that caused me to use YouTube and conceptual diagrams like the one in Figure 9.1 in my own instructional practice. After teaching two semesters at Illinois State University I realized that I needed to alter my pedagogical approach when working with my mostly white, middle-class, female students (Goodman, 2000). Using YouTube to teach my students critical media studies is highly strategic because I know that my students are familiar with it.

The Mindset List is an annual compilation of the values that shape the worldview (or mind-set) of students around 18 years of age who are entering college and, to a lesser extent, adulthood. It is compiled by Ron Nief and Tom McBride of Beloit College in Wisconsin (Gibbs, 2009). Notably, number five on The Mindset List for the Class of 2016 is the following: "If they miss *The Daily Show*, they can always get their news on *YouTube*" (Beloit College, 2012, emphasis added). These are college students who were born in 1994 or later and have always known Kurt Cobain, Jacqueline Kennedy Onassis, Richard Nixon, and John Wayne Gacy to be dead.

Critical Media Studies Conceptualizations

Ira Shor conceptualizes critical media studies by using an interactive field model (see Fig. 9.2) to study the news media. He accomplishes this through what he calls "academic problem posing" (1992, p. 79).

Critical media study encourages professors to teach (and students to learn) that questioning "taken-for-granted" assumptions and "common sense" is vital for establishing democratic and equitable societies. Neil Postman and Charles Weingartner summarize the importance of questioning effectively in their book *Teaching as a Subversive Activity*: "Children enter school as question marks and leave as periods" (1969, p. 60). Being a social foundations of education professor, I feel the same way that Postman and Weingartner did; I do not want my students to become *periods*. I want my students to continue to be (if they already are) or to become (for the first time in their lives) *question marks*. I believe Postman and Weingartner are saying that schooling anesthetizes and socializes children—who are otherwise naturally inquisitive (*question marks*)—to become less inquisitive, and eventually, passive receivers of rote-memorized material (*periods*).

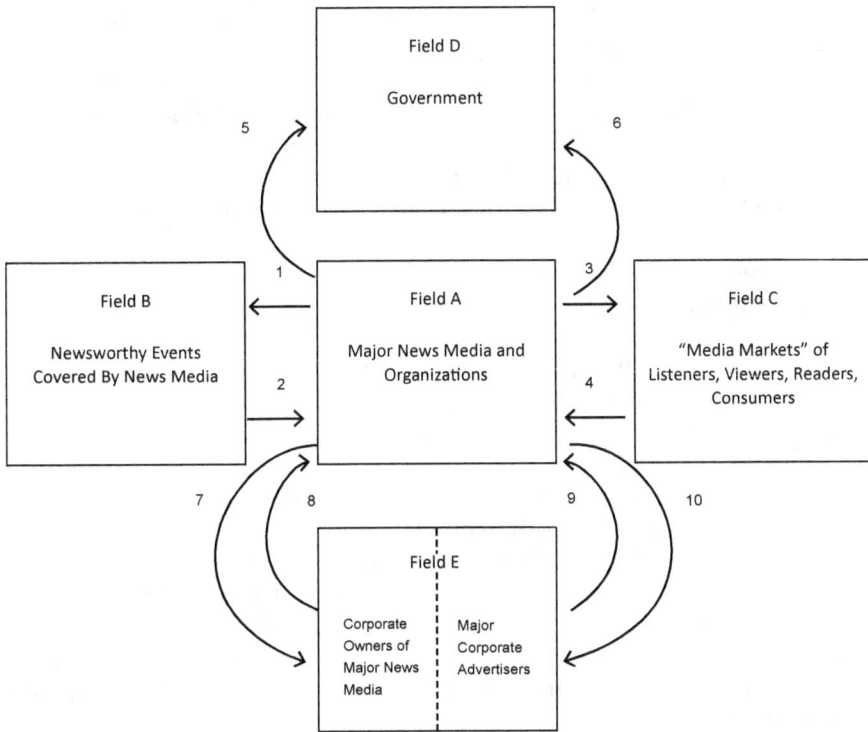

Figure 9.2   The interactive field model of critical media studies.
Source: Shor, 1992, p. 80; reprinted with the permission of Ira Shor.

THREE LESSONS USING YOUTUBE

In the spirit of becoming a critical questioner—to use Postman and Weingartner's language, a "question mark"—I would like to share three lessons in which I have used YouTube to facilitate critical dialogue and critical media literacy. The first lesson is about Vincent Chin, a young Chinese American man who was beaten to death in 1982 in what was generally perceived to be a racially motivated attack. The second is an introductory lesson on the model minority stereotype. The third lesson, also introductory in nature, exposes students to the critical race theoretical fundamental concepts of *white interest convergence* and *false empathy*. Finally, I summarize the three lessons before concluding the chapter.

Miscarriage of Justice: Introducing Students to Vincent Chin

I use a YouTube music video for the song "Vincent Chin" by hip-hop group Model Minority to introduce my teacher education students to the Vincent

Chin case. This introduction is important because many of my students have never heard of Chin.

I find the music video to be an impressive way to introduce the miscarriage of justice that makes the Chin case so infamous and widely recognized. Not only are Model Minority's song lyrics powerful, they are accentuated by clips in the video that are taken from the documentary *Who Killed Vincent Chin?* The introductory lyrics of the song are sampled below:

> *Downtown Detroit, Motor City*
> *Recession time, not lookin' pretty*

Model Minority's "Vincent Chin" uses the beat of Fort Minor's "Kenji," an effective song for introducing students to the internment of Japanese Americans during World War II. I introduce students to the Chin case with this particular song and music video because my students frequently believe that music is apolitical. By hearing politicized music, they begin to become curious about other mainstream songs that they recite and sing, often being clueless about the words that they are singing. After playing the video for the song "Vincent Chin" I show Christine Choy and Renee Tajima-Peña's 1989 Academy Award–nominated documentary *Who Killed Vincent Chin?* Once they have heard the song and viewed the documentary, we begin to unpack the details of the Chin murder and murder trial.

Vincent Chin was a 27-year-old Chinese American who was murdered one week before his wedding. In the summer of 1982, Chin was murdered by two white men (Ronald Ebens and his stepson, Michael Nitz) in Detroit after all three had been in the same strip club. Chin's death was the result of an ethnic mistaken identity. Despite his being Chinese American, Ebens and Nitz mistook Chin for being Japanese. Ebens and Nitz were autoworkers; they reportedly yelled at Chin, "It's because of you motherfuckers that we're out of work!" Discussion of Chin's death and the subsequent trial highlights several miscarriages of justice, facts on which critical literacy sheds light for students.

The first fact is that although Ebens and Nitz were sentenced to three years of probation and each was fined less than $3,000 in the criminal case, neither spent a single day behind bars.

The second fact is that in the civil suit, despite the fact that Ebens was sentenced to 25 years in prison, his conviction was overturned on a technicality, and Nitz was not found guilty at all. Even more egregious was that although a subsequent civil suit ruled that Ebens had to pay $1.5 million to the Chin family, he successfully eluded the authorities and never paid one cent.

In the face of these facts, the case of Vincent Chin can only be labeled a miscarriage of justice because, according to Elaine Low (2008), "At the crime scene, police had found a combination of Chin's spinal fluid, blood and brain matter" (p. 13) and "[s]everal people witnessed the incident, including two off-duty *police officers*" (p. 12, emphasis added).

After *reading the word and the world*, frequently my students are left depressed and upset. This is not all bad; Diane J. Goodman writes, "When someone considers something morally or spiritually wrong, it provides an impetus to act to remedy that situation" (2000, p. 1067). The case of Chin provides a strong segue for introducing my students to the model minority stereotype (Hartlep, 2013b, 2014).

Introducing Students to the Model Minority Stereotype

The Coalition for Asian American Children and Families (CACF) writes,

> The Model Minority Myth is a stereotype that ignores the histories, capacities, cultures, and personalities of an incredibly diverse group of APA children and youth that is larger than the entire enrollment of many other urban systems across the United States. The Myth imposes unrealistic expectations on young people and justifies official and unofficial policies and practices that fail to meet their educational and developmental needs. (2011, p. 45)

Whereas the CACF's report *"We're Not Even Allowed to Ask for Help": Debunking the Myth of the Model Minority* (2011) is highly important, it is not meaningful to my students; they find the report dry, too long, and removed from their life experiences. Therefore, instead of discussing the deleterious model minority stereotype in depth after reading academic writings about it (Hartlep, 2013b), I prefer introducing the stereotype to my students by showing the clip of Alexandra Wallace, a white female University of California–Los Angeles student, who posted a YouTube video in which she rants about what she felt were the culturally inappropriate practices of Asians and Asian Americans in the library and in her apartment complex. Not surprisingly, her video went viral, and she withdrew from UCLA soon after its release. Showing the video to my students exposes them to the reality that cultural, social, and societal stereotypes are many times internally contradictory. In the case of the model minority stereotype of Asian Americans, if they were so well respected and successful, why would they be the subject of the hatred and disdain revealed by Wallace's words and attitude (Hartlep, 2013a, 2013b, 2014)?

I find the YouTube clip of Wallace to be particularly effective for my students because Wallace herself seems to embody many social and societal stereotypes to many viewers, specifically that of a superficial "Valley girl"—a blond, big-breasted bimbo. After my students view the clip, they discuss in small groups whether and why her comments are racist. When they begin to *read the word and the world* in this activity, they often restrict their critiques of her statements in ways that reveal limited contextual understandings. For instance, they will point out how racist her comment was about the Tsunami that impacted many Japanese people. The students' conversations and dialogues, however, eventually move toward a more systems-level or institutional analysis. It is during this period of the lesson that I know I can situate the micro (stereotypes) within the macro (society).

After discussion concludes about the Wallace video clip, I play an audio clip that captures the most macabre form of anti-Asian hatred I have ever heard—a racist death threat that was left on California state senator Leland Yee's answering machine. The following is a transcription of that call[3]:

> I saw on the news that you want people to boycott Rush Limbaugh 'cause he made a . . . a joke, something about a Chinaman or something and president or whatever-the-deal's name is from China. Well, I don't really listen to Rush Limbaugh very . . . uh . . . hardly ever cause I think he's a *duh* . . . a . . . a dope. But I'm gonna listen, so I'm gonna start listening to Rush Limbaugh, 'cause I think you're just a little cry baby, you little chink . . . eh . . . uh . . . duke-headed . . . uh . . . piss-ass. That's fucking stupid, a Chink, Chink, Chink . . . ah so, ohihaoh . . . Good God! What a cry-baby. Dude, why don't you just resign from office—*orffice*, rather—and go get a . . . uh . . . uhm . . . whatchamacallit, an eggroll and an unfortunate cookie, and eat it. God, what a Chink-headed cheatin' duker, really man, ya know, you're just . . . that's pathetic, boycott Rush, ya know the Chinese president that was here can go fuck himself, he should burn in hell. I hope he has a heart attack. That goddamn Chinaman. Fuck China! I hope China just falls on down to the damn river, or the ocean or whatever. Fuck China! I hate China! Fuck China! Fuck China! And fuck you, you Chink! Fuck China! Fuck China! Fuck China! You got it? Fuck China! Fuck China! I hope China goes under. You got it? Chink! (Seitz-Wald, 2011)

In order to cultivate critical media literacy, students sometimes need to experience (by hearing and viewing) jolting media that textual material is incapable of providing. Consequently, affective, dispositional, and sensorial (visual and auditory) media are frequently used in my classroom in order to elicit socioemotional responses from my students. These media may cause my students to feel uncomfortable, something some scholars label as the "pedagogy of discomfort" (Boler & Zemblyas, 2003), but it also ensures that my students are learning because it fosters empathy (Goodman, 2000). One example of student discomfort typically comes after I play the 1995 movie *White Man's Burden*, starring John Travolta and Harry Belafonte, in my class. My students typically have a hard time viewing a film where black and European white Americans have reversed cultural roles due to the fact it causes cognitive dissonance.

Introducing Students to White Interest Convergence and False Empathy

According to Deanna Hill, "Critical Race Theory (CRT) emerged in the legal academy in response to growing dissatisfaction with Critical Legal

Studies (CLS) and its inability to adequately address race and racism in its critique of U.S. jurisprudence" (2009, p. 1). Gloria Ladson-Billings and William F. Tate (1995) were responsible for introducing CRT to the field of education; in their 1995 article they argue for a critical race theoretical perspective in education similar to that of CRT in legal scholarship. According to Ladson-Billings and Tate, (1) race continues to be significant in the United States; (2) U.S. society is based on property rights rather than human rights; and (3) the intersection of race and property creates an analytical tool for understanding inequity (1995, p. 48).

I frequently use YouTube videos to introduce two CRT concepts: *white interest convergence* (Bell, 1980) and *false empathy* (Delgado, 1996). *White interest convergence* is the concept that white people will support issues of social justice when they benefit from its support; in other words, whites act only when there is a *convergence* between their interests and issues of justice. Meanwhile, *false empathy* is Richard Delgado's concept of white liberals pretending "to understand and sympathize with a black" (1996, p. 71).

Teaching my students about CRT creates a complex "*Rashomon* effect" in the classroom , a problem arising during the process of inquiry: there are many contradictory interpretations of the same events from different students. For instance, in order to illustrate white interest convergence in action, I show my students the video *The Space Traders*, which is available on YouTube.[4] *The Space Traders* is a parable in which white America sells its black citizens to extraterrestrial aliens in return for three gifts of great value: (1) enough gold and precious metals to settle America's debts and return it to its former glory, (2) machines that can clean the air, and (3) cold fusion technology that can produce cheap and clean power (Delgado & Stefancic, 1991). After viewing the 30-minute video, my students interpret the same events but in contradictory ways. Some say that it is not racist for the government to send the black people to the space traders because the government does not know what will happen to them in space. Others interpret the parable differently, decrying the U.S. government's action as deplorable. *The Space Traders* video relates nicely with Delgado's (1996) concept of *false empathy* because both the video and article share how white interest convergence and false empathy are grounded in the white experience.

False empathy takes place when a "white [person] believes that he or she is identifying with a person of color, but in fact is doing so only in a slight, superficial way" (Delgado, 1996, p. 70). As I see it, false empathy on the part of white teachers is highly problematic in teacher instruction and student learning because if an individual teacher unsympathetically believes he or she has empathy with students who have a radically different background, the teacher can easily end up hurting them.

I use YouTube to share *The Space Traders* with my students because I recognize that student attention can be captured through the familiar, thereby engaging their interests and values. In this way, YouTube can serve both as a window *and* a mirror for preservice teachers.

Curriculum as a Window and as a Mirror

The Space Traders video allows my white students to see racism (through a window), but also to see how they themselves, as white people, may be modestly culpable for the oppression of minorities, even though they do not feel as though they are oppressors or oppressive to people of color (in a mirror). Many of my students believe that education can transform society, but as Edith E. Baldwin notes, "The education system cannot transform society, for society 'molds' education to conform to the established values and interests of [the elite]" (1987, p. 18). Consequently, as I have already noted, I believe praxis to be the nexus between theory and practice. Ultimately, curriculum that is both a window and a mirror is transformational.

CONCLUDING REMARKS

In this chapter have attempted to show how I have used YouTube in my Social Foundations of Education course at Illinois State University in order to facilitate critical media literacy, embodied best in Freire and Macedo's (1987) concept of *reading the word and the world*. Too often critical media literacy receives short shrift in an era of high-stakes tests and neoliberal dominance (Hammer, 2009). In fact, educational studies departments have closed at major teacher/research universities—Emory University being just one example (DeSantis, 2012).

I feel strongly that preparation of preservice teachers should include critical media literacy. According to the Standards for Academic and Professional Instruction in Foundations of Education (Tutwiler et al., 2013), P–12 teachers must teach their students "reflective, deliberative, and participatory citizenship skills for self-governance and self-empowerment in a democratic society" (p. 114).

Social foundations of education faculty, to cite Postman and Weingartner's idea one last time, should *not* prepare teacher candidates who are themselves, or who will teach children to become *periods*. A commitment to critical literacy is vital; it is a much better alternative to traditional teaching, and a pedagogy that empowers students to be critical media literate—that is, *question marks*. The distinction between periods and question marks is best summarized in my mind as *reading the word and the world*. Finally, critical media literacy must include a critical understanding of technology and how technology can be used as a conduit to foster critical literacy.

I will conclude with Paulo Freire's own words: "No matter the level or the age of the students we teach, from preschool to graduate school, reading critically is absolutely important and fundamental" (1985b, p. 19).

NOTES

1. My colleague (and fellow foundations of education assistant professor) Dr. Karla Martin recently left for a postdoctoral fellowship at Arizona State University. She is a few months younger than me.
2. According to "Meet Gen C" (2013), the "YouTube Generation" spans all ages, but 65% of its composition are people under 35.
3. http://thinkprogress.org/politics/2011/01/27/141079/yee-limbaugh-death-threat/
4. *The Space Traders*, http://www.youtube.com/watch?v=K0BtFWwHOmQ

REFERENCES

Baldwin, E. E. (1987). Theory vs. ideology in the practice of teacher education. *Journal of Teacher Education, 38*(1), 16–19.

Bell, D. A. (1980). *Brown v. Board of Education* and the interest-convergence dilemma. *Harvard Law Review, 93*(3), 518–534. Retrieved from http://pscfiles.tamu.edu/links/div-com/bell-interest%20convergence.pdf

Beloit College. (2012). The Mindset List for the Class of 2016. Retrieved from https://www.beloit.edu/mindset/2016/

Boler, M., & Zembylas, M. (2003). Discomforting truths: The emotional terrain of understanding difference. In P. P. Trifonas (Ed.), *Pedagogies of difference: Rethinking education for social change* (pp. 110–136). New York: RoutledgeFalmer.

Brown, E. L., & Gibbons, P. E. (2011). *Ethnicity: Creating educational opportunities around the globe*. Charlotte, NC: Information Age.

Cellan, R. (2012, December 21). Gangnam Style hits one billion views on YouTube. Retrieved from http://www.bbc.co.uk/news /technology-20812870

Coalition for Asian American Children and Families. (2011). *"We're not even allowed to ask for help": Debunking the myth of the model minority*. New York: Pumphouse Projects.

Delgado, R. (1996). Rodrigo's eleventh chronicle: Empathy and false empathy. *California Law Review, 84*(1), 61–99.

Delgado, R., & Stefancic, J. (1991). Derrick Bell's chronicle of the space traders: Would the U.S. sacrifice people of color if the price was right? *University of Colorado Law Review, 62*, 321–328.

DeSantis, N. (2012, September 14). Emory U. will close 3 departments as part of broad academic restructuring. Retrieved from http://chronicle.com/ blogs/ticker/emory-u-will-close-3-departments-as-part-of-broad-academic-restruct uring/48872

Dewey, J. (1962). *The relation of theory to practice in education*. Cedar Falls, IA: Association for Student Teaching.

Freire, P. (1985a). *The politics of education*. (D. Macedo, Trans.) Boston: Bergin and Garvey.

Freire, P. (1985b). Reading the world and reading the word: An interview with Paulo Freire. *Language Arts, 62*(1), 15–21.

Freire, P. (2005). *Pedagogy of the oppressed* (30th-anniversary ed.) (M. Bergman Ramos, Trans.). New York: Continuum. Retrieved from http://www.users.humboldt.edu/jwpowell/edreformFriere_pedagogy.pdf

Freire, P., & Macedo, D. (1987). *Literacy: Reading the word and the world*. Westport, CT: Bergin and Garvey.

Gibbs, N. (2009, September 21). What college students don't know. *Time*. Retrieved from http://www.time.com/time/magazine/article/0,9171,1921587,00.html

Goodman, D. J. (2000). Motivating people from privileged groups to support social justice. *Teachers College Record, 102*(6), 1061–1085.

Hammer, R. (2009). This won't be on the final: Reflections on teaching critical media literacy. In R. Hammer & D. Kellner (Eds.), *Media/cultural studies: Critical approaches* (pp. 164–193). New York: Peter Lang.

Hartlep, N. D. (2013a). The model minority? *Diverse: Issues in Higher Education, 30*(2), 14–15.

Hartlep, N. D. (2013b). *The model minority stereotype: Demystifying Asian American success*. Charlotte, NC: Information Age.

Hartlep, N. D. (2014). *The model minority stereotype reader: Critical and challenging readings for the 21st century*. San Diego, CA: Cognella.

Hill, D. (2009). *Critical race theory in education: Introduction and selected works*. Retrieved from http://westwinded.com/lib/mats/Critical%20Race%20Theory%20Selected%20Works.pdf

Ladson-Billings, G., & Tate, W. F., IV. (1995). Toward a critical race theory of education. *Teachers College Record, 97*(1), 47–68.

Low, E. (2008). *An unnoticed struggle: A concise history of Asian American civil rights issues*. San Francisco, CA: Japanese American Citizens League. Retrieved from http://www.jacl.org/public_policy/documents/An%20Unnoticed%20Struggle.pdf

Meet gen C: The YouTube generation . . . in their own words. (2013, May 1). Retrieved from http://ssl.gstatic.com/think/docs/meet-gen-c-youtube-generation-in-own-words_articles.pdf

O'malley, G. (2006, July 21). YouTube is the fastest growing website. *Advertising Age*. Retrieved from http://adage.com/article/digital/youtube-fastest-growing-website/110632/

Phelps, P. H., & Ryan, P. M. (1995). Synthesizing theory and practice: Praxis for professors. *Thought and Action: The NEA Higher Education Journal*. Retrieved from http://www.nea.org/assets/img/PubThoughtAndAction/TAA_95Spr_06.pdf

Postman, N., & Weingartner, C. (1969). *Teaching as a subversive activity*. New York: Delacorte.

Seitz-Wald, A. (2011, January 27). California lawmaker receives racist death threat warning "Rush Limbaugh will kick your Ch-nk ass." Retrieved from http://thinkprogress.org/politics/2011/01/27/141079/yee-limbaugh-death-threat/#

Shor, I. (1992). *Empowering education: Critical teaching for social change*. Chicago: University of Chicago Press.

Sorkin, A. R., & Peters, J. W. (2006, October 9). Google to acquire YouTube for $1.65 billion. *New York Times*. Retrieved from http://www.nytimes.com/2006/10/09/business/09cnd-deal.html?_r=0

Thomas, G. (2007). *Education and theory: Strangers in paradigms*. New York: McGraw-Hill Education.

Tutwiler, S. W., DeMarrais, K., Gabbard, D., Hyde, A., Konkol, P., Li, H., Medina, Y., Rayle, J., & Swain, A. (2013). Standards for academic and professional instruction in foundations of education, educational studies, and educational policy studies third edition, 2012, draft presented to the educational community by the American Educational Studies Association's Committee on Academic

Standards and Accreditation. *Educational Studies: Journal of the American Educational Studies Association, 49*(2), 107–118.

U.S. Department of Commerce. (1999, July). *Falling through the net: Defining the digital divide: A report on the telecommunications and information technology gap in America.* Washington, DC: U.S. Department of Commerce. Retrieved from http://www.ntia.doc.gov/legacy/ntiahome/fttn99/FTTN.pdf

10 Developing a User-Friendly, Community-Based Higher Education

Rebecca Collins-Nelsen and
Randle W. Nelsen

INTRODUCTION

The focus of this chapter is upon creating educational contexts in university classrooms that encourage students to take charge of their own learning. The learning environments we describe are classroom-based reforms that take into account the diversity to be found among today's students in a manner that emphasizes equity and opportunity. At their best these reforms empower students, creating classroom contexts that run counter to the current obsession with professionalism and accountability education. Our reforms take the focus away from compiling numbers for statistical comparisons useful to administrators in search of funding and status recognition and away from a university version of teaching to the test. Rather, our suggestions for classroom-based reform are meant to encourage students to focus less on test outcomes in a competition for grades and more on inspiring themselves and others (teachers included) to be creative in approaching their course subject matter. Our goal is to show that university classrooms can empower students, be user-friendly, build social contexts of inclusion, and build creative opportunities of long-term value both to self and community.

We have organized our remarks into three sections. The first section analyzes higher education as professional certification; the second provides a summary understanding of the importance of intersectional analysis in creating a user-friendly classroom; the third discusses several "experiments" that, taken together, offer an exploratory illustration of the benefits to university students and faculty of creating a user-friendly classroom context. These sections are followed by a brief concluding statement that underscores the role of amateurism in constructing alternative learning environments.

HIGHER EDUCATION AS PROFESSIONAL CERTIFICATION

Today's university education is as much about fulfilling the demands for certification in a credential society (Collins, 1979) as it is about satisfying the desires of scholarly curiosity. Thus, today's university is centrally about socialization that trains students according to the dictates of professionalism. Socialization in understanding what it means to be a "professional" is a common thread that runs through all university faculties, whether students are enrolled in disciplines designated as "professional schools," such as business, engineering, education, law, medicine, and nursing, or enrolled in science, social science, arts, or humanities disciplines. It is important to state at the outset that we are not opposed to students being taught skills for possible future careers as purveyors of professional services. We are, however, against what seems to be a training trend that undermines the university's primary and proper role in producing and transmitting general knowledge. This knowledge is useful in helping to define oneself—answering "who am I " questions—and in learning how to think critically about one's surroundings. This includes unmasking or demystifying ideologies, professionalism included, that hinder opportunities for developing a more diverse and democratic society.

Following in the tradition of Paulo Freire (1970), the late David Noble has spoken for education analysts and observers who make a distinction between training and education. This emphasis upon education that encourages self-development is critical, so we quote him at some length:

> In essence, training involves the honing of a person's mind so that his or her mind can be used for the purposes of someone other than that person. Training thus typically entails a radical divorce between knowledge and the self. Here knowledge is usually defined as a set of skills or a body of information designed to be put to use, to become operational, only in a context determined by someone other than the trained person; in this context the assertion of self is not only counterproductive, it is subversive to the enterprise. Education is the exact opposite of training in that it entails not the disassociation but the utter integration of knowledge and the self, in a word, self-knowledge. Here knowledge is defined by and, in turn, helps to define, the self. Knowledge and the knowledgeable person are basically inseparable. Education is a process that necessarily entails an interpersonal (not merely interactive) relationship between people—student and teacher (and student and student) that aims at individual and collective self-knowledge. . . . Education is a process of becoming for all parties, based upon mutual recognition and validation and centering upon the formation and evolution of identity. The actual content of the educational experience is defined by this relationship between people and the chief determinant of quality education is the establishment and enrichment of this relationship. (Noble, 2002, p. 2)

More than forty years ago Ivan Illich (1970) pointed out the link between school certification and upward social mobility for those with the opportunity and the willingness to climb the school ladder. He argued that with each level successfully attained, the graduating student might reasonably expect individual benefits in terms of better job opportunities and ever higher levels of personal consumption—a change in individual circumstance of dubious benefit to society as a whole. Today's glut of university graduates, along with the relative reduction in high-quality professional jobs available, gives one pause to reconsider and somewhat amend Illich's observation. Illich's general concern, however, has been echoed recently by Sheldon Ungar (2003), who argues that increasingly specialized university training designed to prepare students for work as part of an expanding "knowledge industry" has led to their uncritical ignorance of, and perhaps even a lack of curiosity about, the broader society that surrounds them. This troubling development, along with several others, can be found in Jeff Schmidt's (2000) trenchant analysis of the soul-battering grind that constitutes professional graduate training in the modern university. He uses the delightfully descriptive and truth-telling term "assignable curiosity" to summarize the role played by schooling in professional ideology that reproduces status quo arrangements and routinely blunts creative thinking about alternatives. Schmidt's review facilitates understanding about how Illich's desire to radically reform the social context of learning, even to deschool society, is something more than simple hyperbole.

The assigned curiosity that characterizes professional training in university is an important outcome of a much more all-encompassing and deep-seated set of beliefs that constitute the ideology of professionalism. This ideology is characterized by nonrecognition of the limitations of professorial and administrative attitudes and practice grounded on a fantasy. This fantasy is a package of lingering beliefs in so-called scholarly objectivity, value neutrality, and institutional autonomy that does not match today's socioeconomic reality. In university classrooms this fanciful and limiting ideology is covered over, masked by commitment to a particular academic discipline. This is devotion masquerading as responsibility to the acquisition of specialized and technical expertise (see Nelsen, 1975; 1991).

Elsewhere Randle W. Nelsen (2011, 2012) has shown how adherence to this professional ideology is useful in maintaining status quo arrangements and thus the privileged position of professors. A large part of becoming "professional" has to do with learning how to become adept at minimizing potential conflict between professional and bureaucratic norms. This is done by learning how to switch from one set of reference group norms to the other (from the professional to the bureaucratic, and vice versa) as the situation dictates—a balancing act that frustrates and obstructs alternative visions. Rather than empowering themselves and their students to change academic structures and the larger social system, professors protect their privileged position within it and the status quo is maintained. Student boredom and dissatisfaction grow apace (Mann and Robinson, 2009; Nelsen, 1985), alongside a debilitating addiction to school authority and academic standardization. This addiction is self-perpetuating, for another characteristic of professionalism, perhaps the key norm, is that admission as a colleague into a particular profession is governed (read: controlled) in club-like fashion by colleagues already in the club. Our "fix" for this addiction, as the learning experiments described below should make clear, involves transforming the university classroom environment—the social context of learning—to make it more user-friendly in a manner that empowers both students and their professors.

Education should be about both development of self and relationships with others around us, both in transient communities and in those that are more long-term. At bottom, all learning, formal schooling included, is grounded in sociability and social context. Social media observer Clay Shirky (2009) provides evidence regarding the power of today's rapidly changing web-based technology that shows the significant effect it has on the way groups form and function in altering the social contexts of communication. For our analysis here what is most interesting about Shirky's (2009, pp. 25–80) work are his contentions that "sharing anchors community" and that "everyone is a media outlet." We see these two contentions as the heart of what he calls "mass amateurization," an amateurism that offers a learning counter in support of our criticism of professional training outlined above and that is central to our discussions of the several classroom learning experiments reviewed below.

Professionalism as the prevailing social context in today's higher education makes the university a place where administrators, as well as faculty and students, are expected to be accountable for fostering and maintaining a type of monoculture. What might appear on the surface as encouragement of diversity through the development of product lines that feature many specializations has become a university-certified monopoly, the commodification of a learning monoculture united under the umbrella of professionalized training. Those involved in formal education understand that this approach is deeply flawed. As student author Nikhil Goyal (2012) has pointed out, "one size does not fit all." In the next section we develop a line of thought that supports Goyal's thesis. We argue that the key to creating a user-friendly university curriculum is to understand the benefits of an intersectional analysis that takes us beyond the limitations of training and professional ideology, providing the groundwork for taking seriously important differences in the student population with regard to social class, gender, race and ethnicity, and life experience.

DIVERSITY, INTERSECTIONAL ANALYSIS, AND THE NEED FOR USER-FRIENDLY CLASSROOMS

Current university student populations are much larger and much more diverse than they have ever been before. As more people have enrolled, higher education has become the new standard of schooling so that a high school diploma is no longer sufficient to secure a well-paying job (Burris, 1983). This surge in the number of people attending postsecondary institutions has been echoed by a similar trend in relation to graduate school. Further, the expectation of a university education has grown to reach a variety of working sectors, which has resulted in more diversity around social class, gender, race, and age among university student populations (Densen and Chang 2009; Grayson, 1997; Jacobs, 1995; Trueman and Hartley, 1996). The changes in relation to social class can be seen in the dramatic increases in the percentage of first-generation postsecondary graduates (Grayson, 1997). The ever-shifting gender dynamics and increases in racial and ethnic diversity in postsecondary institutions have also been well-documented (Densen and Chang, 2009; Jacobs, 1995). Additionally, increased pressures to have a university degree mean that a variety of generations are returning to postsecondary education in order to receive the necessary credentials (Trueman and Hartley, 1996). These changes in the demographic makeup of university classrooms mean that there is a much broader spectrum of life experiences coming together. We argue that this new university reality reinforces the need for less-structured and more user-friendly classrooms.

Research indicates that standardized testing tends to be an inaccurate measure of future success as well as a false predictor of competence for any kind of practical task (Sacks, 1999). This is largely because it presumes a single-track model for people that tends to be based upon the experiences of white, middle-class, Western males. For these reasons the one-size-fits-all educational system has been highly criticized for negating the assortment of student experiences and failing to meet the needs of a diversified student population. Recently, literature in the area of intersectionality has further complicated the ways in which we understand difference by demonstrating that axes of identity interact in complex matrices of domination and privilege (Collins, 2000). Therefore, no single dimension of inequality can justifiably depict the multiple, intersecting, and conflicting dimensions that contribute to the entire structure (McCall, 2005). Whereas some have argued for schools that cater to a particular axis of identity such as Afrocentric schools (which seek to address racism in the curriculum in an effort to better engage black students) and "pink triangle" schools (which appeal to the needs of lesbian, gay, bisexual, transgender, and queer/questioning youth), we argue that these efforts are valiant but insufficient. In line with intersectional theory, teaching strategies that attempt to account for specific sociodemographic differences are flawed because these differences are not isolated but are instead interconnected in complex and unique ways. Further, research has shown that there are educational benefits associated with a diverse student population (Densen and Chang, 2009). For these reasons it is not simply enough for the current model of education to be *expanded* from a one-track to a multiple-track system; instead, *systemic change* is required. We argue that this change needs to come in the form of classrooms that put students' voices and experiences at the forefront.

With this in mind, it is useful to explore some of the theoretical frameworks that stress the importance of considering difference and differing experiences. *Standpoint theory*, for instance, considers the ways in which people's perspectives are created and shaped by their experiences in their respective cultural and social locations as well as their social groups (Harding, 2004; Smith, 1987). This perspective acknowledges and validates the ways in which people construct their own realities and considers these realities to be intelligible and important contributions to knowledge. In a similar vein, Dorothy Smith's (1987; 2005) conception, known as *institutional ethnography*, asks researchers to better situate and problematize local, everyday experiences within broader global contexts of inequality and power. We argue that this idea is particularly helpful as a pedagogical strategy because it begins by valuing the experiences of individual students and then extends this approach by encouraging them to think critically about how these experiences intersect with and are impacted by broader societal institutions and structures.

These ideas relate to those espoused by bell hooks in *Teaching to Transgress: Education as the Practice of Freedom* (1994). Like us, hooks also calls for an eradication of traditional pedagogical boundaries and argues that personal experiences should be the basis for theory making. She sees the power dynamics in the classroom, particularly between teachers and students, as one of the barriers to appreciating people's voices. Thus, hooks argues, teachers and students alike must learn to be reflective and reach their own self-actualization in order for honest communication and engagement to occur. According to hooks, these types of strategies will allow students to transgress and ultimately make education the practice of freedom. Education as the practice of freedom today occurs at a time when more information is at our fingertips than ever before. The new social context of information technology leads to an increased reliance on cooperative networks, an emphasis on learning collaboration that we argue needs to be more present in our university classrooms.

The increased diversity and sheer size of student populations in higher education have created the need for new styles of teaching and learning. These changes are coupled with the literature that shows the many downfalls of a standardized educational system, the movement toward intersectional considerations, and a novel contemporary social context. All of these phenomena, taken together, strengthen the need for rethinking the ways in which higher education is structured. We argue that the current postsecondary education system would greatly benefit from an approach that emphasizes less-structured classrooms, community connections and involvement, and storytelling. Some of the ways in which these ideas have played out in classroom contexts will be outlined below.

EXPERIMENTS IN CREATING A USER-FRIENDLY UNIVERSITY CLASSROOM

In the following exposition we offer details about teaching experiments in four courses that created a social context that in each case made the university classroom more user-friendly. Taken together, these student-centered approaches sought to reverse a well-documented research finding (see Gross, 1968, for an early example) that professors and the universities that employ them have historically placed student wishes and needs near the bottom of their hierarchy of concerns, taking every opportunity to insulate themselves and their elite position from the "unwashed" (read: uncertified) masses that make up the student body. Beginning in the early 1990s, educational leaders began to attend more closely to the concerns of students—or, more precisely, the role they play as fee-paying consumers. As a result, there have been urgent calls to initiate university teaching reforms that would put more energy and resources into redressing the historic imbalance that emphasizes and privileges research over teaching (see Smith, 1991). The sample of learning initiatives we describe addresses the call to reevaluate and reenergize teaching, providing at least a partial answer to Goyal's (2012) one-size-does-not-fit-all criticism of today's schools.

We recognize that our classroom restructures are baby steps that are undoubtedly patchwork reforms rather than the revolution called for in Goyal's manifesto. In sharing our classroom experiments we hope to promote Noble's conception of education as an ongoing process of awareness that increases both individual self-knowledge and collective self-knowledge. A significant outcome for classroom participants is to make us all more aware of an important parenthetical observation Noble offered when delineating his distinction between training and education:

> (Whenever people recall their educational experiences they tend to remember above all not courses or subjects or the information imparted but people, people who changed their minds or their lives, people who made a difference in their developing sense of themselves. It is a sign of our current confusion about education that we must be reminded of this obvious fact: that the relationship between people is central to the educational experience.) (2002, p. 2)

Relationships constitute the heart and soul of teaching and learning. It is these connections among people that must be remembered and reenergized if we are to succeed in transforming learning experiences for both our young people and ourselves.

The Less-Structured Classroom

Our first attempt to make the university classroom more user-friendly has been extensively reported upon (see Nelsen, 1981), and here we offer only a summary of what took place. It occurred early in my (Nelsen's) teaching career when I saw an opportunity to do something different in a third-year sociology of education evening course I was assigned to teach in three-hour sessions meeting only one time each week. As a questionnaire administered on the last night of class confirmed, the class comprised a diverse group of 19 mature (average age just under 30) students, most of whom were employed in either full- or part-time day jobs. My plan was to encourage a seminar-type, give-and-take experience in a less-structured classroom context, a learning environment where the teacher, acting more as a facilitator than an instructor, becomes a student and the students become teachers in the fullest and best sense of these terms. Some ten years later, City University of New York professor Ira Shor (1992; 1996), drawing upon his work with activist educator Paulo Freire, would persuasively articulate this vision. Shor's work shows how the key to critical teaching for social change involves participatory problem posing that creates what he calls "generative themes" drawn from the everyday lives of students that are capable of empowering them.

At the first meeting of the class, I made specific reference to my research interests and teaching background in the sociology of education and I told the students what I did *not* have for them—a course outline to be covered, required texts to be read, and so on. I then offered a succinct and carefully prepared statement, as follows:

> For the record, I would rather not run this as a traditional course. I'd like to help make this course a "happening." In other words, I'd like this course to become what we as a group want it to become. I would prefer that this course be as much "an open book" to begin with as possible.

I elaborated by voicing my hope that the group as a whole might construct a process-oriented, always provisional "learning agenda" together that might lead to readings and discussions centered upon shared problems and issues. I finished with these pointed sentences: "As far as I am concerned, it's open. There is an unwritten agenda here to be filled in."

The rest of that first evening was spent in animated discussion, introducing ourselves to one another and talking about potential learning projects, what we were going to do in the following week's class session and for the remainder of the year; the matter of evaluation was discussed as well, but the usual concern with marks or grades was not a focal point. The fear that comes with moving away from a teacher-centered classroom began to diminish as we began to acclimate ourselves to the exciting prospect of trying together to create something new, a different learning environment. Something akin to fear—certainly a large helping of uncertainty—peaked for me when, 30 minutes into the course, two students got up and walked out, leaving the distinct impression that this attempt to create a new learning environment was an unexpected surprise that was not for them. I immediately shared my reaction to this with the remaining students. I spoke to my emotional feelings regarding this rather abrupt student departure by talking about my confidence in relation to teaching, my ego involvement as a teacher, and the leaps of faith required for both myself and the remaining students as they let this classroom process of change unfold.

Talking about personal involvement in our learning gradually became commonplace among all of us in this less-structured classroom. It was just this kind of openness that permitted us to overcome some of the most debilitating effects of the ever-present hidden curriculum of cultural capital biases and inequities resting upon background differences with regard to social class, race and ethnicity, and gender. For example, discussion contributions from the few class members—predominantly women—from working-class families were able to give the other 80% of us from middle- or upper-middle class backgrounds a better understanding of these women's struggles to obtain a university education and how much they appreciated their schooling. Feedback confirmed that class members benefitted, as two of these women thought through and told their stories of being raised in "union families" by parents active in promoting the rights of workers. Through class discussion we were compelled to rethink not only the important role that immigrants played in building Canada but also commonly held views such as the one that sees unions as socialist-tinged organizations that have outlived their usefulness. Two other women, one French Canadian and the other a First Nations woman with a background that included extensive experience as a client of the welfare system, struggled to explain their ethnic and cultural differences to the majority remainder of us representing English, English Canadian, and American ancestry. Again, as was the case with social class, their explanations of the contributions of their people in creating the modern Canadian mosaic were generally acknowledged by the students as beneficial, helping us to better understand and bridge racial and ethnic differences.

The less-structured classroom, in revealing and countering the hidden curriculum, also had an effect with regard to gender. The gender split, at one time often discussed in sociological literature, emphasizes that men are more "instrumental" and less "expressive" in their view of the world than are women. If answers to the end-of-course questionnaire can be taken as a reliable guide, then the less-structured student-centered classroom environment tended to even things out in this regard, with the men in particular feeling more comfortable in expressing their feelings and emotions in front of class members. This came about because we had become somewhat "known" to each other, encouraging each other to not be afraid of our diversities and to recognize, confront, and express our feelings about difference. We developed a sense of knowing each other as "real people"—what Noble talked about as "individual and collective self-knowledge" and Abraham Maslow (1970) infamously referred to as "self-actualization." As I noted at the time, our classroom interaction was vitally and positively affected: "In short, there was a tie between us, a sense of relationship among us, **not** often found in other more highly-structured and traditional courses that made this class special for *everyone*, including myself" (Nelsen, 1981, p. 237)

This unusual classroom learning atmosphere of a group-organized and directed curriculum not only made collective use of the combined resources and experience of everyone in the seminar but also informed the personalized learning agendas on display in the students' (and the instructor's) year-long projects. These did not constitute a "culminating activity" in the way that many of today's education professors use this phrase in reference to an end-of-term production of a learned commodity. Rather, the great majority of our projects constituted not a finished product but an ongoing process of learning and self-development that did not end when the course ended in April. Two of the best projects were typical in showcasing this process.

The first project was undertaken by a government employee who was moved by a class discussion and some readings on adult education and retraining to come to grips with his strong feelings concerning the inadequacy of training programs he administered in his job at Canada Employment and Immigration. Not only did he believe the programs to be largely a waste of taxpayers' money, but for him they had long constituted a frustrating block to doing his job properly. In gathering supportive evidence from his work experience and researching why and how various nongovernmental agencies had become involved with government-initiated training, he began to develop a clearer and more refined picture of the situation he was confronting daily at work. This new understanding both lessened his frustration and served as a springboard for thinking about alternative procedures and policies that might make the training programs more effective for his clients.

The other project was undertaken by a mother on leave from her profession and working in the home taking care of two young children. One of her children was exhibiting what she referred to as "severe behavior problems." Her project began to take shape after class discussions and readings about the practice of drugging into submission "hyperactive" children. She revealed to the class that one of her children had been so diagnosed and was having problems both at school and at home. Her reading motivated her to closely observe her child's behavior and gave her confidence to make significant changes in the child's diet and to start using megavitamin and naturopathic therapy in place of Ritalin and other amphetamines, all the while keeping a detailed record of the effects of these changes. Not only was she able to help her child make some necessary and healthy adjustments that considerably reduced tensions among family members and consequently her level of frustration, but in the process she and our whole class began to develop a broader sociological understanding regarding the appropriateness (the "normalness") of some responses of hyperactive students to the many intolerable situations the institution of formal schooling creates for all children.

These two projects and others that came out of this experiment in creating a less-structured classroom benefitted all course members. The manner in which this course was organized helped us all to develop greater individual and community awareness, a self-knowledge necessary to overcome the limits of business-as-usual thinking dominated by taken-for-granted polarizations that separate learning form from content, theory from practice, and political from personal matters. In essence, this course encouraged the growth of what C. Wright Mills (1960) called the "sociological imagination," analysis that works at that creative intersection where individual biography meets institutional social structure at a particular historical moment.

Community Connections and Volunteerism

This imagination was also at work in two other, smaller classes, each with a dozen students. These were senior-level courses, one taught by Randle Nelsen alone and the other a collaborative effort with Rebecca Collins-Nelsen. They were organized in a slightly more structured fashion, with (somewhat provisional) course outlines and some required specialized readings. In both courses the instructors made a conscious attempt to encourage students to engage by starting with their personal experiences; most were then able to follow up by developing learning projects with the objective of bringing the community outside academia into their work. Everyone in these courses, including the two instructors, wound up doing volunteer work related to the projects.

As supervising faculty, we found this volunteerism to be critically important in engaging students and in bridging the several gulfs that often separate them from the larger community surrounding the university. The personal and institutional connections created by volunteerism offer many teachable learning moments that make the strange and strangers familiar, helping cement new community ties that affect our everyday lives. Our volunteer activity created a different, livelier classroom social context than is usually the case, and the benefits of volunteerism were clearly reflected in student projects. Two students collaborated in turning in thoughtful diaries dealing with difficulties in balancing their academic and sports lives as well as their joy in participating as members of their respective teams in community outreach programs. These programs involved donation drives and an on-site shelter house service designed to improve the lot of the stereotyped and stigmatized homeless. Stereotypes and stigma were not unknown to these athletes, who were used to regularly confronting the "dumb jock" label. Another project involved a health care professional's reflections, which showed us how and why she was engaged translating and transferring her work experience in "third world" conditions in an African country to her work in a Frontier College–like literacy program with people in the Canadian north. A third project, the work of a Greenpeace volunteer, was based on an autoethnography of her job as a tree planter. She turned her diary of summer employment in the forest industry into a reflection on her hobbies of jewelry crafting and hemp clothes making that sparked creative discussion regarding the potential of sustainable employment opportunities. It also provided an interesting lesson in environmental conservation.

Volunteerism also played a key role in the graduate course where we as instructors went along with a majority of class members who in the first session voiced their desire to make this course on community and culture "more real" by bringing the surrounding community into the classroom and vice versa. We all agreed to volunteer and keep a participant observation record of our experiences. Class members volunteered in a variety of capacities with agencies and programs that included an adult literacy agency, a home for senior adults, a diversity center that helped immigrants in transitioning in their new and unfamiliar environment, an elementary school breakfast program, the executive board of a nursery preschool, a soup kitchen, and a church-sponsored group engaged in community social work activities. Again, this volunteerism helped to empower students and change the social context of the classroom, making it more user-friendly in serving the diversity of experience present among the students and further enlarging the scope of that diversity.

Storytelling

In our fourth and final instance of classroom experimentation, both of us were involved in using a storytelling approach. The pedagogy of storytelling has been insightfully conveyed by Debbie Storrs (2009), and we shall not repeat her delineation; instead we offer our comments on how effective we found this approach to be in teaching large lecture sections of Introductory Sociology to several hundred first-year students. Rather than speaking in abstractions we used stories, several of them autobiographical, of everyday interactions as starting points. Only after these stories were told did we help our student listeners reconsider them by introducing sociological concepts and theories teased out of the telling. For example, Randle Nelsen related a story of a former colleague who wanted to abandon his university teaching career but needed to figure out a way to replace his rather handsome professor's salary. This financial pressure was made more intense by the fact that in recent years leading up to this decision he and his wife had fostered and adopted, as additions to the family of three children from their union, three hard-to-place preschoolers. The story, then, turns on their solution: clever adherence to and legal manipulation of bureaucratic rules both at the federal government employment office and at a state-controlled county child welfare office in Albany, New York. This resulted in the former agency sponsoring the couple's strategy of shared and permanent unemployment that allowed one or the other parent on a continual basis to stay out of the paid labor force and remain at home, looking after child care and family matters. It also resulted in the latter agency agreeing to continue providing child subsidy payments even when this blended family decided to move all the way across the United States to settle near their childhood homes outside Seattle, Washington. This state-to-state payment continuation with regard to child adoption subsidies was one of the first, if not the first, agreement of this kind—and yes, moving expenses were included.

As one might imagine, this story was met with ethical and moral questions as well as some outrage directed at "pogey" and "welfare" cheaters. But the tone of our discussion changed when the instructor proceeded to tie the literacy provided by many years of formal schooling to enhanced abilities in filling out forms properly so that some clients with potentially legitimate claims on the services of a bureaucracy might be better equipped than others in presenting a "normal" case—that is, one meeting with the approval of bureaucratic officials. The story sparked further discussion about how schools and other bureaucracies function but also about how social class inequalities and differences in cultural capital are connectable to favorable and unfavorable outcomes for clients serviced by various bureaucratic organizations. Students joined in with bureaucratic tales drawn from their own experiences, involving everything from university registration protocol to job searches, unemployment income rules, cell phone company hassles, online dating, and more. A veritable smorgasbord of student experience was routinely presented in class as we encouraged students to make sociological use of their stories both in verbal exchanges and in their term papers.

At bottom this storytelling approach, as is the case with our other approaches designed to alter the standard teacher-centered classroom, was an effort encouraging students to take seriously their everyday life experiences, to do the best they could to seriously reflect upon and incorporate them as part of the course material. Simply put, students were enticed and encouraged to take on—to at least partially assume—the role of noncertified experts in the subject matter at hand; that is, to move from being professional students to amateur professors. This is a makeover that makes courses and the classroom more user-friendly and thus stimulates and facilitates learning that can be intriguing, fascinating and fun—a renewable cycle of reinforcement that keeps on giving.

Taken together, our learning experiments can be viewed as putting Shirky's (2009) previously mentioned insights regarding social media to the test. We downplayed professional certification and put our trust in the developing abilities of our students as creditable amateur observers. The change in classroom social context that we fostered can be viewed as an experiment that emulates Shirky's analysis of today's networked communication where he describes everyone, each individual, as "a media outlet" with the communication potential to produce a kind of sharing that "anchors community"—or, in our case, serves to anchor a classroom group of university students. In sum, the experimental approaches outlined here constitute an early non-computer-based trial run of the feasibility and general valuableness of encouraging classroom diversity grounded upon equity and opportunity.

CONCLUSION

There are several things that the experiments related in this chapter have in common. First, fundamentally and perhaps most obviously, they all transform the learning environment, the social context of the university classroom. Second, in all cases students are newly empowered, with professors relinquishing some professional authority of office in favor of encouraging the amateurism of students as they begin to take greater control of their classroom learning. Third, in each case this is initiated by professors modeling and encouraging students to use their personal life experiences to explore the subject matter of the course. (Admittedly this is a task and outcome often more easily accomplished in the social sciences and humanities than in the so-called natural sciences.) Fourth, this emphasis on life experiences results in all cases in an opportunity for individual reflection and self-transformative growth but also—and just as important—a related opportunity to bring the wider community into the university classroom. Here there is potential for unifying what is often referred to as an alienating split between "town" and "gown" or the "real world" and the "ivory tower." Fifth, in each experiment a healthy sustaining diversity is served and the deleterious effects of a one-size-fits-all training monoculture grounded on professional ideology are limited.

In sum, all these experimental learning initiatives change the social context of the classroom, and all contain self-revelatory and storytelling elements. Our hope is that the learning approaches described herein constitute a beginning in transforming learning from drudgery into a more fun and more playfully exploratory experience. Learning becomes an engaging emergent process rather than a routinized and limited finished product. In a word, the university classroom becomes more *user-friendly.*

REFERENCES

Burris, V. (1983). The social and political consequences of overeducation. *American Sociological Review, 48*(4), 454–467.

Collins, P. H. (2000). *Black feminist thought.* New York: Routledge.

Collins, R. (1979). *The credential society: A historical sociology of education and stratification.* New York: Academic Press.

Densen, N., & Chang, M. J. (2009). Racial diversity matters: The impact of diversity-related student engagement and institutional context. *American Educational Research Journal, 46*(2), 322–353.

Freire, P. (1970). *Pedagogy of the oppressed.* (M. Bergman Ramos, Trans.) New York: Herder and Herder.

Goyal, N. (2012). *One size does not fit all: A student's assessment of school.* Roslyn Heights, NY: Alternative Education Resource Organization.

Grayson, J. P. (1997). Academic achievement of first-generation students in a Canadian University. *Research in Higher Education, 38*(6), 659–676.

Gross, E. (1968). Universities as organizations: A research approach. *American Sociological Review, 33*, 518–544.

Harding, S. G. (2004). *The feminist standpoint theory reader: Intellectual and political controversies.* New York: Routledge.

hooks, b. (1994). *Teaching to transgress: Education as the practice of freedom.* New York: Routledge.

Illich, I. (1970). *Deschooling society.* New York: Harper and Row.

Jacobs, J. (1995). Gender and academic specialties: Trends among recipients of college degrees in the 1980s. *Sociology of Education, 68*, 81–98.

Mann, S. & Robinson, A. (2009). Boredom in the lecture theatre: An investigation into the contributors, moderators and outcomes of boredom amongst university students. *British Educational Research Journal, 25*(2), 243–258.

Maslow, A. H. (1970). *Motivation and personality* (2nd ed.). New York: Harper and Row.

McCall, L. (2005). The complexity of intersectionality. *Signs: Journal of Women in Culture and Society, 30*(3), 1771–1800.

Mills, C. W. (1960). *The sociological imagination.* New York: Oxford University Press.

Nelsen, R. W. (1975). *Growth of the modern university and the development of a sociology of higher education in the United States.* (PhD dissertation, McMaster University, Hamilton, Ontario, Canada.)

Nelsen, R. W. (1981). Reading, writing and relationship: Towards overcoming the hidden curriculum of gender, ethnicity, and socio-economic class. *Interchange, 12*(2–3), 229–242.

Nelsen, R. W. (1985). Books, boredom and behind bars: An explanation of apathy and hostility in our schools. *Canadian Journal of Education, 10*(2), 136–160.

Nelsen, R. W. (1991). *Miseducating: Death of the sensible.* Kingston, ON, Canada: Cedarcreek.

Nelsen, R. W. (2011). The community college con: "Changing your life through learning." In S. E. Bosanac & M. A. Jacobs (Eds.), *Work, occupations and professionalization* (pp. 259–275). Whitby, ON, Canada: De Sitter.

Nelsen, R. W. (2012). The military-industrial-university complex and social science: A brief history and current update of a professional contribution to war. In P. R. Carr & B. J. Porfilio (Eds.), *Educating for peace in a time of "permanent war": Are schools part of the solution or the problem?* (pp. 148–162). London: Routledge.

Noble, D. F. (2002). *Digital diploma mills: The automation of higher education.* Toronto: Between the Lines.

Sacks, P. (1999). *Standardized minds: The high price of America's testing culture and what we can do to change it.* New York: Da Capo.

Schmidt, J. (2000). *Disciplined minds: A critical look at salaried professionals and the soul-battering system that shapes their lives.* New York: Rowman and Littlefield.

Shirky, C. (2009). *Here comes everybody: The power of organizing without organizations.* New York: Penguin.

Shor, I. (1992). *Empowering education: Critical teaching for social change.* Chicago: University of Chicago Press.

Shor, I. (1996). *When students have power: Negotiating authority in a critical pedagogy.* Chicago: University of Chicago Press.

Smith, D. E. (1987). *The everyday world as problematic: A feminist sociology.* Toronto: University of Toronto Press.

Smith, D. E. (2005). *Institutional ethnography: A sociology for the people.* Oxford, England: AltaMira.

Smith, S. (1991). *Report: Commission of inquiry on Canadian university education.* Ottawa, ON, Canada: Association of Universities and Colleges in Canada.

Storrs, D. (2009). Teaching Mills in Tokyo: Developing a sociological imagination through storytelling. *Teaching Sociology, 37*(1), 31–46.

Trueman, M., & Hartley, J. (1996). A comparison between the time management skills and academic performance of mature and traditional-entry university students. *Higher Education, 32,* 199–215.

Ungar, S. (2003). Misplaced metaphor: A critical analysis of the knowledge industry. *Canadian Review of Sociology and Anthropology, 40,* 331–347.

11 Transcending the Standard

One Teacher's Effort to Explore the World Beyond the Curriculum

Christopher R. Leahey

Throughout the last decade, federal policies fixated on standardizing curriculum, instruction, and assessment have dominated education reform in the United States. No Child Left Behind (NCLB) requires public schools to test all K–8 students in math, English, science, and social studies. Using standardized tests as the centerpiece of education reform, NCLB mandates that schools make adequate yearly progress toward the larger requirement that all students be proficient in core areas by 2014. Now that 2014 has arrived, federal school reformers have quietly abandoned this goal, and allowed states to apply for waivers. The administration of president Barack Obama has created the Race to the Top program, through which individual states may apply for hundreds of millions of dollars in federal funds for designing and implementing reforms that include comprehensive teacher and principal evaluation systems, using data and test scores to improve instruction, and adopting and implementing the Common Core State Standards.

Far from novel, these recent reform initiatives are deeply rooted in the American system of schooling, where the use of local, state, and, more recently, federal bureaucratic structures have been the primary tool to leverage change and increase external control of curriculum, instruction, and assessment. Starting with the social efficiency movements of the 1920s, American school reform efforts have drawn upon scientific management systems to quantify and rationalize teaching and learning (Callahan, 1964). Addressing these continuous efforts to control and manage education, Jal Mehta (2013) explains that although the state and federal governments have become increasingly involved in school reform, the same rationalization principles that rely on external control, scientific management, and imposing policy initiatives that rely on bureaucratic reforms have been used from the Progressive Era to the Obama administration's Race to the Top (RTTT) program. Throughout the 20th century, elite policy makers have devised education reforms rationalizing learning and regulating teaching to gain power over schools and knowledge production and to maintain social and economic privileges and iniquities. Whereas there has been much criticism of these more recent reform initiatives (Meier & Wood, 2004; Nichols & Berliner, 2008; Ravitch, 2010; Sacks, 1999), this chapter explores the ways in which bureaucratic accountability systems perpetuate the status quo, depriving students of opportunities to critically investigate the past and explore the social, political, and economic forces shaping their lives. Pointing the way toward a more authentic, democratic form of social studies education, this chapter also explores how a deliberative framework and a critical stance can be used to humanize the world history curriculum, complicate the past, and create authentic opportunities to question dominant narratives and critically investigate the world history.

ACCOUNTABILITY AND SOCIAL STUDIES

Viewed from the K–12 classroom, NCLB and RTTT have limited value for strengthening instruction or improving student outcomes. Setting aside the bureaucratic nature of such reforms, their concomitant control mechanisms, and inherent rationalization of teaching and learning, such reforms may be inappropriate ways to improve disciplines and activities for which they were not designed. As a discipline, social studies cannot be standardized. Whereas social studies necessarily involve all of the social sciences, Alan Singer (2011) suggests that social studies education should be designed to support the development of an active, participatory citizenry. In this sense, students' questions, interests, and values are at the center of social studies instruction:

> [A] social studies approach to studying world history starts with student questions, questions about why the world is the way it is today. It organizes the curriculum, units, and individual lessons in order to go back and forth across time, to examine case studies from the past, to help us gain insights into the human condition, and to stimulate questions about the present. Everyone in our class is not going to become a historian; in fact, very few will. But educated citizens in a democratic society need to think about the past and raise questions about the present so they can be informed and active participants in shaping the future. (Singer, 2011, p. 5)

If we take Singer's notion that social studies are preparation for citizenship seriously, it appears that standardized curriculum, tests, and federal policies designed to closely monitor and regulate classroom instruction have very little to offer social studies teachers interested in this type of instruction and working with students to explore the world. Further, if we take the goals of social studies seriously and work with our students to develop both academic and social skills, providing opportunities to experience and understand the meaning of citizenship and community, then we should be opening students to the world and opening the world to our students (Singer, 2009). Accountability systems that serve to rationalize student performance and regulate classroom instruction, however, make this type of authentic social studies difficult, if not altogether impossible.

The Weight of the Educational Bureaucracy

Perhaps this is the greatest tension experienced by K–12 classroom teachers: the tension between the goals of the discipline and the demands of state and federal policies and the way standardized curriculum, tests, and accountability mechanisms impinge upon these goals. Consider that the New York State Education Department organizes the world history curriculum into eight units of instruction, 51 general topics, and 280 subtopics (NYSED, 1999). In addition to this exhaustive outline of curriculum content, the Common Core Learning Standards require teachers to implement "instructional shifts" requiring students to demonstrate evidence of analyzing texts and identifying and understanding textual evidence, key ideas, themes, and supporting details (Common Core Learning Standards, 2011a). On top of these two sets of standards, New York has also implemented teaching standards delineating how curricular content is to be planned, delivered, and assessed (NYSED, 2011b). Taken together, each set of standards places its own set of constraints on social studies teachers, with each set of standards further proscribing a teacher's creativity and ability to offer authentic, meaningful instruction.

To illustrate, curricular standards—whether they be state content standards or Common Core standards prescribing what skills are valued—establish parameters about what is and what is not permissible to teach and what does and does not count as evidence of learning. Given the exhaustive list of content to be taught, these standards also preclude teachers from allowing students to explore content area in depth. When standardized tests are designed to measure a sample of curriculum content, teachers are pressured to cover material superficially (Horn, 2006). In his research on teaching and accountability in the state of Michigan, Avner Segall found that student performance on standardized tests had a significant influence on teachers' instructional decisions. He explains:

> Under pressure from the district and school administrators as well as from the media and parents, the teachers in this study view the MEAP [Michigan Evaluation Assessment Program] as a force they cannot afford to ignore. At the broad level, this means that teachers constantly think of MEAP as they plan for and teach. "Every time we step into the classroom to start the school year," Susan [a teacher included in this study] explains, "one of the end results needs to be: Are these kids going to be ready to take the MEAP? And are they going to do well?" Although this sense does not mean teachers spend the year simply teaching to the MEAP, she adds, "you always teach with some pressure of the MEAP hovering over you" (Segall, 2006, p. 115).

Marginalizing Students

By surrendering to the demands for shallow coverage and the ritual of pursuing acceptable test scores, the teacher also becomes part of the bureaucracy, diminishing his value as a social being and surrendering his commitment to learning and exploring the world with students. Under the weight of multiple layers of standards, and enforced by bureaucratic procedures and accountability mechanisms, students too are valued in relation to their ability or desire to meet the demands of the bureaucracy: idiosyncrasy is replaced with sameness, authenticity is replaced with plasticity, and free thought is replaced with compliance. In essence, sameness—or the illusion of similarity—is the foundation upon which accountability systems are built. Students are not valued by who they are or what they bring to the classroom, but what they can take from the classroom. As Wayne Au (2009) explains, accountability systems that hinge on student performance on standardized exams value students not for their humanity but for their ability to produce acceptable test scores, which represent a limited, commoditized abstraction of the child sitting in the classroom. The end result is an enterprise that implicitly dehumanizes students as it reduces children to data points. "Hence students' lives, home cultures, histories, educational differences, and socioeconomic conditions mean nothing within the logics of high-stakes standardized testing," writes Au (2009, p. 43).

In our efforts to standardize the curriculum, the teacher is devalued and delimited in his ability to work and teach in authentic, meaningful ways. Rather than learning alongside students, allowing student interest to guide inquiry and exploration, social studies becomes a bureaucratic ritual in building allegiance to the technical elements of accountability systems at the expense of attending to the needs and interest of the students themselves (Leahey, 2013). As a consequence, social studies loses its value; dynamic events, people, and concepts are reduced to a static litany of things to identify and superficially understand, all for the purpose of demonstrating learning on a standardized test. Within this system, the teacher's primary goal is to acclimate the student to the rules and procedures required to successfully navigate the corridors of the bureaucracy; authentic learning becomes a secondary function. In doing so, the student is taken further and further from the complex social, political, and economic world that the social studies were originally designed to investigate. We trade the complex and sometimes ambiguous world for the familiar procedures and routines established by the hierarchical bureaucracy that has increasingly come to influence schooling. The irony is that the better the teacher becomes at navigating the bureaucracy, the more distance she may experience between herself and her students, and the more powerless she may become in influencing her pedagogy. Ralph P. Hummel is worth quoting at length as he explains the power of the bureaucracy:

In bureaucratic society—the modern organization—my social identity is organizational identity. The person becomes a case. Social identity was originally developed between myself and others. While social identity defined the range of my social being (my rights), what I am as organizational identity defines the range of permissible activity: the size of my *cage*. As a case, I am defined by my two-way relations with other people, but by one-way definition of the organization's architects and designers. For example, official relations between offices are not defined by people in them. They are defined by those who organize relations from the top down. The totality of such relations between offices or bureaus makes up the bureaucracy—the power of the office (*bureau* + *kratos*).

Society yields to an artificial structure populated by cases, types, cut-outs. These make up the work organization centrally conceived and centrally run. Who we are socially is replaced by what we are to the organization. The power of bureaucracy derives and running of the organization. The organization becomes a power instrument without compare for those who run it. (2005, pp. 52–53)

Hummel's assessment of the power of the bureaucracy is an accurate description of the prevailing movement to standardize the public school experience. As we continue to pursue test scores and implement new teacher evaluation systems, both teachers and students are precluded from designing and influencing the educational experience. Teachers' work is limited to working within the constraints of the system, and their value is mostly determined by their ability to motivate students to generate acceptable test scores. Similarly, students' value is determined by their ability to comply with reasonable requests and accept test scores as evidence of learning. In this sense, the relationship between teacher and student is ultimately defined by their ability to successfully negotiate the system of standardized curriculum, teaching, and tests. In the end, a quality teacher is one who thrives within Hummel's "bureaucratic society" and willfully works to organize classroom life to reflect externally developed state and national imperatives.

Table 11.1   Bureaucratic Pedagogy vis-à-vis Humanistic Pedagogy

Bureaucratic Pedagogy	Humanistic Pedagogy
1. Commitment to system of standardized curricula and tests	1. Commitment to students exploring the world
2. Teaches to impose standardized curriculum	2. Teaches for understanding of complex world
3. Students treated as passive recipients of school knowledge	3. Students treated as thoughtful, sentient beings
4. Simplifies social studies curriculum	4. Complicates social studies curriculum
5. Mastering measurable outcomes as ideal practice	5. Sustained, thoughtful inquiry as ideal practice
6. Commercial tests provide evidence of learning	6. Authentic student products provide evidence of learning
7. Teacher's primary function is to efficiently teach content	7. Teacher's primary function is to facilitate learning
8. External authorities determine learning and growth	8. Learning and growth determined within local context

TOWARD AUTHENTICITY

As a classroom teacher who has worked within a standard-based environment for more than a decade, I have found that perhaps the most effective way to build a classroom dedicated to humanistic values is to develop a deep faith and understanding of the power and importance of social studies for democratic life. At the center of a democratic form of social studies is the concept of community. John Dewey reminds us that a community "involves not merely a variety of associative ties which hold persons together in diverse ways, but an organization of all elements by an integrated principle" (1927/1954, p. 38). For me (and for my students) the organizational element is democratic social relationships. Our classroom is a community of learners who work together to explore and experience the world history curriculum. As a democratic community, we honor and encourage diverse perspectives that shed light on ourselves and our values and strengthen our understandings of who we are (Sleeter, 2005). Unlike the educational bureaucracy and the layers of standards that seek to reduce difference, our personal experiences and sense of justice, equality, and freedom are acknowledged and validated as we explore the history of the world.

To embark on a democratically oriented form of social studies, the first step is to abandon the notion that learning should be reduced to that which can be measured on paper and pencil tests. Rather, democratically oriented social studies treat knowledge as dynamic and conceptualize the curriculum as an object to be manipulated and conceptualized to reflect the interests of teachers and students (Thornton, 2005). In each class, students' values, experiences, and ideas influence the way the course is presented, the voices to which we attend, and the meaning and significance we draw from the past. No two classes are alike, as each student and each combination of students create idiosyncratic environments that read the curriculum and the world differently. Honoring students' lived experiences is a counterbalance to the regiment of standardized curricula, tests, and teaching evaluations and other such bureaucratic instruments of control.

Honoring students as active participants in reading the curriculum also allows us to problematize knowledge construction and create opportunities to diverge from the well-worn path of the standardized curriculum and textbook narratives. By placing the curriculum as the centerpiece of critical inquiry, power relationships and classroom authority are recast. Rather than deriving authority from credentials and state certificates, teachers derive authority from their ability to sit alongside their students, critically examine the past, and pose questions about implications for today. By working in this fashion, teachers and students participate in a dialogue about the past in which teachers pose questions, facilitate the pursuit of inquiry projects, and participate in a continuous discussion about the lessons to be drawn from past and what it means for us today (Kincheloe, 2008).

A Deliberative Approach

In place of treating social studies as a static list of past events figures, dates, and concepts, a democratic approach to social studies prepares students to critically interrogate the past, wrestle with complexity, and make meaning within a public context. Thus, a democratic form of social studies reflects the central elements of deliberative politics. James Bohman defines public deliberation as

> a dialogical process of exchanging reasons for the purpose of resolving problematic situations that cannot be settled without interpersonal coordination and cooperation. On this definition, deliberation is not so much a form of discourse or argumentation as much as a joint, cooperative activity. (2000, p. 27)

Approaching social studies instruction within a dialogical framework underscores both the values and views we possess and allows us to see history as series of episodes that we can only begin to understand when we study as a community of learners, drawing upon the past to further our understanding of the present. Working from the classroom outward, democratically oriented social studies prepare students for more than sporadic participation in elections. They prepare students for a thicker, more vibrant form of democracy in which ordinary citizens play a significant role in shaping the future. Paul R. Carr suggests that such a critical pedagogy of democracy is "an ethos, an ideology, a set of values, a philosophy, a contested terrain of action and debate, and a complex, problematic, dynamic framework and terrain in which diverse forces, interests, and experiences, continue to evolve" (2011, p. 83).

Problematizing the curriculum, interrogating the past, and building a community of learners is to prepare students for the complex world of democratic citizenship. Within this framework, the goal is not to teach students about the social world or to explore the historical record. Rather, the goal is to use past human experiences such as oppression, tyranny, resistance, revolution, and reform to prepare students to address the injustices of the future. Lying at the center of this form of social studies education are concepts such as power, authority, oppression, and change. Whether studying the highly stratified social structure of ancient Egypt or the injustices embedded within Hammurabi's Code, students can explore the contours of power and the myriads ways it has regulated and defined human relationships throughout time and space.

Beyond gaining a critical understanding of the historical record, democratically oriented social studies treat studying the past as important but subordinate to the larger goal of preparing students to be thoughtful, engaged citizens who possess public values and the ability to identify iniquities and work collectively to confront and challenge social, political, and economic injustices. As Joe L. Kincheloe explains, a pedagogy founded on "critical democratic civics operates to protect the oppressed from exploitative power wielders, to intervene on the side of the subjugated" (2011, p. 64). As progressive educators interested in empowering students to participate in the political arena, we must create opportunities for students to come face to face with past injustices, identify and explore moments of triumph and defeat, and view the historical record as a series of signposts marking contested terrain and pointing out the uneven, unpredictable road to a more secure, just future. Each historical episode, from the fall of Athens to the fall of the Soviet Union, reveals much about imperial hubris, injustice, and power. As teachers we can also confront the injustices that have created our own sociocultural values. Starting with the horrors of slavery and tracing oppression and injustice through Jim Crow laws, the civil rights struggle, and the social policies that have led to crumbling inner city schools and a disproportionate number of minorities being locked in prisons, we can see that the struggles of the past continue to influence and shape who we are and what U.S. society has become. Failing to connect the present with the past is to misrepresent the past and to prepare students for the prevailing culture of entertainment and consumerism and the politics of intellectual dependence and compliance (Saltman, 2000; Zinn & Macedo, 2005). In the end, a democratically oriented social studies education may prove futile if it fails to connect the past to the present, the curriculum to the contemporary world, and the struggles of the past to the struggles of the present. Without this connection, social studies have little democratic value.

CREATING DEMOCRATIC SPACES

Rather than limit the discussion to social studies education under the weight of multiple layers of state and federal standards, we might also consider the possibilities for negotiating a form of social studies education that can be democratic and humanistic despite these constraints. In her celebrated work *The Dialect of Freedom* (1988), Maxine Greene contends that the language and purpose of contemporary school reform compels students to discount their personal stories and experiences and attend to the external world as defined by curricular objectives and outlines. In this sense, students' minds are in a perpetual state of reaching for the external, striving to understand that which is beyond their lived experiences. This striving places students in a state of perpetual dependence on external authorities—in this case teachers or curriculum designers—for understanding the identified body of information and the requisite skills that allow students access to that body of information. The result is, as Greene thoughtfully suggests, the tendency to ritualize the practice of faithfully accepting what is given, and that which is externally defined as real, without regard or respect for the reality of the student. Pushing forward, Greene suggests that this ritual of emphasizing the external world, without attention to our students' place in it or our interpretation of it, has a tendency to turn our students away from themselves, depriving them of personal freedom:

> Finding it difficult to stand forth for what is officially (or by means of the media) defined as real, unable to perceive themselves in interpretive relation to it, the young (like the elders) are all too likely to remain immersed in the taken-for-granted and the everyday. For many, this means an unreflective consumerism; for others, it means a preoccupation with *having* more rather than *being* more. If freedom comes to mind, it is ordinarily associated with a individualist stance: It signifies a self-dependence rather than relationship; self-regarding and self-regulated behavior rather than involvement with others. Above all, it means an absence of interference or . . . a deregulation. People consider themselves free if the road is open before them—to secure success, or security, to "get ahead." (Greene, 1988, p. 7)

To make social studies democratic in nature, there must be a renewed emphasis on students' experience and interpretation of their lives, the past, and the connection between the two. The curriculum must be conceived as a key to unlock the doors to understanding their world rather than an obstacle to understanding and appreciating their experiences. To pry open the doors and create opportunities for democratic engagement, teachers must consciously plan for critical encounters and present the curriculum in a way that fosters thoughtful deliberation.

Prioritizing the Social Studies Curriculum

For my world history course, we set out to gain an understanding of social, political, and economic forces and how they serve to oppress and liberate. The course is taught thematically, highlighting how recurring themes such as political power and social inequality have shaped history and created circumstances that can at times oppress and at other times lead to liberation. For instance, when studying the feudal system, students explore the variegated ways military and legal obligations worked to keep peasants in a continuous state of dependence, tied to the land, while maintaining social and economic privileges for the landed nobility. We explore how the Magna Carta redefined the political landscape, wresting power from King John, securing basic rights for English men, and paving the way for the development of the British Parliament. We also investigate how the onset of the Black Plague that killed approximately one-third of Europe's population shifted some degree of economic power to the peasants, who could demand more wages and, in some cases, land for their services.

Throughout the course, students are invited to examine critical developments and follow the path of change and transformation. As we study primary sources that include artwork, codes of laws, speeches, maps, photographs, and literature, we draw upon our experiences and values as we study the past. Each historical development is juxtaposed to lived experiences, and we explore how each historical development presents new problems as well as opportunities for critical engagement.

Table 11.2   Teaching Social Studies with Recurring Themes

Historical Event	Theme(s) Supporting Critical Discourse
Hammurabi's Code	Political and economic inequality
Pericles's Funeral Oration	Political power
Twelve Tables of Rome	Political inequality
Development of the Silk Road	Economic expansion
Rise and fall of the Roman Empire	Military expansion, political inequality
Justinian Code	Political and economic inequality
European Crusades	Religious conflict, economic expansion
Japanese and European feudalism	Social inequality, military conflict
Rise and fall of the Mongol Empire	Military expansion, economic imperialism
Columbian Exchange	Economic imperialism
Development of Timbuktu	Social inequality, economic expansion
European Renaissance	Cultural conflict, political repression
Spanish Inquisition	Political, social, economic conflict
Protestant Reformation	Religious oppression, economic injustice
Ming dynasty	Political oppression, economic expansion
Scientific Revolution	Political inequality and oppression
European absolutism	Political and economic power
Magna Carta and the English Bill of Rights	Political and social struggle
French Revolution	Political and economic power
French, American, and Latin American Revolutions	Political, social, and economic power

NURTURING A COMMUNITY OF LEARNERS

Whereas approaching the curriculum from a critical perspective is one step that could be taken to transcend standardized curriculum, teachers must also be thoughtful about the way students interact. All too often, the social dynamics of the classroom represent the values of the marketplace, where students are required to be passive consumers of information, competing for grades and recognition. Within these environments creativity, identity, and difference are mitigated for the sake of efficiency and order (Olson, 2009). Democratic classrooms, however, view students as valuable members of a learning community, working alongside other students and the teacher to explore the world. Within these democratic learning communities, each student's ideas are valued and treated as necessary, essential elements for creating and sustaining an inclusive learning environment. What we value is not intellectual compliance and dependence on the teacher and textbook to define our encounters with the past; rather, it is intellectual diversity that can only be tapped when our purposes are to develop democratic thinkers and engage enduring themes centered on real problems, not merely efficient delivery of the curriculum. In her thoughtful work on using controversy to foster deep thinking and intellectual encounters within the classroom, Diana E. Hess explains why diversity matters in preparing students for democratic life:

> As a backdrop, it is important to recognize that the heart of the deliberative enterprise is the foundational belief that multiple perspectives are an asset—not a hindrance—to democratic thinking, participation, and governance. After all, if people agree on what should be done about important problems, what would be the purpose of deliberation. In such a circumstance, it would be logical to move forward to putting into place the solution that enjoyed such widespread support. But we know that many of the public's problems do, in fact, involve controversy because there are fundamental disagreements about which problems deserve attention in the first place, what has caused the problem, how much of a problem it really is, for whom it is a problem, what the strengths and weaknesses of proposed solutions are . . . and the list goes on. In short, while there are some things vast majorities of things people agree on in communities, it is also the case that there are many disagreements—as one would expect in democratic nations. In fact, the extent to which there are multiple and competing perspectives voiced about what "we" the people should do to address a problem facing the community is not a flaw of democracy, but a marker of how democratic a community is in practice. (2009, pp. 77–78)

Hess's words are important because they are rooted in a democratic way of thinking that is focused on solving problems and using our diversity as an asset to draw upon as we work together to confront challenges. Within the classroom, this means making problems the centerpiece of the curriculum and allowing students the space and time to think through problems, explore possible solutions, deliberate with one another about the best of all possible solutions, and to learn from the deliberative experience. More specifically, such deliberation can be nurtured by debates, mock trials, problem-solving activities, and—perhaps most important—assignments and projects that require students to work collaboratively to engage and demonstrate understanding of the problems and conflicts associated with democratic life (Loewen, 2010; Singer, 2009, 2011). In the end, teachers must strive to make critical inquiry, problem-solving, and deliberative discourse an essential part of curricula, a regular part of instructional practices, and the focal point of authentic assessments.

BUILDING DIGITAL DEMOCRATIC COMMUNITIES

Whereas classroom spaces can be made less hierarchical, and based on mutual respect for diverse viewpoints, digital technology has made it possible to create democratic spaces online. Alan Collins and Richard Halverson (2009) explain that with the advent of digital programs that can customize activities and tasks to meet student goals and interests, teachers can create powerful learning experiences that were not possible a decade ago. They point out that commercials games such as *Civilization*, *Railroad Tycoon*, and *The Sims* allow students to learn about historical progress and conflict, and allow for flexible responses and problem solving that could not be made possible in a traditional teacher-directed learning environment. By allowing for more student control, institutional control is eroded and, Collins and Halverson suggest, traditional assumptions are challenged. For example, digital technologies can potentially offer instruction at a pace that meets individual student needs. Digital technologies can also provide students with material written at the appropriate level. Further, digital technologies can allow more access than a teacher and textbooks assigned ten months of the school year, challenging the assumption that students must learn with their class cohort, with the school calendar dictating the pace of instruction and the state curriculum regulating what can and cannot be taught (Leahey, 2010).

Whereas these technologies offer fascinating new possibilities for the ways in which curriculum can be taught, a democratic form of social studies seeks to understand how these technologies can bring students together to investigate the curriculum, make sense of human experience and, when possible, to solve long-standing problems. In his discussion of digital media, David Buckingham (2009) points the way toward a more democratic form of social studies education in which student experience and democratic discourse are situated at the center. Buckingham suggests that digital media can be used to extend students' knowledge of themselves gained through deliberation and dialogue. He explains that media learning could be conceptualized as a three-stage process whereby students start by making their existing knowledge explicit, then move to formal knowledge embodied in the curriculum, and, in the final stage, apply what they have learned to their lived experience. He goes on to explain that each stage is a collaborative process; "through the encounter with their peers and with the academic knowledge of the teacher, students progressively move towards greater control of their own thought processes" (Buckingham, 2009, p. 143).

Within my pedagogical practice I have found the digital program Edmodo to be a useful tool to initiate and sustain a rich dialogue over the world history curriculum. A commercial resource, Edmodo allows students to create accounts and participate in online discussions. Teachers have the ability to create discussion groups that can consist of an entire class or create subgroups comprised of students with common interests. Once students are placed in subgroups, the teacher can post social studies materials; these may include videos as well as primary and secondary sources. Or, alternatively, students can facilitate and lead their subgroups in investigating such materials.

What I find particularly valuable is that Edmodo allows students to understand course content socially because they are provided the opportunity to influence one another's understanding. Similarly, the interactive nature allows me to challenge students to appreciate the connection between the past and the present. For example, my first post includes an annotated version of Hammurabi's Code. Once posted, students are asked to analyze the code in terms of fairness and equality. As the facilitator of the discussion, I can participate by acknowledging divergent viewpoints, challenging students to support their assertions, and prodding students to extend their understanding of Hammurabi's Code to recent legal disputes. By using this tool, I can create democratic spaces centered on recurring themes, as mentioned above, as well as series of interactions in which students can experience deliberative discourse firsthand.

CONCLUSION

In the end, a vigorous form of social studies education requires teachers to negotiate the bureaucratic world of standards-based learning where outcomes are predetermined and students' lived experiences are marginalized or all together discounted. This requires us to think deeply about the ways in which we present the curriculum, the manner in which we interact with students while engaging the past, and the ways in which we allow students to interact as they develop a richer, deeper understanding of the curriculum and the complex world they have been given. Perhaps the truest, most significant measure of learning social studies may not be found in test scores but instead may be better demonstrated in students' willingness to unlock the past and draw upon one another to build a sophisticated understanding of the history of the world and a desire to apply what they have learned beyond the classroom. It is only then that students will see social studies as viable subject matter that not only provides the time and space to make sense of historical complexity but also points the way toward a more equitable future. Connecting past injustices to the present is, of course, the precondition to working collectively to dream of and work toward a more just, more humane, social world.

REFERENCES

Au, W. (2010). *Unequal by design: High-stakes testing and the standardization of inequality.* New York: Routledge.

Bohman, J. (2000). *Public deliberation: Pluralism, complexity, and democracy.* Cambridge, MA: MIT Press.

Buckingham, D. (2009). *Media education: Literacy, learning, and contemporary culture.* Malden, MA: Polity.

Callahan, R. (1964). *Education and the cult of efficiency: A study of the social forces that have shaped the administration of public schools.* Chicago: University of Chicago Press.

Carr, P. R. (2011). *Does your vote count? Critical pedagogy and democracy.* New York: Lang.

Collins, A., & Halverson, R. (2009). *Rethinking education in the age of technology: The digital revolution and schooling in America.* New York: Teachers College Press.

Dewey, J. (1954). *The public and its problems.* Athens, OH: Swallow Press/Ohio University Press. (Original work published 1927)

Greene, M. (1988). *The dialect of freedom.* New York: Teachers College Press.

Hess, D. E. (2009). *Controversy in the classroom: The democratic power of discussion.* New York: Routledge.

Horn, C. (2006). The technical realities of measuring history. In S. G. Grant (Ed.), *Measuring history: Cases of state-level testing across the United States* (pp. 57–74). Greenwich, CT: Information Age.

Hummel, R. P. (2008). *The bureaucratic experience: The post-modern challenge* (5th ed.). Armonk, NY: Sharpe.

Kincheloe, J. L. (2008). *Critical pedagogy* (2nd ed.). New York: Lang.

Kincheloe, J. L. (2011). Civics in the social studies: Critical democratic citizenship education in a corporatized hyperreality. In J. DeVitis (Ed.), *Critical civic literacy: A reader* (pp. 63–80). New York: Lang.

Leahey, C. (2010). *Whitewashing war: Historical myth, corporate textbooks, and possibilities for democratic education.* New York: Teachers College Press.

Leahey, C. (2013). Catch-22 and the paradox of teaching in the age of accountability. *Critical Education, 4*(6), 1–18.

Loewen, J. (2010). *Teaching what really happened: How to avoid the tyranny of textbooks and get students excited about doing history.* New York: Teachers College Press.

Mehta, J. (2013). *The allure of order: High hopes, dashed expectations, and the troubled quest to remake American schooling.* New York: Oxford University Press.

Meier, D., & Wood, G. (Eds.). (2004). *Many children left behind: How the No Child Left Behind Act is damaging our children and schools.* Boston, MA: Beacon.

NYSED (New York State Education Department). (2011a). Common Core State Standards for English language arts and literacy in history/social studies, science, and technical subjects. Retrieved August 4, 2013 from http://www.core-standards.org/assets/Appendix_A.pdf

NYSED (New York State Education Department). (2011b). The New York State teaching standards. Retrieved July 14, 2013 from http://www.highered.nysed.gov/tcert/pdf/teachingstandards9122011.pdf

NYSED (New York State Education Department). (2009). Social studies resource guide. Retrieved July 14, 2013 from http://www.p12.nysed.gov/ciai/socst/pub/sscore2.pdf

Nichols, S. L., & Berliner, D. C. (2008). *Collateral damage: How high-stakes testing corrupts America's schools.* Cambridge, MA: Harvard Education Press.

Olson, K. (2009). *Wounded by school: Recapturing the joy in learning and standing up to old school culture.* New York: Teachers College Press.

Ravitch, D. (2010). *The death and life of the great American school system: How testing and choice are undermining education.* New York: Basic Books.

Sacks, P. (1999). *Standardized minds: The high price of America's testing culture and what we can do to change it.* Cambridge, MA: Perseus.

Saltman, K. (2000). *Collateral damage: Corporatizing public schools—A threat to democracy.* New York: Rowman and Littlefield.

Segall, A. (2006). Teaching history in the age of accountability: Measuring history or measuring up to it? In S. G. Grant (Ed.), *Measuring history: Cases of state-level testing across the United   States* (pp. 105–132). Greenwich, CT: Information Age.

Singer, A.J.J. (2009). *Social studies for secondary schools.* New York: Routledge.

Singer, A.J.J. (2011). *Teaching global history: A social studies approach.* New York: Routledge.

Sleeter, C. (2005). *Unstandardizing the curriculum: Multicultural teaching in the standards-based classroom.* New York: Teachers College Press.

Thornton., S. (2005). *Teaching social studies that matters: Curriculum for learning.* New York: Teachers College Press.

Zinn, H., & Macedo, D. (2005). *Howard Zinn on democratic education.* Boulder, CO: Paradigm.

Conclusion
Learning and Teaching in Scarcity

P. L. Thomas

Recent reports on Southern and urban schools are disturbing harbingers about the growing weight being shouldered by U.S. public education: the rise in segregation (Siegel-Hawley & Frankenber, 2012) and a new majority in public school—students living in poverty (Southern Education Foundation, 2013). These in-school patterns reflect similar conditions of inequity in the wider society. As Harvard University professor of social sciences Robert J. Sampson (2013) notes, race and class remain powerful markers for the imbalance of opportunity in the U.S.:

> Fifty years after the Rev. Dr. Martin Luther King Jr. pointed to African-Americans on a "lonely island of poverty in the midst of a vast ocean of material prosperity," racial and economic disparities by place not only remain but are closely connected. Nationwide, close to a third of African-American children born between 1985 and 2000 were raised in high-poverty neighborhoods compared with just 1 percent of whites. Crucially, income does not erase place-based racial inequality—affluent blacks typically live in poorer neighborhoods than the average lower-income white resident.

In the 21st century, the U.S. stands as a stratified society, and public schools tend to reflect that inequity (Thomas, 2012). Moreover, race and class disparities are reflected in not only educational inequity but also the current 30-year cycle of mass incarceration (Thomas, 2013b). As Sampson (2013) explains,

> What many have come to call "mass incarceration" has a local face as well—only a small proportion of communities have experienced America's prisoner boom whereas others are relatively untouched. I was taken aback to learn that the highest incarceration rate among African-American communities in Chicago was over 40 times higher than the highest ranked white community. This is a staggering difference of kind, not degree. And it does not go unnoticed, even by children. In one neighborhood I came across a wall behind a school with sketches of the grim faces of black men behind prison bars. An

open book and diploma were drawn underneath—hope to be sure, but against a backdrop of despair.

Children are impacted directly and indirectly by the destiny of their births—in their homes, their communities, and their schools. Yet, most education policies and advocates of those policies represent the belief that *in-school-only* reform—calling for "no excuses" from teachers and schools, as well as "grit" from students—is the sole workable option. U.S. secretary of education Arne Duncan has aligned president Barack Obama's education agenda with the in-school-only stance (Horton, 2013)—a perspective articulated by educational consultant Grant Wiggins (2013):

> My point was merely to ask those who speak only of forces outside of our immediate control as educators to attend to what is not only in our control but can make a big difference. . . .
> *Teachers and schools make a difference, a significant one.* And we are better off improving teaching, learning, and schooling than anything else as educators because that's what is in our control. (emphasis in the original)

For Duncan and Wiggins—as well as a legion of reformers and elected officials—education reform should address teacher quality, increase choices for parents, implement Common Core (CC) standards, and depend on the next generation of high-stakes tests aligned with CC.

In the few years since the start of CC implementation, the narrative and policies among reformers have shifted slightly away from the hardline "ZIP code is not destiny" (How to Fix Our Schools, 2010)—likely in response to scholarly and public challenges to CC—but remained mired an ideology that goes something like this: "poverty matters, but educators and schools must focus on only what educators and schools can control—measurable school and teacher quality." Yet considering that re-segregation and rising poverty have plagued public schools (Reardon, 2011) during the same three decades as intense accountability-based reform driven by standards and high-stakes testing, it may be well-past time to accept that in-school-only reform is not only deeply misguided but also part of the problem.

SCARCITY AND SLACK OFTEN DETERMINE ACHIEVEMENT

"Poverty is surely the most widespread and important example of scarcity," explain Sendhil Mullainathan and Eldar Shafir (2013, p. 147). Today, poverty in the U.S. is not just widespread (Rank, 2013)—it is expanding. Despite the rise in poverty, what hasn't changed are public and political views of poverty and the poor, nor claims that public institutions such as schools can overcome *alone* negative and powerful social inequity.

For example, stereotypes of people in poverty (see Paul Gorski's work, excerpted in Strauss, 2013)—such as not appreciating education, being lazy (and thus deserving their poverty), and lacking parenting skills—help perpetuate the belief that schools are reform mechanisms, especially for those in poverty whom we view through a deficit perspective: if people in poverty had the qualities middle-class and affluent people have they would then flourish. The logical conclusion of these assumptions? School must give "other people's children" (Delpit, 2006) those qualities they lack. The stereotype of laziness among the impoverished is especially corrosive for education and education reform because reformers tend to suggest that low student achievement in high-poverty schools is the result of poor students lacking "grit" and their teachers using poverty as an excuse for failure, sometimes called "fatalism" by reformers like Wiggins (2013).

Yet Kerris Cooper and Kitty Stewart (2013) show that money in the lives of poor children may be at least as powerful as in-school reform:

The impact of increases in income on cognitive development appears roughly comparable with that of spending similar amounts on school or early education programmes. Increasing household income could substantially reduce differences in schooling outcomes, while also improving wider aspects of children's well-being.

This contradicts the in-school-only stance of reformers in two ways: first, by showing the effectiveness of addressing poverty directly in order to raise academic achievement, and second, by showing that social reform is likely to enhance in-school reform, if that social reform comes first; and such is the argument of many educators and scholars calling for addressing the opportunity gap in order to close the achievement gap (Carter & Welner, 2013).

However, whereas money is important, it isn't, on its own, enough. "The poor are not just short on cash," Mullainathan and Shafir (2013) clarify:

They are also short on bandwidth. This is exactly what we saw in the mall studies and in the harvest studies [discussed earlier in Mullainathan and Shafir's book]. The same person when experiencing poverty— or primed to think about his monetary troubles—did significantly worse on several tests. He showed less flexible intelligence. He showed less executive control. With scarcity on his mind, he simply had less mind for everything else. (p. 157)

The synthesis and analysis by Mullainathan and Shafir, then, provide a perspective on poverty that exposes the essential failure of in-school-only education reform, including the key concepts and terms at the heart of their thesis:

- "By scarcity, we mean *having less than you feel you need*" (p. 4); thus, scarcity is a condition, but not a decision made by anyone or necessarily a consequence of inherent behaviors by anyone. As a result, Mullainathan and Shafir argue, "Scarcity captures the mind" (p. 7).

- "Bandwidth" is the term they use for mental capacity: "Being poor, for example, reduces a person's cognitive capacity more than going one full night without sleep. It is not that the poor have less bandwidth as individuals. Rather, it is that the experience of poverty reduces anyone's bandwidth" (p. 13).
- Whereas Mullainathan and Shafir admit scarcity can have some shortterm benefits (e.g., focus), they warn that tunneling is a much greater and negative result of scarcity—"to *tunnel*: to focus single-mindedly on managing the scarcity at hand" (p. 29).
- Mullainathan and Shafir caution against drawing conclusions about personal qualities from behaviors. For example, they show that abundance allows people "slack," space that doesn't force anyone to consider trade-offs. Conversely, scarcity removes slack (p. 83). In moments of abundance, then, people behave differently than in moments of scarcity. The consequences for people in poverty are thus much greater than the consequences for people in affluence.

For education reform, understanding the pervasive influence of poverty as an intense form of scarcity requires that we address poverty systemically in all children's lives. In-school-only reform is, therefore, an indirect, and ultimately inadequate, approach to targeting achievement gaps. In the context of calls for "grit" among poor children and "no excuses" attitudes among teachers and schools, Mullainathan and Shafir's (2013) concept of slack helps show that whereas policies focusing on "grit" and "no excuses" may produce rare and short-term success, the margins are so slim and the behavior so taxing that these attitudes will ultimately intensify, not eradicate, low achievement among impoverished students. Evidence, for example, from 20 years of accountability-based reform in Massachusetts shows that such reform measures have been ineffective in closing test score gaps, and high-poverty students remain left behind (French, Guisbond, & Jehlen, 2013).

Instead, efforts to afford all students the slack that the affluent enjoy are likely to produce effective and lasting outcomes (Carr, 2013). Just as Mullainathan and Shafir (2013) detail how changing the conditions of scarcity impacts behavior for all people, education reform is likely to succeed once the conditions of poverty in children's lives and inequity in their learning are alleviated (Carter & Welner, 2013). For example, Sarah Carr highlights a move among some schools in New Orleans to offer all children the opportunities the affluent enjoy:

Across the country, the number of charter schools that are diverse by design has been steadily rising in recent years, in cities including New York, Denver, and Washington D.C. Scholars at the Century Foundation in

Washington D.C., a nonpartisan research organization, estimate that about two dozen such charters have opened in recent years although they still comprise only a tiny fraction of charter schools. . . .

Josh Densen, the founder of Bricolage Academy in New Orleans, says he has a lot of respect for charter schools targeted at low-income students with the explicit goal of closing the achievement gap.

But "what we saw was one type of school model that was offered to kids living in poverty and a very different school model offered to kids living in affluence," he said. "And this to me . . . seemed inherently inequitable."

Ultimately, according to Mullainathan and Shafir, education reformers must accept, as the reformers above have, that "[o]ne cannot take a vacation from poverty. Simply deciding not to be poor—even for a bit—is never an option," adding, "Our data suggest . . . that poverty—the scarcity mindset—causes failure" (pp. 148, 155). Children in poverty and their teachers cannot simply pretend the impact of scarcity doesn't exist during the school day. Scarcity and its consequences are engulfing and ever-present—and directly connected to low performance in school.

IT'S SLACK, NOT GRIT, THAT MATTERS

Finally, the most disturbing aspect of education reform committed to in-school-only policy and "no excuses" ideologies is that many of these policies and ideologies create additional types of stress that exacerbate the scarcity already experienced in the lives of impoverished students. For example, one element of the scarcity trap exposed by Mullainathan and Shafir (2013) explores how lonely people portray themselves to potential companions: "Their problem was that they performed badly when they thought it mattered" (p. 141). Scarcity (loneliness) creates stress, and that stress causes failure. Accountability policies, by their high-stakes nature, similarly increase the likelihood of failure because the punitive consequences for teachers and students increase stress.

The current era of education reform is characterized by demands that students and teachers do more with less (increasing class sizes, cutting education funding, reducing instruction time that is taken by testing and test preparation), while elevating the stakes attached to teaching and learning, all to improve achievement. But these features actually reinforce the disadvantages of scarcity by heightening stress, reducing the cognitive capacity of teachers and students—in effect, cultivating failure. To that end, what children and adults learning and teaching in high-poverty schools really need are education reform measures that *reduce,* not heighten, stress.

Broadly, Mullainathan and Shafir's (2013) work shows that living and learning in a state of scarcity or abundance creates predictable behaviors; therefore, traditional assumptions that poverty and wealth are the result of individual character and (lack of) effort are deeply misguided. "The failures of the poor are part and parcel of the misfortune of being poor in the first place," they write. "Under these conditions, we all would have (and have!) failed" (p. 161). In the context of high-stakes, "no excuses" practices, many students and teachers are likely to fail not as a result of a *lack* of effort or ability but as a result of the stressful conditions themselves.

The accountability era of in-school-only education reform is built on the premise that students and teachers lack motivation; this is a flawed and corrosive assumption. The affluent live and learn in abundance with adequate slack for risk and failure; those in poverty, however, live and learn within razor-thin margins not of their making and often beyond their control to change. Children from affluent homes who attend affluent schools aren't succeeding because of grit but because of the slack created by their relative privilege. And children from impoverished homes, attending high-poverty schools, are not struggling because they lack grit but because they embody the consequences of scarcity.

As Mullainathan and Shafir (2013) detail, addressing scarcity in the lives and schools of children *directly* "can liberate bandwidth, boost IQ, firm up self-control, enhance clarity of thinking, and even improve sleep" (p. 180). To make this transition, however, we must shift our accusing gaze away from the people trapped in scarcity and toward social and educational inequity, the conditions of living and learning that drive the outcomes. If we truly want all children to achieve, to thrive and not just survive, education reform must acknowledge that academic success is about slack, not grit. And this volume has sought ways in which we can all strive to achieve that equitable end.

EDITOR'S NOTE

This volume's conclusion is adapted from an article of the same title published in *AlterNet* (Thomas 2013b).

REFERENCES

Carr, S. (2013, November 5). In New Orleans and nationally, a growing number of charter schools aspire to be "diverse by design." *Hechinger Report*. Retrieved from http://hechingerreport.org/content/in-new-orleans-and-nationally-a-growing-number-of-charter-schools-aspire-to-be-diverse-by-design_13756/

Carter, P. L., & Welner, K. G. (Eds.). (2013). *Closing the opportunity gap: What America must do to give every child an even chance*. New York: Oxford University Press.

Cooper, K., & Stewart, K. (2013, October 21). *Does money affect children's outcomes?* York, England: Joseph Rowntree Foundation. Retrieved from http://www.jrf.org.uk/publications/does-money-affect-childrens-outcomes

Delpit, L. (2006). *Other people's children: Cultural conflict in the classroom*. New York: New Press.

French, D., Guisbond, L., & Jehlen, A. (2013, June). Twenty years after education reform: Choosing a path forward to equity and excellence for all. Boston: Citizens for Public Schools.

Horton, P. (2013, October 28). Pseudo democracy: Duncan double dribbles in Chicago. *Education Week Teacher*. Retrieved from http://blogs.edweek.org/teachers/living-in-dialogue/2013/10/paul_horton_pseudo_democracy_d.html

Klein, J., Rhee, M. et al. (2010, October 10). How to fix our schools: A manifesto by Joel Klein, Michelle Rhee and other education leaders. *Washington Post*. Retrieved from http://www.washingtonpost.com/wp-dyn/content/article/2010/10/07/AR2010100705078.html

Mullainathan, S., & Shafir, E. (2013). *Scarcity: Why having too little means so much*. New York: Holt.

Rank, M. R. (2013, November 2). Poverty in America is mainstream. *New York Times*. Retrieved from http://opinionator.blogs.nytimes.com/2013/11/02/poverty-in-america-is-mainstream

Reardon, S. F. (2011, July). The widening academic achievement gap between the rich and the poor: New evidence and possible explanations. Retrieved from http://cepa.stanford.edu/sites/default/files/reardon%20whither%20opportunity%20-%20chapter%205.pdf

Sampson, R. J. (2013, October 26). Division street, U.S.A. *New York Times*. Retrieved from http://opinionator.blogs.nytimes.com/2013/10/26/division-street-u-s-a

Siegel-Hawley, G., & Frankenber, E. (2012, September). Southern slippage: Growing school segregation in the most desegregated region of the country. Los Angeles: UCLA Civil Rights Project. Retrieved from http://civilrightsproject.ucla.edu/research/k-12-education/integration-and-diversity/mlk-national/southern-slippage-growing-school-segregation-in-the-most-desegregated-region-of-the-country/hawley-MLK-South-2012.pdf

Southern Education Foundation. (2013, October). *A new majority: Low income students in the South and nation*. Atlanta: Author. Retrieved from http://www.southerneducation.org/getattachment/0bc70ce1-d375-4ff6-8340-f9b3452ee088/A-New-Majority-Low-Income-Students-in-the-South-an.aspx

Strauss, V. (2013, October 28). Five stereotypes about poor families and education. *Washington Post*. Retrieved from http://www.washingtonpost.com/blogs/answer-sheet/wp/2013/10/28/five-stereotypes-about-poor-families-and-education/

Thomas, P. L. (2012, May 15). Studies suggest economic inequity is built into, and worsened by, school systems. Retrieved from http://truth-out.org/news/item/8993-studies-suggest-economic-inequity-is-built-into-and-worsened-by-school-systems

Thomas, P. L. (2013a, May 17). Education reform in the new Jim Crow era. Retrieved from http://truth-out.org/opinion/item/16406-education-reform-in-the-new-jim-crow-era

Thomas, P. L. (2013b, November 8). Learning and teaching in scarcity. *AlterNet*. Retrieved from http://www.alternet.org/education/learning-and-teaching-scarcity-how-high-stakes-accountability-cultivates-failure

Wiggins, G. (2013, October 26). To my critics. Retrieved from http://grantwiggins.wordpress.com/2013/10/26/to-my-critics/

Contributors

Paul Berger is an associate professor at Lakehead University in Thunder Bay, Ontario, Canada. A former grade 7 teacher in Nunavut, he has maintained ties to Nunavut through collaborative research with Inuit teacher education students on Inuit uses of mathematics and Inuit teacher recruitment. He is also involved with research on schooling in the western Arctic with the Inuvialuit communities in the Beaufort delta. His other interests include teacher education, the faltering Canadian democracy, accelerating climate change, and ice kayak construction.

Paul R. Carr is professor in the Department of Education at the Université du Québec en Outaouais, Canada. His research is focused on political sociology, democracy, peace studies, media literacy, and transformative education. Carr's most recent book, coedited with Ali A. Abdi, is *Educating for Democratic Consciousness: Counter-Hegemonic Possibilities* (New York: Lang), and was a recipient of the 2013 American Educational Studies Association's Critic's Choice Award. He is the Principal Investigator of the *Democracy, Political Literacy and Transformative Education* research project (www.education4democracy. net), which involves collaborations in several countries.

Mary Christianakis is an associate professor of critical theory and social justice at Occidental College. Having received her Ph.D. in language, literacy, and culture from UC Berkeley, she studies literacy development from a critical sociocultural perspective, primarily in urban and multilingual school contexts. Professor Christianakis' article, "Children's Text Development: Drawing, Pictures, and Writing," was the recipient of the 2012 Alan C. Purves Award. Currently, she is conducting research on youth who are tried as adults. Her scholarship has been published in *Journal of Educational Controversy, Journal of Inquiry and Action in Education, Perspectives on Urban Education, Urban Education, Journal of Literacy Research, Issues in Teacher Education, Research in the*

Teaching of English, *Teacher Education Quarterly*, and included in numerous edited volumes.

Rebecca Collins-Nelsen is a PhD student at McMaster University in Hamilton, Ontario, Canada. Her scholastic interests revolve mainly around the areas of gender, work, technology, intersectionality, social inequality, and the politics of materiality. Her master's thesis (2010) was titled "Retooling Gender? A Constructivist Analysis of *Tomboy Tools.*" Her current dissertation work explores the processes through which women negotiate careers in comedy. She has teaching experience in the courses Introduction to Sociology, Communication and Media, Sociological Theory, and Technology and Society. She is currently President of CUPE local 3906 at McMaster University.

Robert L. Dahlgren is an assistant professor of social studies education at the State University of New York–Fredonia. He teaches undergraduate and graduate courses in social studies methods, contemporary issues in education, and the philosophy of education. Dahlgren's primary research area is the nexus between the history and conceptions of academic freedom and strategies for teaching controversial public policy issues in K–12 social studies classes. Recent projects include longitudinal studies of the experiences of students participating in a summer institute on human rights, and the self-efficacy of student activists involved in a Gay-Straight Alliance Network chapter in Florida.

Christopher J. Frey is an assistant professor of social foundations of education at Bowling Green State University. He teaches courses in multicultural education, international education policy, comparative education, and history of education, and coordinates the Master of Arts in Cross-Cultural and International Education program. A former social studies teacher for the Navajo Nation, Frey's research interests focus on comparative histories of indigenous and minority education policy, particularly in the U.S. and Japan. He has published in *Comparative Education Review*, the *Journal of American Indian Education*, and the *Journal of Curriculum Studies*. Frey is completing work on a book about the development of education policy in 19th-century Japan, and is an associate editor for the journal *Diaspora, Indigenous and Minority Education*.

Julie Gorlewski is an assistant professor of secondary education at the State University of New York–New Paltz and a former public school teacher. Her research focuses on the experiences of students, teachers, and teacher candidates as they navigate the challenges constructing identities in a neoliberal era. Gorlewski is author of *Power, Resistance, and Literacy: Writing for Social Justice* (2011), and coauthor (with David Gorlewski) of *Making It Real: Case Stories for Secondary Teachers* (2012) and (with David Gorlewski and Thomas Ramming) of *Theory into Practice: Case Stories for School Leaders* (2012). She is currently coeditor (with David Gorlewski) of the *English Journal*.

Nicholas D. Hartlep is an assistant professor of educational foundations at Illinois State University and editor of the Urban Education Studies book series (Information Age Publishers). Hartlep edited *The Model Minority Stereotype Reader: Critical and Challenging Readings for the 21st Century* (2014) and coedited (with Cleveland Hayes) *Unhooking from Whiteness: The Key to Dismantling Racism in the United States* (2013). As the author of *The Model Minority Stereotype: Demystifying Asian American Success* (2013), he recently launched the Model Minority Stereotype Project (http://my.ilstu.edu/blogs/ndhartl/). Follow his work on Twitter (@nhartlep) and at the Illinois State University website, http://ilstu.academia.edu/NicholasHartlep.

Randy L. Hoover, PhD, is emeritus professor of graduate studies in teacher education at Youngstown State University. He is coauthor (with Richard Kindsvatter) of *Democratic Discipline: Foundations and Practice* (1997) and, more recently, has been involved in No Child Left Behind test performance research in terms of educator accountability, value-added metrics, and the impact of accountability mandates on public schooling and democracy. Hoover is the author of two major empirical studies of high-stakes test performance and statistical validity in Ohio. He holds degrees in political science and teacher education from Ohio State University and a master's degree in educational administration from Edinboro State University. He was a 2012 winner of the NCTE/SLATE Intellectual Freedom Award.

Allison L. Hurst is an associate professor of sociology at Furman University, where she teaches courses on the sociology of education, class, and qualitative methods. She is also one of the founders and the current acting president of the Association of Working-Class Academics, an organization composed of college faculty and staff who were the first in their families to graduate from college. She has written two books on the experiences and identity reformations of working-class college students, *The Burden of Academic Success: Loyalists, Renegades, and Double Agents* (2010) and *College and the Working Class* (2012).

Christopher R. Leahey's research interests include democratic education, critical theory, and civic literacy. He is the author of *Whitewashing War: Historical Myth, Corporate Textbooks, and Possibilities for Democratic Education* (2010), and his articles have appeared in *Social Education*,

Critical Education, and *The Social Studies*. He has also contributed essays to *Critical Civic Literacy: A Reader* (2011), *Educating for Peace in a Time of Permanent War* (2012), *School Reform Critics* (2013), *and The Social Studies Curriculum: Purposes, Problems, and Possibilities* (2014). He is currently an adjunct professor at the State University of New York–Oswego and a full-time teacher in North Syracuse, New York, public schools.

Barbara Madeloni is a teacher educator and activist, and is currently running for president of the Massachusetts Teachers Association under the banner of its progressive caucus, Educators for a Democratic Union. As a member of the education activist groups Can't Be Neutral and Reclaiming the Conversation on Education she has developed conferences and led workshops designed to educate and organize resistance against the neoliberal assault on education. Her recent publications include articles in the journals *Rethinking Schools* and *Schools: Studies in Education* and book chapters in *Left Behind in the Race to the Top: Realities of School Reform* (2013), and *Policing the Campus: Academic Repression, Surveillance, and the Occupy Movement* (2013). Madeloni blogs at @The Chalk Face (http://atthechalkface.com) and hosts a monthly radio program on WXOJ in Northampton, Massachusetts.

Richard Mora is an associate professor of sociology at Occidental College. He has a B.A. in Sociology from Harvard College. Professor Mora also holds a M.A. in education from the University of Michigan, an M.A. in sociology from Harvard University, and a Ph.D. in sociology and social policy from Harvard University. His areas of research interest include masculinity, schooling, and juvenile justice. Currently, Professor Mora is conducting research on youth who are tried as adults. His scholarship has been published in *Journal of Educational Controversy, Journal of Inquiry and Action in Education, Perspectives on Urban Education, Gender and Education, Gender & Society, THYMOS: Journal of Boyhood Studies*, and included in numerous edited volumes.

Randle W. Nelsen is professor emeritus of sociology at Lakehead University, Thunder Bay, Ontario, Canada. He has published mostly in the areas of higher education, bureaucracy and the professions, and popular culture. His book *Fun & Games & Higher Education* (2007) incorporates Reuel Denney's classic studies of American popular culture to comment on conformity and rebellion by analyzing university classroom edutainment alongside college football and its accompanying tailgate parties; the follow-up book, *Life of the Party* (2012), examines sociability, community, and social inequality in parties across various social contexts. His latest publication is an e-book of poetry, *Haiku Montreal: Metropolitan Musings* (2013). Nelsen's chapter in this volume continues his interest in our human search for knowledge, sociability, and community and the role these play in the complicated nterrelation of social stability and social change.

Kysa Nygreen is an assistant professor of teacher education and school improvement in the College of Education at the University of Massachusetts–Amherst. Her research and teaching focus on diversity and multicultural education, urban schooling, teacher education, immigration, educational ethnography, and participatory action research. Nygreen is the author of *These Kids: Identity, Agency, and Social Justice at a Last Chance High School* (2013). She formerly worked as an English and Spanish teacher at an alternative high school.

Nancy C. Patterson is an associate professor of social studies education at Bowling Green State University. Her research interests include beginning teacher retention, urban school reform, digital democracy, and democratic citizenship education. Dr. Patterson is participating in three grants: Gear Up (Gaining Awareness and Readiness for Undergraduate Programs) is currently focusing on high school reform; A Civics Mosaic is a curriculum-writing effort and teacher exchange program with Russia; and History Links is a social studies teacher professional development program.

Brad Porfilio is an associate professor of education at Lewis University in Romeoville, Illinois, where he conducts research and instructs doctoral students in becoming critical scholars, social advocates, and multicultural educators. He has published numerous peer-reviewed articles, book chapters, edited volumes, and conference papers in the field of education. Dr. Porfilio earned his PhD in sociology of education at the State University of New York–Buffalo in 2005.

William M. Reynolds teaches in the Department of Curriculum, Foundations, and Reading at Georgia Southern University. He has authored, coauthored, and coedited numerous books, including *Curriculum: A River Runs Through It* (2003), *Expanding Curriculum Theory: Dis/positions and Lines of Flight* (2004), *The Civic Gospel: A Political Cartography of Christianity* (2009), and *A Curriculum of Place: Understandings Emerging Through the Southern Mist* (2013). He has also published many articles and chapters on issues in curriculum, the politics of education, critical media literacy, critical pedagogy, and cultural studies.

P. L. Thomas is an associate professor of education at Furman University, and taught high school English in rural South Carolina before moving to teacher education. The National Council of Teachers of English recognized his blogging with the 2013 George Orwell Award, and he is currently a column editor for *English Journal* and series editor for the Critical Literacy Teaching Series: Challenging Authors and Genres. Recent edited volumes include *Becoming and Being a Teacher* (2013) and, coedited with Joe Bower, *De-Testing and De-Grading Schools* (2013). His teaching and scholarship focus on literacy and the impact of poverty on education as well as confronting the political dynamics influencing public education in the U.S. Follow his work on Twitter (@plthomasEdD) and at The Becoming Radical (http://radicalscholarship. wordpress.com/).

Index

For Product Safety Concerns and Information please contact our EU
representative GPSR@taylorandfrancis.com
Taylor & Francis Verlag GmbH, Kaufingerstraße 24, 80331 München, Germany

www.ingramcontent.com/pod-product-compliance
Lightning Source LLC
Chambersburg PA
CBHW071855270326
41929CB00013B/2238